CONFIDENCE IN WRITING

A BASIC TEXT

CONFIDENCE IN WRITING

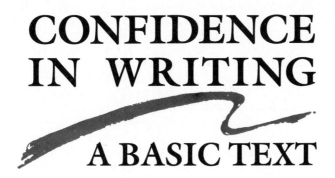

A BASIC TEXT

Ed Reynolds
Spokane Falls Community College

Marcia Mixdorf
Everett Community College

HARCOURT BRACE JOVANOVICH, PUBLISHERS
San Diego   New York   Chicago   Austin
London   Sydney   Tokyo   Toronto

COPYRIGHTS AND ACKNOWLEDGMENTS

22 Excerpt from *Blue Highways: A Journey into America* by William Least Heat Moon. Copyright © 1982 by William Least Heat Moon. Reprinted by permission of Little, Brown and Company, in association with The Atlantic Monthly Press. **54** Excerpt from *The Edge of the Sea* by Rachel Carson. Copyright © 1955 by Rachel L. Carson. Copyright © renewed 1983 by Roger Christie. Reprinted by permission of Houghton Mifflin Company. **122** "Team Slighted," letter to the editor by Kirsten Riegel. Originally appeared in *The Spokesman-Review*, March 11, 1984. Reprinted by permission. **132–33** Excerpts from *Tactics in Reading I* by O. S. Niles, et al. Copyright © 1961 by Scott, Foresman and Company. Reprinted by permission. **138, 142** "Warning: TV Can be Hazardous to Children," by Vance Packard. Condensed in *Reader's Digest*, May 1986. Reprinted by permission of the author. **151** "Battling the Blahs When a Job Seems Routine," by Peggy Schmidt. First appeared in *Family Weekly*, November 18, 1984. Reprinted by permission of the author. **160** "To Have and to Hold," by Alan Meyers. Adapted from pp. 864–65 and 870–71 of *The People's Almanac* by David Wallechinsky and Irving Wallace. Copyright © 1978 David Wallechinsky and Irving Wallace. Reprinted by permission of William Morrow and Company. **162** "Leaving the Office Behind" by Dr. Barbara Mackoff. First appeared in *VIEW* magazine, March 1985. Reprinted by permission of the Group Health Cooperative of Puget Sound. **167** "Climbing Kilimanjaro" by Charles Bracelon Flood. Reprinted by permission of The Sterling Lord Agency, Inc. Copyright © 1959 by Charles Bracelon Flood. **174** "What Is Language?" Adapted from *Introduction to Linguistic Structures—from Sound to Sentence in English*, by Archibald Hill. Copyright © 1958 by Harcourt Brace Jovanovich, Inc.; renewed 1986 by Archibald Hill. Reprinted by permission of the publisher. **178** "How Pro Football Was Ruined" by Roland Merullo. Copyright 1984, by Newsweek, Inc. All rights reserved. Reprinted by permission. **182** "The Bad News Grizzlies," by Jon R. Luoma. Copyright © 1984 by Jon R. Luoma. Reprinted by permission of the author.

Text and cover illustrations by Jan Reynolds.

Copyright © 1987 by Harcourt Brace Jovanovich, Inc.

ISBN: 0-15-512985-6
Library of Congress Catalog Card Number: 86-80767
Printed in the United States of America

For Bill, Jim, and Jan
Those were the days

TO THE INSTRUCTOR

Basic writing students form one of the most diverse groups on a school campus, yet they share two characteristics: they have little writing experience, and they have even less confidence in their writing abilities. In *Confidence in Writing: A Basic Text*, we have attempted to give you a book that addresses both of these characteristics. We address the first by making writing the students' primary activity, and we address the second by teaching a writing process that has discrete steps, each carefully modeled. From the beginning of the first chapter, students put their own ideas, observations, and experiences on paper, and because they are shown exactly how to do this, their first writing activity can bring them nothing but success. Subsequent steps and writing activities are similarly described and modeled, so the students' chances for success are always high. This success builds confidence.

This book continually emphasizes writing and offers an approach that has grown out of many years of success in a writing lab in which students work at their own pace and freely consult an instructor. The book's format and design, however, make it equally useful in either a writing lab or a conventional classroom setting.

We have designed the appendix to be used by students as they work to improve given pieces of their own writing, and we rely heavily on the instructor to refer students to appropriate sections.

We gratefully acknowledge the following reviewers for their comments on this book: Donald Cruickshank of University of Illinois, Urbana-Champaign; Jack Hartley of Glendale Community College; and Carolyn A. Simonson of Tacoma Community College. We also thank former students Victor O. Adams, Lawrence C. Browning, Nelda M. Eichstaedt, Rod Foster, Manuel R. Gollihue, Tammy Hamilton, Nona Jones, David A. Knight, Gregg Larson, Deborah L. Peters, Donna Quale, and Nikolaos Roussos for permission to reprint their work.

We have enjoyed creating this book. Our hope is that you and your students will enjoy using it.

ED REYNOLDS

MARCIA MIXDORF   VII

TO THE STUDENT

Writing is a skill that, like any other skill, can be learned. You don't need talent, and you don't need to have been "good in English" in school. But you do need to be willing to follow instructions and to work hard.

This book will take you, step by step, through the process of writing a paragraph, and it will give you plenty of opportunity to practice your skills as you learn them. We begin with writing the paragraph because it's short and therefore easy to work with and talk about. Also, writing paragraphs allows you to practice nearly all the skills necessary for any writing assignment. Other sections of this book give you practice in writing summaries, in taking essay examinations, and in writing essays.

Most of this book talks about school writing assignments, but you will find many other uses for your developing writing skills. Most jobs that graduates take require writing skills, and, in fact, most job applications must be written. Letters to the editor about issues that concern you, letters to friends about important events, and letters to companies or government officials are all examples of the many demands on your writing skills. But you will also write just for yourself. You may keep a journal or diary, write poems or other pieces to express your feelings, or just jot down ideas so you can remember them. As your writing skills improve, you will find that your daily writing becomes not only easier but also more enjoyable.

ED REYNOLDS
MARCIA MIXDORF

CONTENTS

CONFIDENCE IN WRITING

A BASIC TEXT

I

WRITING THE PARAGRAPH

Preview for Chapter 1

Before you begin reading Chapter 1, read the following list of terms which you will find in this chapter.

1. Audience
2. Voice
3. Paragraph
4. Brainstorming
5. Writing process
6. Topic sentence
7. Controlling idea
8. First draft
9. Development
10. Unity
11. Coherence
12. Revision
13. Proofread

Before you read this chapter, preview it. You have already looked at the list of important vocabulary words you will find in the chapter. Now count the pages in the chapter to get an estimate of how long it will take you to read it. Next, quickly look through and notice the main ideas that are being presented. Main headings, usually in bold type, divide chapters into sections, and in this book you'll see that the headings show the steps in the writing process. You will also see that the vocabulary words are defined at the end of the chapter.

You are ready to start reading when you know what special terms you need to watch for, how long the chapter is, and the main ideas you need to learn.

1

GETTING STARTED: WRITING ABOUT A PERSON

Writing helps us to explore our own experiences and ideas. We write to discover what we have to say.

As you write, always remember that you are a real person with real ideas and concerns. You are unique—there has never been and will never be anyone exactly like you. As a result, even what you see as common and ordinary may be new to someone else.

Sharing your ideas with someone else is another important reason for writing. As you write, keep your reader in mind and remember that you and your reader see the world differently. Thus you must express your ideas to your reading **audience** as clearly as you can so that the reader can understand your view of the world.

It is important that you write about what you know—your friends and family, your environment, your activities, and your understanding of new things you see and learn. Writing about what you know will help you to write honestly and in your own **voice**. Just as you have an individual style of speaking, you will develop your own style and voice in writing.

As we said in the introduction to this book, writing is a skill. The only way you can learn any skill is by doing it, so let's start writing. Because it's important that you write about familiar subjects, your first exercise will be a paragraph about someone you know. A **paragraph** is a unit of writing that states and explains a single idea, and we'll take you step by step through a process of paragraph writing. The first step is to identify the idea that the paragraph will explain, and we'll do this by **brainstorming**.

3

STEP 1:
Brainstorming for Ideas

First, think of a specific person you know or remember very well. What does the person look like? What do you do together? What do you like about this person? What don't you like? How does he dress? Where does she live? What is special about this person? There are hundreds of questions you can ask and answer about people you know, and that's the first step in the **writing process**. We call it pre-writing, brainstorming, or exploring what you know about your subject. As you think of questions and answers to them, write down words or phrases that come to your mind. Here is a list of details we made as we thought about our friend Ariadne.

1. wears flattering clothes
2. eats Triscuits and vanilla yogurt
3. always has a new joke to tell
4. short (5'1")
5. wears glasses
6. likes to watch "Muppet Show"
7. blonde (light)
8. blue eyes
9. can laugh at herself
10. likes to read Edgar Allan Poe
11. likes "Doonesbury"
12. 30 years old
13. lives in apartment next door
14. likes plants
15. collects rocks
16. go to movies together
17. go to lunch together
18. has math anxiety
19. wears interesting jewelry
20. loves the snow
21. allergic to cats
22. works at Burger King
23. has three brothers we've never met
24. is optimistic
25. have psych class together
26. good cook
27. we laugh a lot
28. is a Taurus
29. wants to go camping together
30. gets us to try new things with her

Writing Activity 1.1

- ☐ Think carefully now about the person you've chosen to write about.
- ☐ Quickly list as many ideas about that person as you can, without worrying about spelling, punctuation or the way things sound.
- ☐ List at least twenty or thirty ideas. Include anything that comes to mind about this person, ignoring whether one idea relates to another. Your purpose at this time is to explore all the possibilities.

STEP 2:
Writing the Topic Sentence

As we said earlier, a paragraph states and explains a single idea. The **topic sentence** is the statement of that idea. We also refer to the topic sentence as the **controlling idea** because it controls what goes into the paragraph and what stays out. In the first draft of this paragraph, we'll make the first sentence our topic sentence. (That's not always true of paragraphs, but it's easiest to start this way.) Because it's a statement of the main idea, the topic sentence is simply a one-sentence summary of what the rest of the paragraph will say. We will let some of the details from our brainstorming list suggest a topic sentence to us.

Look back at our list. The list gives us far more information than we can use in a paragraph, and that's good. It helps us to explore a subject thoroughly, to see the most interesting features about our subject, and to discover what we'd like to say about the subject. As we looked back through our list, we grouped items that seemed to have something in common. For example, items 3, 9, 11, 24, and 27 all involve Ariadne's personality, so they can be grouped together:

3. **She always has a new joke to tell.**

9. **She can laugh at herself.**

11. **She likes "Doonesbury."**

24. **She is optimistic.**

27. **We laugh a lot.**

These similar items suggest a topic sentence like this:

Our friend Ariadne has a good sense of humor.

A different set of details will, of course, give us a different topic sentence. For example, items 6, 10, 11, 14, 15, 20, 26, and 30 involve things Ariadne enjoys doing, so they also can be grouped:

6. **She likes to watch the "Muppet Show."**
10. **She likes to read Edgar Allan Poe.**
11. **She likes "Doonesbury."**
14. **She likes plants.**
15. **She collects rocks.**
20. **She loves the snow.**
26. **She is a good cook.**
30. **She gets us to try new things with her.**

These items could lead to this topic sentence:

Ariadne likes a wide variety of activities.

In turn, items 1, 4, 5, 7, 8, 12, and 19 deal with Ariadne's looks:

1. **She wears flattering clothes.**
4. **She is short (5′1″).**
5. **She wears glasses.**
7. **She is blonde (light).**
8. **She has blue eyes.**
12. **She is 30 years old.**
19. **She wears interesting jewelry.**

We thought that her looks might be really interesting to write about. We liked this topic sentence:

Our friend Ariadne is as striking as her name.

Writing Activity 1.2

- ▫ Look closely at your list from activity 1.1. Read it several times to get a good "feel" for what you know about this person. Are some ideas more vivid than others? Are some items especially significant about this person?

- ▫ Next, as we did in the examples above, choose several related items that interest you and that might interest others. Group these items together so you can analyze their relationship. What do they say about this person?

- ▫ Now write a statement which expresses the main idea of the group of related items.

- ▫ Try working with more than one group of related ideas and writing a topic sentence for each group.

STEP 3:
Outlining the Paragraph

Outlining is an excellent way to plan and organize your writing. An outline includes the topic sentence and the most important details that will go into the paragraph. Our method of outlining is very simple. First, turn your topic sentence into a question that begins with *who, what, when, where, why, how,* or *in what way.* Be sure to use the words from your topic sentence as you write your question. For example, our first topic sentence would become

In what ways is Ariadne's sense of humor good?

Our second topic sentence would give us

What are some of the wide variety of things Ariadne likes to do?

For the paragraph we're going to write, our topic sentence question will be this:

How is Ariadne striking?

Writing Activity 1.3

□ Choose one of the topic sentences you have written for activity 1.2 and turn it into a question. Be sure to use the same words from your topic sentence in your topic sentence question. Add one of the question words in front of your topic sentence and rewrite the sentence to change it into a question. With this step you're almost ready to finish your outline.

The second outline step is to answer the question you have asked. Be sure that your answers directly answer the question and that each answer is a complete sentence. Our outline looks like this:

Topic Sentence:

Our friend Ariadne is as striking as her name.

Topic sentence question (The question won't appear in our paragraph. We put it here only as an aid in planning the paragraph.):

How is Ariadne striking?

Answers:

1. **She is short but carries herself well.**
2. **She chooses clothes that flatter her.**
3. **Her glasses give her a look of intelligence and self-confidence.**
4. **Her hair is light blonde and her eyes are a deep, vivid blue.**
5. **She seems ageless.**

Writing Activity 1.4

□ Look carefully at your topic sentence question, and answer the question as directly as you can.

□ Write at least three answers. Be sure to use complete sentences for your answers, and make sure your answers do, in fact, answer the question you've asked. These answers will become the main details of your paragraph.

☐ Make your outline as complete as you can. This step of the writing process may seem time-consuming, but careful work at this stage will save you from headaches, sweat, and tears in the later stages of the writing process.

STEP 4:
Writing the First Draft

The words **first draft** simply mean that it's your first try at writing. It's very rare for any writer to do something perfectly (or even nearly perfectly) the first time, so get used to the idea that you'll need to do two or three or more drafts of just about everything you write except letters to your mother (unless you're asking for money). We promised that writing is hard work, but it's also interesting and sometimes exciting to see what happens as your writing goes through various drafts.

We'll use the outline as our guide, but we won't just copy it, since doing that would give us a paragraph that looks like this:

> **Our friend Ariadne is as striking as her name. She is short but carries herself well. She chooses clothes that flatter her. Her glasses give her a look of intelligence and self-confidence. Her hair is light blonde and her eyes are a deep, vivid blue. She seems ageless.**

This is pretty dull, isn't it? Since we're writing for a reading audience that has never seen Ariadne, we'll have to work on **development** or the explanation of the details we identified in our outline. To help us do that developing, let's ask some questions about our details. Our thinking might go something like this:

She is short but carries herself well.   What does "short" mean? Short to a pro basketball player? To a third grader?

She chooses clothes that flatter her.   How can we give the reader a picture of her clothes?

Her glasses give her a look of intelligence and self-confidence.   Do we need to explain more about how her glasses make her look striking?

Her hair is light blonde and her eyes are a deep, vivid blue.   Her eyes sound striking, but what's striking about light blonde hair?

She seems ageless.   Can we say more about this idea to help the reader see Ariadne more clearly?

We'll show you our first draft before you write yours. Remember, it's not perfect; in fact, you might try to pick out some of the things that are wrong with it as you read it. Here it is:

> **Our friend Ariadne is as striking as her name. She carries herself like the heroine she's named after, even though she's only five feet one. Another thing she does is to choose clothes that flatter her. Her clothes aren't always new, but she uses colors and lines in a way that immediately catches your eye. Her glasses give her a look of intelligence and self-confidence. Up closer, you can see her vivid, deep blue eyes that look nice with her light blonde hair. She's 30 years old, but you'd never know it by looking at her. She seems ageless.**

That's our try. Now let's review the process so far. First we explored our subject by listing all the details that came to mind. We hadn't decided what we were going to say; we were only trying to figure out what the possibilities were. Second, we reviewed those possibilities, decided what we wanted to say, and wrote a topic sentence that would help guide our selection of details. Third, we outlined the paragraph to make sure that the details were clearly related to the topic sentence. Finally, we wrote a draft of our paragraph.

 Writing Activity 1.5

□ Write your own first draft of your paragraph. As you write, focus on the controlling idea expressed in your topic sentence. Remember that every detail you include in your paragraph must, in some way, explain that controlling idea. In other words, your paragraph must have

unity. As you write about each answer to your topic sentence question, try to develop the idea further.

☐ Do as we did in our paragraph about Ariadne: ask questions about each item in your outline to help you expand the idea. You might, for example, add a quote from the person you're writing about. A bit of conversation can often tell much about a person's character.

☐ Try to use words and phrases that help your reader see how one idea leads to the next idea. "First," "next," and "finally" are examples of words that show how ideas relate to each other; they give the paragraph **coherence**.

☐ Put your rough draft aside and let it sit overnight so you can come to it fresh when we go through the last step of the writing process.

STEP 5:
Revising the Paragraph

Revision of your work means that you will write a second, third, or fourth draft, and even professional writers sometimes go through many more drafts than that. It depends on the subject, the writer, and the intended audience. Still, there are questions we can ask to help us through the revising step.

There is a widely agreed upon set of standards for judging writing. The eight categories listed below and the questions in each reflect those standards. Read them through right now so that you'll become familiar with them. Plan to refer back to them each time you revise something you've written.

Standards for Judging Writing

1. *Controlling Idea*—Is the topic sentence clearly stated? If this is one of those paragraphs without a stated topic sentence, can the reader tell what your controlling idea is?

2. *Unity*—Does the paragraph contain only one central idea? Have you stayed with your subject? Does all of your material relate directly to your original topic?

3. *Development*—Do the details adequately develop or support the main idea? Have you provided enough information for your reader to see or feel or understand what you're talking about?

4. *Audience*—Is your presentation appropriate for this intended audience? Nearly everything is written to give information to someone else. Most school papers are written for a teacher, a specific class, a committee, or the readers of a journal or newspaper. Much other writing is written for a general audience, but the writer can usually make some good guesses about the audience's education, level of information about the subject, and so on. Who is your reading audience? How must you present your ideas so your audience can best understand them?

5. *Vocabulary*—Is your phrasing clear, precise, accurate? Are your words direct and to the point? Are you using the kind of vocabulary your subject requires?

6. *Coherence*—Does it all make sense? Are relationships among the ideas clear? Is the paper logically sound? Have you used necessary or helpful transitional words or phrases? Can your reader follow your line of thought without getting confused?

7. *Sentence Structure*—Have you used complete sentences? Is there some variety in your sentence structures? Are there sentences you could combine to make your ideas flow more smoothly and effectively?

8. *Mechanics*—Is your writing free of serious problems in spelling and punctuation? Are capital letters, quotation marks, apostrophes, and other punctuation marks turning up in the right places?

There may be some terms in that list that you don't understand right now. Don't worry. If you have trouble with some of these terms, your instructor can explain them to you. You'll probably know most of these terms by the time you've finished this book, and you'll certainly come across them again in later writing courses. Also, in the appendix of this book, we discuss some of the most common errors students make in sentence structure and punctuation, and we show you how to correct them.

Now let's see how using the above questions can help us revise our paragraph. Look back at the first draft of the paragraph about Ariadne. The *controlling idea* seems clearly stated and neither too broad nor too narrow to control the paragraph effectively. Our reading *audience* might need more information about the heroine Ariadne. Our reading audience might also appreciate a more lively *vocabulary* in our paragraph. Words like "new," "uses," and "look nice" don't do much to excite the imagination, do they? How about *unity*? We have talked about one subject, Ariadne's striking looks, but our last detail doesn't seem to fit quite clearly enough into our description. This might be a problem in unity, but it might also be a problem in *development*; we might just need to explain our idea in more detail. As experienced writers, we know that *coherence* and *sentence structure* often improve automatically as one revises to improve unity and development, so since we don't see any glaring problems, we won't worry much about these for now. Finally, we'll look through the paragraph for obvious errors in *mechanics*—sentence fragments, poor punctuation, faulty capitalization, and so on. Here's the original draft, followed by our revision with some notes about the changes we made.

Draft 1

Our friend Ariadne is as striking as her name. She carries herself like the heroine she's named after, even though she's only five feet one. Another thing she does is to choose clothes that flatter her. Her clothes aren't always new, but she uses colors and lines in a way that immediately catches your eye. Her glasses give her a look of intelligence and self-confidence. Up closer, you can see her vivid, deep blue eyes that look nice with her light blonde hair. She's 30 years old, but you'd never know it by looking at her. She seems ageless.

Draft 2 (with notes)

Our friend Ariadne is as striking as her name. (She knows that the original Ariadne was a heroine in a Greek myth,) and she carries herself like a heroine even

added information about heroine

though she's only five feet one. (But her
posture isn't the only thing that catches
your eye.) (Her skillful use of jewelry,
scarves, and other accessories and the
way she blends the colors and lines of her
clothes) (make her stand out in any group
of people.) It doesn't matter that her
clothes aren't always in the current fashion. They are right for her. (Even glasses
look good on her;) they give her a look of
intelligence and self-confidence. Up
closer, you can see her vivid, deep blue
eyes that contrast strikingly with her light
blonde hair. (The effect of all of these features is to make her seem as ageless as
the myth that gave her her name.)

makes smoother connection between ideas

added information shows more clearly how she dresses

another way of saying she's striking

smoother connection of ideas

makes paragraph end smoothly by relating last detail back to topic sentence

Draft 2 (without notes)

Our friend Ariadne is as striking as her name. She
knows that the original Ariadne was a heroine in a
Greek myth, and she carries herself like a heroine even
though she's only five feet one. But her posture isn't the
only thing that catches your eye. Her skillful use of jewelry, scarves, and other accessories and the way she
blends the colors and lines of her clothes make her
stand out in any group of people. It doesn't matter that
her clothes aren't always in the current fashion. They
are right for her. Even glasses look good on her; they
give her a look of intelligence and self-confidence. Up
closer, you can see her vivid, deep blue eyes that contrast strikingly with her light blonde hair. The effect of
all of these features is to make her seem as ageless as
the myth that gave her her name.

The information that Ariadne was a heroine in a Greek myth clarifies
who the original Ariadne was. We've added specific details to help the
audience see how Ariadne is striking, and we've chosen more specific
words such as "blends" for "uses," "current fashion" for "new," and "contrasts strikingly" for "looks nice." The more specific words help a reader
to see Ariadne as we see her.

Writing Activity 1.6

☐ Reread your first draft, asking the questions listed in the "Standards for Judging Writing" section (pages 11–12).

☐ Write your second draft, making any changes you think will improve it. If you need to, change your topic sentence to make the controlling idea clearer. Add specific details to develop your ideas fully. Remove any idea that strays from your controlling idea. Always keep your audience in mind as you write, and try to make changes that will help your readers understand your meaning.

☐ Write additional drafts until you are satisfied with the paragraph.

☐ Finally, before you share your draft with your instructor, **proofread** it carefully. Read it aloud and exaggerate the pauses after each period or question mark. These pauses will help you be sure that each of your sentences expresses a complete thought. Look carefully at spelling and punctuation. You have worked hard at expressing your ideas; don't let simple mechanical errors interfere with a reader's understanding of what you have written.

You have now completed the five steps of the writing process, and the result is a paragraph you can be proud to have written. First you brainstormed ideas to explore what you might say about your subject. Next, you reviewed your list of details and grouped ideas that seemed to relate to each other. That led you to a topic sentence, an idea that would control your paragraph. Third, you outlined your paragraph in order to plan how you would present your ideas to your readers. Fourth, you wrote a first draft and let it sit for a time. Finally, you reviewed the first draft by asking a series of questions about it, and then you wrote one or more revisions of your paragraph, letting the questions guide you as you added, subtracted, or changed material. These five steps form the writing process which we will use throughout this book.

Other Suggestions for Writing

1. Read pages 105–107 and do Writing Activity 7.1, page 107.
2. Write about someone you remember well from your childhood—someone you especially liked or disliked.
3. Write about a person you care about who has a habit that annoys you. Give examples to show how the person annoys you.
4. Write about a public figure whom you admire or don't admire.
5. Write about an elderly relative who has had an influence on your life.
6. Write about a character on a television program that you enjoy.

Terms to Remember

audience   A person or group of people who might be interested in your subject. Your choice of a reading audience will help determine your vocabulary, sentence structures, details, and so on.

brainstorming   A method of discovering what you want to say or what you know about a subject. In this chapter we used listing as our method of brainstorming.

coherence   The relationships among ideas in your writing. A paragraph has coherence when these relationships are clear.

controlling idea   The idea that summarizes what the paragraph says.

development   The details that explain and clarify the controlling idea. The paragraph is adequately developed when the reader can see, feel, or otherwise understand the controlling idea.

first draft   A draft is the piece of writing you do after exploring your subject and planning how you might present it. The first version of a paragraph or other piece of writing will be the rough or first draft. Each revision will be another draft. Most writing goes through several drafts before it can be called finished.

paragraph   A unit of writing that states and explains a single idea. The first line is indented to show that a new paragraph has begun.

proofread   To check for and correct errors such as misspellings, missing or misused punctuation, word endings left off, and words left out.

revision   Literally, "seeing again." When you revise, you evaluate your previous draft and rewrite it in an effort to express your ideas more clearly and effectively. The last part of the revision step is to proofread your work carefully, making sure that there are no mechanical errors that interfere with meaning.

topic sentence   The controlling idea of a paragraph. The topic sentence is a one-sentence summary of the paragraph. It controls what goes into the paragraph and what stays out of it.

unity   A paragraph has unity when it talks about or focuses on one idea only.

voice   Your way of expressing yourself. Just as people can recognize your voice on the telephone, readers can recognize your voice when you write.

writing process   The steps you take as you write a paragraph or other piece of writing.

Preview for Chapter 2

These are important words that you will find in Chapter 2.

1. Brainstorming
2. Focused brainstorming
3. Listing
4. Focused listing
5. Clustering
6. Focused clustering
7. Freewriting
8. Focused freewriting

Preview this chapter as you did the last. You will see that the main headings here are different from those in the last chapter, so you can expect this chapter to do something different from Chapter 1. You will also see some similarities in organization such as the definitions of key terms at the end of the chapter.

As an additional preview step, look carefully at the table of contents for this text. The table of contents is an outline of the entire book. Just as seeing how a chapter is organized can help you understand that chapter, seeing how a book is organized can help you use the book more effectively. Notice the topics presented, the progression of ideas from the beginning to the end of the book, and how the chapters relate and connect to one another. Note how Chapter 2 fits into the book's organization.

2

MORE ABOUT BRAINSTORMING FOR IDEAS

For most of us, there is nothing as terrifying as a blank piece of paper. We know that we eventually want to produce a neatly written paragraph with clearly stated ideas, an interesting approach, and no mechanical errors. But that blank page staring up at us sometimes makes this task seem impossible. Just remember, though, that a piece of writing rarely comes out perfectly the first time, even for professional writers. You simply have to start somewhere and work your way through until you've said what you want to say in the best way possible.

Sometimes when you write you will have a clear idea of what you want to say, but that's not always the case. Much of the time, you'll want to start the writing process with **brainstorming**—getting ideas on paper as fast as possible. When you brainstorm, don't worry about your handwriting, how you say something, whether it's interesting, or whether it's properly punctuated. Just get words on paper. This brainstorming does two things: it gets your ideas flowing, and it starts to fill up that blank page.

You can use brainstorming to explore a very general topic, a very specific topic, or anything in between. If you are not given a specific assignment, you can start by brainstorming for a subject. If you are to write from memory, your first step would be to brainstorm about subjects you know well. What do you know about that other people might want to know? Once you've decided on your subject (or if a more specific subject has been assigned), you can do some **focused brainstorming**. This is brainstorming that focuses on a very specific subject. In this chapter we will show you three methods of brainstorming.

Brainstorming by Listing

In Chapter 1 you already made a list of ideas about a person, so you know something about how **listing** is done. There are, however, a few rules to keep in mind when you list ideas to brainstorm a topic.

Rules for Listing

1. Don't worry about spelling, punctuation, sentence structure, or anything else. No one is going to grade or criticize your list. Its only purpose is to help you think about your subject.

2. Don't worry about using phrases or words that other people might not understand. The list is a shorthand note from you to yourself. Its purpose is to help you discover what's in your mind.

3. List as fast as you can. Stopping to think will only give your mind a chance to wander to other things. Also, one idea about a subject can often lead to another idea, and stopping will interrupt that flow.

4. List as much as you can. It doesn't matter how silly or unimportant an idea may seem at the time. Don't evaluate, just write. The more information you get into your list, the more ideas you'll have to choose from when you decide on a subject or a controlling idea.

For the writing assignment in Chapter 1, you had to pick a subject. That is, you had to choose someone to write about. You probably did a mental list of people and were able to choose a subject fairly quickly. Sometimes, though, the choices are harder, and in those cases, writing a list can help you choose your subject. If, for example, you are asked to describe a place on your campus and you can't decide which place to write about, simply begin by listing as many places as you can think of on your campus. Don't stop to ask whether a place is a good subject or not. That comes later. For right now, you're just brainstorming the possible subjects. Here's an example of a brainstorming list we did about places on our campus.

Places on campus

1. **Student Union**
2. **Music Auditorium**
3. **Cafeteria**
4. **Football Field**

5. Social Science Building
6. English Building
7. Bookstore
8. Financial Aid Office
9. Counseling Center
10. Computer Lab
11. Parking Lot
12. Library

In looking over our list, we decided we felt most comfortable with describing the bookstore, so we went there and made a list of things we saw. When we were first brainstorming to find a subject, our list was very general. Our next list of observations about the bookstore was more specific, however, since its purpose was to help us find what's worth writing about in the bookstore. We call this **focused listing** since our attention is focused on a single subject. Your brainstorming in Chapter 1 began with a focused list—a list of details you recalled as you thought about one person. Here's our more detailed brainstorming.

The Bookstore

1. cubbyholes where you must leave your belongings before entering
2. turnstiles
3. T.V. security cameras
4. school stuff for sale—T-shirts, sweatshirts, beer mugs, banners
5. textbook sections—divided by subject
6. many colors of books
7. notebooks, tablets, pencils, writing gear, "pee chee" folders
8. art materials—brushes, frames, canvases, paints, portfolios
9. munchies—candy bars, chips, cookies, Lifesavers
10. checkout counter
11. electronic cash register
12. signs—checks for amount of purchase only, no returns

Several things in this list might call our attention to specific parts of the bookstore. We might, for example, decide to write about how we feel about the security system in the bookstore, or we might choose to write about the food that is available. This focused list helps us explore our subject further and discover what is worth saying about it.

We have seen how listing can help us explore our memories about a person and how it can help us to observe a place, but listing can also help us to explore ideas. In his book *Blue Highways*, William Least Heat Moon includes a list that he made as he observed a place. His purpose in observing was to test the idea that the Texas desert is bare and lifeless.

> It was the Texas some people see as barren waste when they cross it, the part they later describe at the motel bar as "nothing." They say, "There's nothing out there."
>
> Driving through the miles of nothing, I decided to test the hypothesis and stopped somewhere in western Crockett County on the top of a broad mesa, just off Texas 29. At a distance, the land looked so rocky and dry, a religious man could believe that the First Hand never got around to the creation in here. Still, somebody had decided to string barbed wire around it.
>
> No plant grew higher than my head. For a while, I heard only miles of wind against the Ghost [his van]; but after the ringing in my ears stopped, I heard myself breathing, then a bird note, an answering call, another kind of birdsong, and another: mockingbird, mourning dove, an enigma. I heard the high zizz of flies the color of gray flannel and the deep buzz of a blue bumblebee. I made a list of nothing in particular:
>
> 1. mockingbird
> 2. mourning dove
> 3. enigma bird
> 4. gray flies
> 5. blue bumblebee
> 6. two circling buzzards (not yet, boys)
> 7. orange ants
> 8. black ants
> 9. orange-black ants (what's been going on?)
> 10. three species of spiders
> 11. opossum skull
> 12. jackrabbit (chewed on cactus)
> 13. deer (left scat)

14. coyote (left tracks)

15. small rodent (den full of seed hulls under rock)

16. snake (skin hooked on cactus spine)

17. prickly pear cactus (yellow blossoms)

18. hedgehog cactus (orange blossoms)

19. barrel cactus (red blossoms)

20. devil's pincushion (no blossoms)

21. catclaw (no better name)

22. two species of grass (neither green, both alive)

23. yellow flowers (blossoms smaller than peppercorns)

24. sage (indicates alkali-free soil)

25. mesquite (three-foot plants with eighty-foot roots to reach water that fell as rain two thousand years ago)

26. greasewood (oh, yes)

27. joint fir (steeped stems make Brigham Young tea)

28. earth

29. sky

30. wind (always)

That was all the nothing I could identify then, but had I waited until dark when the desert really comes to life, I could have done better. To say nothing is out here is incorrect; to say the desert is stingy with everything except space and light, stone and earth is closer to the truth.

Having used his list as a tool to help him see, the author concludes that the popular opinion is wrong—that the desert is not a lifeless place.

 Writing Activity 2.1

□ List places on your campus that you might describe.

□ Choose one of the places on your list.

□ Go to that place and observe it. As you observe, list your observations. Follow the Rules for Listing on page 20.

Brainstorming by Clustering

A second useful way of brainstorming is called **clustering**. The best way for us to talk about clustering is to show you what a cluster looks like, then to make some suggestions about how you can use this method. Figure 2.1 is a cluster that one student made as she thought of possible subjects for an assignment to write about a childhood memory.

Looking at this cluster, you can see that this method is quite different from listing. It shows how ideas relate to each other, and it does more to help one idea lead to another. There are four basic rules to follow when you brainstorm by clustering.

Rules for Clustering

1. First, in a circle near the center of a page, write the subject you want to brainstorm. This can be just a word, an idea, or a feeling, like "afraid," or it can be something more specific, such as "my first day in college" or "why I should not get married."

2. Next, show other related ideas in other circles. Draw lines to show how those ideas are related to the main idea or to each other. This step can also help you organize your ideas.

3. Again, work quickly. Don't stop to evaluate your idea; don't worry about spelling; don't worry about whether other people can make sense out of what you are doing.

4. When your cluster is finished, look at it. Is one part more detailed or more interesting to you than the rest? That may be the part you'll want to write about. If you're clustering to explore a subject, choose one part of your cluster and make a second cluster on that part to explore your ideas more thoroughly. This will be a focused cluster, and you might decide to do a third or fourth cluster, each more sharply focused than the one before.

In our student's cluster on a childhood memory, the part about the first grade teacher is the most detailed, but she found the Raggedy Ann costume section more interesting. It's what she really wanted to write about, so she chose to explore it further by **focused clustering**. Figure 2.2, then, is the second cluster on a childhood memory. It is focused on a specific memory suggested by the Raggedy Ann costume—Halloween in the fourth grade.

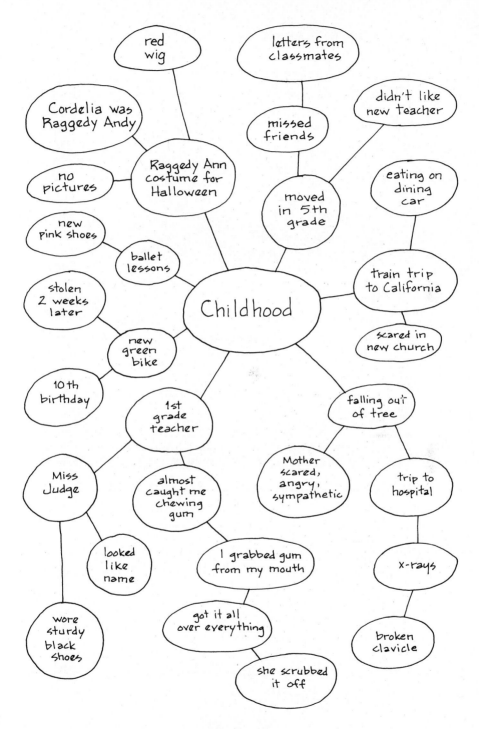

Figure 2.1

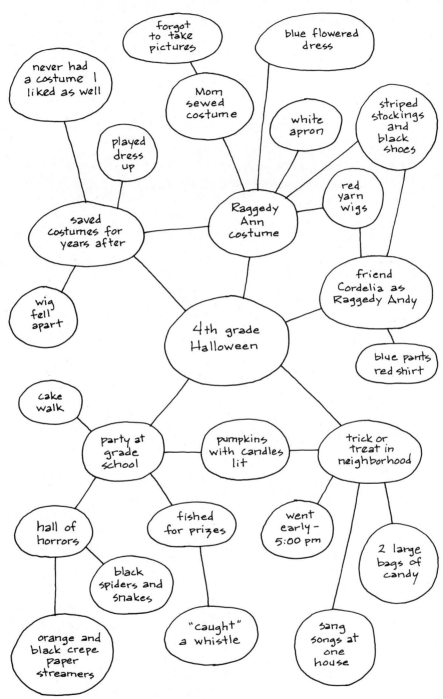

Figure 2.2

As is the case with listing, clustering can be used to explore a variety of topics—ideas, places, memories, and so on. As you continue to use these various brainstorming methods, you will see how useful they can be.

 Writing Activity 2.2

- □ Make a cluster of holiday celebrations you remember.
- □ Choose one celebration and make a focused cluster on that celebration.
- □ Follow the Rules for Clustering on page 24.

Brainstorming by Freewriting

The third method of brainstorming we'll discuss is called **freewriting**. The techniques are simple but effective.

Rules for Freewriting

1. Start writing about anything, and don't stop. Try to write for at least ten minutes without picking up your pen from the paper or your fingers from the keyboard of your word processor. If you need to repeat a word, repeat it. If you need to write nonsense, write nonsense. Just don't stop writing. As one of our colleagues says, "Write your heart and guts out."

2. Don't pay attention to spelling, punctuation, proper language, or anything else like that. No one needs to see this but you, and no one will tell you it's wrong.

3. When you're finished, look over what you've written. Have you repeated an idea several times? Is there anything that stands out as especially interesting? These are possible topics for your writing.

4. To explore one of these topics, select an idea, concentrate on it for a few minutes, then freewrite again for at least ten minutes. This is called **focused freewriting**, and, like the other forms of focused brainstorming, it helps you to explore ideas more fully.

Here's an example of freewriting that one of our students did. Like the clusters assignment, it is about a childhood experience.

Freewrite on a Childhood Experience

Riding horses at grandpa's farm . . riding in the car with my mom and dad, going to the park I liked to lead the ponie . . . riding my bike in the early mornings. My birthday. My surprise birthday party. We were over at a freinds housemyfamily and I. It was my birthday that day. I was telling everyone it was my birthday. going to the party—I was excited. I was always the most excited when we visited grandma and grandpa at there farm. that farm. It was in Alberta. Sleeping upstairs, getting up early, puffed wheat in the kitchen. The barn, the cows, milking the cows killing that chicken messy. Granpa let us ride the horse up and down the road. the time I fell off and had to walk home with dad.

As the student reread her freewrite, she quickly realized that she wanted to write about the times she had at her grandpa's farm. She then continued with a focused freewrite on that more specific subject.

Focused Freewrite on Experiences at the Farm

I remember sleeping upstairs on a soft soft bed with a down quilt over me. Getting up at the crow of the roosters and hurriedly eating breakfast, a bowl of puffed wheat. Grandma bought a great big plastic bag of this cereal. I like it to this day. Then I'd hurry outside and run to the barn with uncle Bob and help him milk the cows, he would let me try to squeeze the utter but I couldn't get much milk out. Then he would give me a squirt of milk in my mouth, but I wasn't too crazy about warm milk. They did have milking machines and I got to put my finger in one—just a nice gentle squeeze. Then it was collecting the eggs and feeding the animals. There were twin calves born just before we got there and my sister and I got to name them. We called them Spic and Span. The mama cow was very gentle

and grandpa would let us ride her around the barnyard. She was bony and very uncomfortable so we didn't ride her very much. I remember the time grandpa had to kill some chickens for our dinner. He let one go after its head was chopped off just so we could see what happened, what a mess but we laughed and screamed with excitement. What a morning it was when my sister and I got to ride on the tractor with my uncle to the cows that were in another pasture down the road. We could see our breath it was so cold. An early frost that year. I remember the flighty young horse, too flighty for young inexperienced children like us. My dad put us on the back of the horse and lead us down the road. I was the smallest and I was on the back . . . I began to slip and held on to my sister and we both ended up in the ditch. I had the wind knocked out of me so I walked back home beside my dad.

This focused freewrite provided a wealth of specific detail for the student. She did not know that she remembered so much about the farm, and she ended with many possible topics from which to choose.

Like listing and clustering, freewriting can be used to brainstorm any subject. We have told you about it and shown you how it works; now try it for yourself.

 Writing Activity 2.3

□ Freewrite to explore possible subjects for a paragraph about a childhood experience.

□ Choose an experience and do a focused freewrite on that experience.

□ In both of these steps, follow the Rules for Freewriting on page 27.

As you wrote your paragraph for Chapter 1, you probably added details that were not on your original brainstorming list, for the flow of ideas continued as you drafted and revised. Brainstorming is, above all, a way to get started, but its usefulness doesn't end there. Writing is a process of dealing with ideas, and ideas change as we deal with them. As a result, you may find yourself going back to the brainstorming step as you draft and revise what you write.

If part of a paragraph gives you trouble, do a list, cluster, or freewrite on that part. Every step of the writing process can lead you to new discoveries about your subject, and a new discovery can take you back to an earlier step in the process. This is good. As you progress through this book, you will develop the ability to see when you need to move from one step to another and back, but what's important right now is that you know how to use the techniques of brainstorming—listing, clustering, and freewriting.

You have had some practice in these techniques, and you will use them throughout this book. You will probably find that you prefer one method over the others, but you will also find that different techniques are useful in different writing situations. The more experience you have in using these techniques, the better you'll be able to choose the right one for you in any situation. Refer back to this chapter whenever you need to refresh your memory.

Terms to Remember

brainstorming   Letting ideas flow freely from your mind without pausing to make judgments about them. This technique is often used when a group of people are trying to solve a problem. People suggest possible solutions as they think of them, no matter how far-fetched or silly the solution may seem, for often a silly idea can suggest a serious possibility that might not have been thought of otherwise. For a writer, brainstorming offers a way to discover and explore ideas.

clustering   A kind of brainstorming that shows in a map-like picture (circles, squares, lines, and so on) how ideas and details relate to one another.

focused brainstorming   Brainstorming may be focused or unfocused. We use unfocused brainstorming when we are just searching for a topic on which to write. When we focus our attention on a single topic and brainstorm just on that topic, we call it focused brainstorming.

focused clustering   Clustering that focuses on a specific detail or topic to help a writer discover and explore more specifically what is worth writing about on that topic.

focused freewriting   Freewriting that focuses on a specific item or idea. The writer spends a few minutes thinking about or focusing his attention on the topic on which he wishes to do a focused freewrite. Then he freewrites about that topic.

focused listing   The more specific form of brainstorming by listing. A writer may list to discover subjects she might write about, but when she has decided on a subject she does a more sharply focused list just on that subject or on some aspect of that subject.

freewriting   Brainstorming by writing without stopping and with no concern for spelling, punctuation, sentence structure, and so on. The aim of freewriting is to let ideas flow from your mind to the paper.

listing   Brainstorming by writing down words and phrases as they come to mind, in much the same way we would write a grocery list.

Preview for Chapter 3

Here are some words and phrases to look for in this chapter.

1. Narrative
2. Dominant impression
3. Point of view
4. Time line
5. Chronological order

As you preview Chapter 3, you will see that this chapter is like Chapter 1. You will again follow the five steps of the writing process in order to write a paragraph. For this chapter, though, we'll add to the preview step to give you some experience in learning word meanings from context. *Context* means the words, phrases, and sentences that surround another word, and the context of a word often contains valuable clues to the word's meaning. Becoming conscious of this fact can help you as a reader and as a writer.

To preview Chapter 3, count the pages so you'll know about how long it will take you to read it, and then go page by page through the chapter. Read each main heading, and when you see one of the words on our vocabulary list, read the sentence just before and just after it (the key words are printed in boldface when they first appear in the chapter). Guess at the meaning, and then read the definition on page 46 or 47 to see whether your guess was right.

Like most chapter surveys, this one should take less than five minutes, and the payoff in learning will be great.

3

WRITING ABOUT AN EXPERIENCE

This chapter will continue the development of your writing skills by taking you once again through the five steps of the writing process you followed in the first chapter:

1. exploring your subject by brainstorming
2. writing the topic sentence
3. outlining or planning the paragraph
4. writing the first draft
5. revising the paragraph

You will be writing a paragraph about an experience you have had, and we'll discuss some of the special things you must do when you write a **narrative**, or story-telling, paragraph. To start writing, begin by brainstorming.

STEP 1:
Brainstorming for Ideas

You have had hundreds of experiences, so your first brainstorming for a topic is an important step. Of all of your experiences, which are worth writing about? Some are dull, some are nobody's business, some are funny, some are exciting, and so on. Figure 3.1 is a cluster that one of our students, Aldin, did as he explored possible topics for this assignment. Even   33

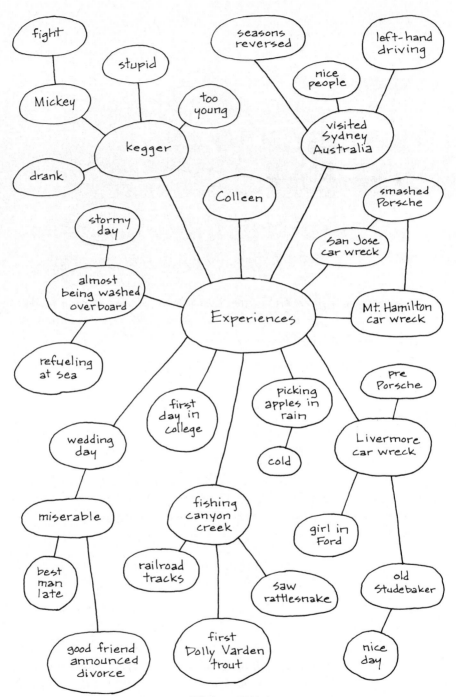

Figure 3.1

without knowing the details of Aldin's experience, you can see how some ideas suggested others and how the writer thought of details and saw connections as he brainstormed.

 Writing Activity 3.1

□ Make a cluster like the one in Figure 3.1 to brainstorm experiences you might write about.

□ Work quickly; write down ideas as they come to you, and don't worry about the order in which the ideas occur. Let your brain work freely.

Looking back at his cluster (Figure 3.1), Aldin decided to do a focused cluster on the Livermore car wreck. He had three car wrecks on his first cluster, and the Livermore wreck seemed to have some good detail in it. It looked like it might be an interesting subject to work with. Figure 3.2 shows his focused cluster.

As Aldin added on more details, they reminded him of others, and he found that he remembered the event more vividly than he had at first thought he would. This will frequently happen as you brainstorm.

 Writing Activity 3.2

□ Choose an experience from your cluster from activity 3.1 and do a focused cluster on that experience.

□ Again, work quickly, letting one idea suggest another.

□ Don't stop to question or criticize your ideas. Your purpose is to discover what is in your memory and to nudge it to the surface.

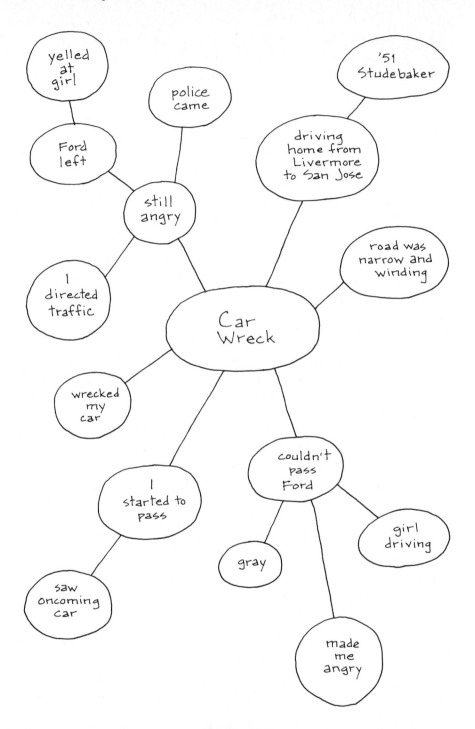

Figure 3.2

STEP 2:
Writing the Topic Sentence

There are two steps in writing a topic sentence for a narrative paragraph. First, you must identify a word or idea that will control the paragraph, and then you must write a topic sentence that contains that word or idea. The word or idea will be your **dominant impression** of the experience. Something that is dominant is something that stands out above everything else. You have been stating your dominant impressions of events all your life. For example, when you say, "That was really fun," you have identified *fun* as the dominant impression of the experience you're talking about. "That was the scariest thing that ever happened to me" is another statement of a dominant impression, and so is, "That lecture totally confused me." *Scary* and *confusing* are the key ideas in the last two examples.

Clustering helps you relive the experience you are exploring, so think about thoughts and emotions you had as you clustered about your experience. There's a good possibility that you have written a word that states your dominant impression or that you have repeated one idea within your cluster. For example, from his second cluster (Figure 3.2), Aldin identified *anger* as the dominant impression.

The second step in writing a topic sentence for a narrative is to state the dominant impression in a complete sentence, like this:

I was angry at the girl in the Ford.

That's a complete sentence, and it certainly focuses on anger. It would make an effective topic sentence for Aldin's paragraph.

 Writing Activity 3.3

- □ Write your own topic sentence about the incident you detailed in activity 3.2.
- □ Check to make sure it's a complete sentence, and be sure that it focuses on the dominant impression you have of the event.

STEP 3:
Outlining the Paragraph

Now we're ready to go on to the next step, outlining the paragraph. Remember that the first step in outlining is to turn your topic sentence into a question that begins with *who, what, when, where, why, how,* or *in what way.* Use the words from your topic sentence to complete your question. This keeps your attention focused on the controlling idea; it helps you to be sure that the controlling idea does, in fact, control the paragraph. Here is Aldin's question.

What made me angry at the girl in the Ford?

He will answer the question by choosing from the details on his cluster. Here, then, is his outline:

Topic sentence:

I was angry at the girl in the Ford.

Topic sentence question:

What made me angry at the girl in the Ford?

Answers (be sure to use complete sentences):

1. **I wanted to go fast in the corners, and she slowed down.**
2. **I wanted to pass her, and she sped up.**
3. **When I finally did get past her, I wrecked my car.**

The outline of a narrative often has only a few main points. When you just sketch the events of an experience, it usually doesn't sound like much of a story. The story can't come to life until you develop it by providing the audience with the details that will let them experience the events.

Writing Activity 3.4   ▫ Now write your outline from your material of activities 3.2 and 3.3.

- ☐ Be sure to use the important words from your topic sentence in your question.
- ☐ Be sure that your answers are complete sentences.

STEP 4:
Writing the First Draft

In the eight categories of "Standards for Judging Writing" (pages 11–12), one question about development asks, "Have you provided enough information for your reader to see or feel or understand what you're talking about?" Your task in writing about an experience is to re-create for your reader what the experience was like for you. You can do this by showing your reader not just *what* happened but also *how* it happened and how you felt about it. If you've chosen an experience you remember well and have done a good job of brainstorming and outlining, you'll be off to a good start.

One more thing you must consider before you begin your first draft is where your story will begin and end. Experiences themselves seldom have clear beginnings and endings: there are always things that happened before and after. When you tell a story, however, you must start and stop somewhere. For his story, Aldin chose not to talk about what happened before he got behind the girl in the Ford, and he decided not to include any information about what happened when the police and the wrecker arrived. Here's his first draft.

Draft 1

One warm, fall afternoon I was hurrying home to San Jose. The road I was on was narrow, and it had a lot of curves. Even though it was a winding road, I was having fun driving fast through the corners. I was about to buy a sports car, and I really wanted to practice cornering. Then I came up behind a gray Ford; the girl driving it braked hard at every turn. And each time we came to a straight stretch, she accelerated so I couldn't pass her. I was becoming angrier by the second. Finally, I started to pass, and just as I did I saw a car coming towards me. I hadn't seen it before because it had been hidden in a small depression in the road. I tried to cut back in, but I didn't make it. My car ran up on the bank and tipped over. Now I was really angry, so when the girl in the Ford stopped, I shouted at her to go on. I directed traffic until the police came.

This draft has a clear starting and stopping point, but it lacks the details that might really make it come to life for a reader. To make it do so, Aldin must help the reader see the experience through his own eyes, that is, from his own **point of view**. It is, after all, Aldin's experience, so the reading audience doesn't know how he sees the events unless he shows them. The details of Aldin's story would change if they were told from the viewpoint of the girl driving the Ford or from that of the highway patrol officer who investigated the wreck. The story would change even if Aldin were writing about the incident from his point of view today, many years after the accident. The topic sentence might then become, "I realize now how foolish I was."

To show his audience how he felt at the time, Aldin must choose details that show more about each of his main points. He has told us of the events, but he hasn't shown us what makes those events live in his mind. The idea of anger does not appear until halfway into the paragraph, and only his use of the detail, "I shouted at her to go on" *shows* his anger. He needs to add more details that will show his emotions, for his emotions are what make him remember the event.

 Writing Activity 3.5

□ Write the first draft of your paragraph you've outlined in activity 3.4. Remember that you were there, but your reader wasn't.

□ Use your cluster to remind yourself about the small details which are still in your head. You might take these images for granted, but your reader needs them in order to understand the event.

Step 5:
Revising the Paragraph

As we discussed Aldin's paragraph with him and looked back at his focused cluster, we suggested he return to the brainstorming step before writing another draft. While his cluster for a subject had been thorough, he had, he said, gotten in a hurry and raced through his focused cluster. The result was that he had not explored his subject thoroughly, so his paragraph lacked the details that he later discovered in his second focused cluster. Figure 3.3 shows the result of his second, closer look at the experience.

The new cluster helped Aldin to remember details he thought he had forgotten, and he soon became so enthusiastic about his subject that he began to experiment with it. The final result was three more drafts in which he showed the events in different orders.

Aldin's three drafts—any one of which could be a final draft—show that a narrative paragraph can re-create events in the order that they actually happened or *in a different order.* In other words, you can control the **time line** of a narrative. In the second draft of his paragraph, for example, Aldin uses strict **chronological order**, starting at the beginning and going straight through to the end, just as events happen in real life. Notice that we see the driver's anger in the second sentence ("I shouted") but that the controlling idea isn't stated until the middle of the paragraph ("By this time I was furious"). It is given again at the end of the paragraph ("I was still angry at the girl in the Ford").

Draft 2

The brake lights on the Ford sedan ahead flashed again as the driver braked hard for another gentle turn. "Drive it or park it!" I shouted, though I knew she couldn't hear me. For no good reason, I was in a hurry to get home, and besides, I enjoyed driving my '51 Studebaker Landcruiser coupe fast through the corners. As we came on to a straight stretch, I accelerated to pass her, but she accelerated too. The old Studebaker just wouldn't do it. Again we crept through a corner at a snail's pace. By this time I was furious. The next straight stretch was short, and I knew she wouldn't accelerate, so I started around her. I almost made it. When the oncoming car

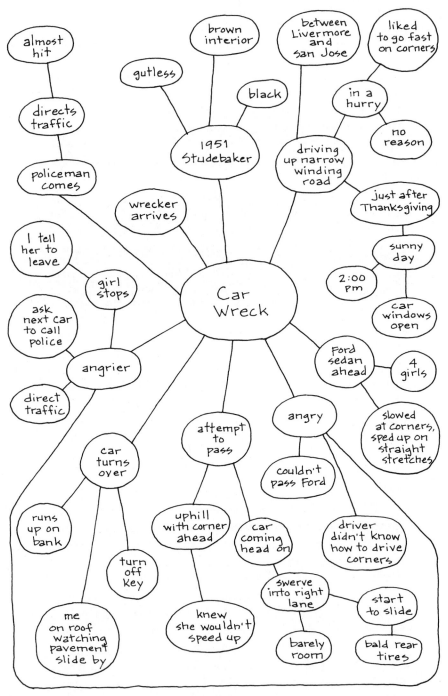

Figure 3.3

suddenly appeared from a small depression in the road, I cut sharply in front of the Ford. I felt the bald rear tires slide toward the bank, corrected, felt the car move up the bank and flip neatly over onto its top. The next thing I knew, I was sitting on the inside of the roof of the car watching the pavement slide by beneath the shattered windshield. The car skidded to a stop, I reached up and turned the key off, then crawled out the partly open door. "Are you all right?" one of the girls shouted from the Ford. "Yes, get out of here," I snarled, and the Ford left. As I directed traffic around the wreck, I was still angry at the girl in the Ford. Even today I remember my frustration at not being able to play "sports car" in the California mountains on a warm fall day.

In the next version of his paragraph, the writer starts in the middle of things, then lets us know how he got into the situation, and finally shows us how it ends. Obviously, events don't happen in this order in real life, but we see this time line in books, in movies, and on television all the time. It draws us immediately into the story and keeps us interested in finding out what will happen next.

In this version, we see the anger in the third sentence ("And it was all that stupid girl's fault"), a version of the controlling idea near the middle ("I was furious at her"), and another version near the end ("my anger died a little"). Though stated specifically in those three places, the dominant impression, anger, is apparent throughout.

Draft 3

Sitting on the roof of my '51 Studebaker Landcruiser coupe watching the pavement slide by beneath the shattered windshield, I felt the car skid to a stop, reached up and turned the key off, then looked for a way out. My car was wrecked; there was no question about that. And it was all that stupid girl's fault! Why had she braked for every corner? Why hadn't she let me pass on a straight stretch? It had started out to be such a nice drive home. For no good reason, I had been in a hurry, and besides, I enjoyed driving my car fast through the corners. I'd gotten behind her Ford just as we started through the pass. She'd braked at the gentlest corners but accelerated hard at each straight stretch. I was furious at her, but my old Studebaker just didn't have the guts to pass until we came to a short straight stretch followed by a sharp turn. I knew she wouldn't speed up for that one. I was nearly around her when the oncoming car suddenly appeared from a small dip in the road. I cut sharply in front of the Ford and felt the bald rear tires slide toward the bank. I corrected, but the car rode up the bank and flipped neatly over onto its top. As I crawled through the partly open door, one of the girls shouted, "Are you all right?" "Yes," I snarled. "Get out of here!" The Ford left. As I directed traffic around the wreck, my anger died a little, but not much. Even today, I remember my frustration at not being able to play "sports car" in the California mountains on a warm fall day.

Notice that the change in order from draft 2 to draft 3 involved much more than just shifting the sentences around. All of the main ideas are still there, and most of the words are the same, but only the last sentence is exactly the same.

The fourth and final version of Aldin's paragraph begins at the end, moves quickly to the beginning, and then gradually returns to the end. The controlling idea is stated in the first sentence ("I was furious"), and it is strongly suggested in the last ("wish that I'd hit her").

Draft 4

As I directed traffic around the remains of my upside down Studebaker, I was furious. I didn't even know the girl, but I wished I had punched her. It was all her fault. If she'd known how a car should be driven, it never would have happened. You don't brake in corners; you accelerate through them. Anyone who's ever wanted to race sports cars knows that. But she had braked for every gentle corner and accelerated on every straight stretch, and my old Studebaker just didn't have the guts to get around her until we came to a short straight stretch followed by a sharp curve. Knowing she wouldn't accelerate, I started around her and almost made it.

When I cut back in to avoid a car that suddenly appeared out of a small depression in the road, the bald back tires let go, and my car drifted up onto the steep bank. It flipped slowly over onto its top, and the next thing I knew I was sitting on its roof watching pavement slide by beneath the shattered windshield. I remember reaching up, turning off the key, and crawling out the partly open door, but mostly I remember my anger when one of the girls in the Ford shouted, "Are you all right?" How dare they even ask? My car was wrecked, and it was all their fault. "Get out of here!" I snarled. Wisely, they left, and I had a few moments to collect my thoughts before the first of the traffic showed up. All I had to do until the police arrived was to direct traffic and wish that I'd hit her.

We have seen Aldin's narrative progress from his original clusters to three very effective versions of a final draft. Let's take a final look at some of the things the writer did to make those drafts effective. First, he was thorough in his exploration of subjects. He had a variety of topics from which to choose, and he was able to choose one with which his audience could probably identify. Most of us have been in similar situations, and we have all experienced anger and frustration. Next, when he did a thorough cluster of his chosen subject, the writer identified details that would help the reader to see his experience as he saw it, and it is those details that make the final drafts come to life. Finally, Aldin was willing to experiment with the time lines of his narrative and with the ways in which he combined the various ideas of his paragraph. The result is a paragraph that lets a reader see the events as the writer saw them, and that's what makes the paragraph work.

 Writing Activity 3.6

□ Revise your paragraph.

□ Review your rough draft and ask yourself whether it begins at the time you want it to and ends when you want it to. Remember that you can present the events in a different order from the one in which they actually happened, but it is probably best to use chronological order, at least until you have a detailed draft you're satisfied with. Then you can start to play with the order of events to make it more exciting.

□ Be sure your dominant impression is evident throughout your paragraph. In other words, be sure that your controlling idea controls what goes into the paragraph and what stays out.

□ Finally, be consistent in your point of view. Obviously, you are telling the story, but are you telling it as you saw it then or as you see it now?

Other Suggestions for Writing

1. Read pages 110–13 and do Writing Activity 7.4 (page 110), 7.5 (page 112) or 7.6 (page 113).
2. Write about a frightening experience you have had.
3. Write about a mistake you once made and what happened as a result.
4. Write about something that happened to you recently that made you feel glad to be alive.
5. Write about a time when everything seemed to go wrong at home, at work, or at school.
6. Write about your first day in a new school.
7. Write about a time you performed exceptionally well in a sporting event.

Terms to Remember

chronological order   The order in which events actually happen. A paragraph with its details presented in chronological order will start with the first thing that happened and end with the last.

dominant impression   The overall or most important feeling about something. Your dominant impression of a person, place, or event will usually be the controlling word in your topic sentence.

narrative   A re-telling of an experience or series of events, usually in chronological order.

point of view   The standpoint from which ideas are presented. A story, for example, might be told from the point of view of the person doing the action, the person to whom the action is being done, a person observing the action, a person hearing about the action later, and so on.

time line   The time order in which ideas are presented. Your time line may be chronological, but it may also begin somewhere in the middle or be completely reversed. By changing the time line, the writer changes the order in which the reader sees the events.

Preview for Chapter 4

The list of important words for this chapter is short.

1. Lead
2. Thesaurus
3. Sentence structure
4. Wordiness

Because you have already previewed and read three chapters of this book, you are familiar with the organization of each chapter. You have seen that each one begins with a list of important words to look for as you read; you know how to look for context clues to the meaning of those words; and you know that the words are formally defined at the end of each chapter. By now you realize that the more you know about a chapter *before* you read it, the more easily you will understand that chapter as you read. Thus, another helpful preview technique is to read the end material such as chapter summaries, vocabulary definitions, and writing assignments before you read the chapter. These things can tell you what you should know by the time you finish reading a chapter, and you will read any textbook chapter more quickly and with better understanding when you know the important things to look for as you read.

4

![decorative line marking]

More about Revising

In Chapter 2 we explored the task of brainstorming, one of the most important of the five steps of the writing process. In this chapter, we will focus on the task of revising. To *revise*, remember, means to "see again" and then to make the changes that you see need to be made. We will show you some ways to "see" your work again so that you can decide what changes will help your audience better understand what you have to say.

You may often be reluctant to go back and change what you have written, but the truth is that most of us seldom do our best job on our first try. Also, as we work on a piece of writing, we develop a kind of "pride of ownership" and, at the same time, an inability to see how something might be said differently. Although it takes time and effort, revision leads to clearer communication, pride in a job well done, and higher grades.

The most common form of communication is talking, but writing is different from talking. When you talk, you almost always have an audience who will respond to you. Likewise, you can respond to them. They can ask you questions when they don't understand, they can look puzzled, or they can rephrase what you have said, repeating it back to you in their own words to make sure they understand. You, in turn, can back up to provide information you forgot, can pick up where you left off after an interruption, and can use facial expressions, body movements, and voice changes to help express your meaning. When you write, however, you don't have the advantage of this give and take with your readers. They must be able to understand clearly your ideas and feelings only from your printed words.

As a writer, you must picture your audience in your mind, and you must try to communicate your ideas to that audience. Even for professionals, this is sometimes not easy. A major purpose of revision, then, is   49 to make sure that you have expressed yourself so your reading audience can clearly follow your ideas.

As the first step in revision, let your writing get cold before you begin to revise. That is, don't look at it for twenty-four hours before you start your revision. This waiting period lets you approach your work with a fresh eye and mind. Of course, given deadlines and due dates, waiting a day is not always possible, but try to give it at least a few hours' rest.

When your work is cold, reread it and ask yourself whether you are really discussing what you want to discuss. Because the process of writing is a process of discovery, sometimes as you write, you may discover that your ideas have changed. Here, for example, is a paragraph in which a student began with one idea and, after letting her work get cold, decided that she really wanted to discuss only a small part of her original topic.

Marla's First Rough Draft

Being Homecoming Queen was a thrilling experience for me. The night after I was crowned queen, I was at the Homecoming Dance. My four princesses were there on stage with me. We all wore long dresses, but I was the only one with a crown, and that was exciting. It was a great honor to represent my school as Homecoming Queen, but I was nervous. I knew that the Master of Ceremonies was going to call me to come and give the welcoming speech, and I started to sweat. When he did, I walked across the stage, and my knees were shaking. When I finished, I was glad to have it over with. I knew I'd share the first dance with the captain of the football team.

When we first discussed this rough draft with Marla, we suggested that she might want to drop the sentences about being nervous since they didn't seem to support the controlling word, "thrilling." We suggested that she add more details about what made the evening thrilling. Marla, however, said that as she thought about it, being nervous was the main thing she remembered, and she thought it would be better to use "nervous" as her dominant impression.

After brainstorming about her nervousness, Marla revised her paragraph, and the revision became the first draft of a paragraph with a new controlling idea.

Marla's Second Rough Draft

Giving the welcoming speech at the homecoming dance made me very nervous. As I sat with my princesses on stage, I knew it was only a matter of minutes before the master of ceremonies was going to call my name. I started to sweat and was afraid I would ruin my gown. I repeated my speech over and over in my head. When I heard my name, I stood up and attempted to walk across the stage, but my knees were shaking and I could hardly walk. Standing at the microphone, I looked out at what seemed to be hundreds of faces that blurred in front of me. I forgot my speech. I opened my mouth, squeaked a hello, a thank you, something I can't remember, and then I fled back to the safety of my chair. It wasn't until later when I was dancing the first dance with the captain of the football team that I started to relax and have a good time.

This second draft has some of the same elements of the first draft, but it's a very different paragraph. Having revised her paragraph so that it focused on the topic she really wanted to discuss, Marla was ready to begin a more detailed revision.

As we promised, we will show you some ways of deciding what changes will improve your paragraph, so when your paragraph is ready for a detailed revision, begin by doing the following steps:

1. *Listen to it.* There are two ways of listening to your paper. One is to read it aloud to yourself, and the other is to have someone read it to you. Try both of these methods and see which one works better for you. Hearing how your ideas sound in spoken language is an amazingly effective way to find places where you haven't expressed yourself clearly enough. It also helps you spot when you're using stuffy or phony language, rather than writing in your own, natural voice.

2. *Read it with a different eye.* Pretend you are someone whose opinion you respect and would ask for. Spend a few minutes thinking about how that person might look at your paper, then read it as if you were that person. Seeing your writing from a different point of view can help you evaluate it more objectively.

3. *Analyze it.* Review the criteria for judging writing we listed in Chapter 1 (pages 11–12), and read your paper, asking the suggested questions.

As you do these steps, make notes in the margins of your paper about problems you see or things you might change. When you're finished, you are ready to begin the actual revision of your work. As you revise, you will see that when you make one change, others are necessary; these other changes often occur naturally. It is probably not possible to tell you everything you should look for as you revise. Writing is too individual an activity for that. However, we can tell you that good writers often play with their writing. They experiment with words, sentences, and ideas. That fact, then, leads us to a list of things you should try to achieve in your revision:

1. an interesting opening
2. developed ideas
3. effective vocabulary
4. varied sentence structure

Revising for Interesting Openings

As you revise, pay particular attention to the introduction or opening of your paragraphs. The opening sentence, or **lead**, is especially important because it should catch your readers' attention enough to make them interested in reading further. In effect, it "grabs" your readers and draws them into your writing.

Effective leads come in many forms. In Chapter 3 we saw three different openings of the same story when the writer began at a different place in the action. One reason for changing time order might be to catch reader interest by starting at a dramatic moment. Some other ways to catch reader interest might be to open with a startling fact, a quotation, a brief story to illustrate your point, or a detailed description to set the scene. Consider this lead from Lewis Thomas' essay, "On Warts."

> Warts are wonderful structures. They can appear overnight on any part of the skin, like mushrooms on a damp lawn, full grown and splendid in the complexity of their architecture.

This is an effective opening, a real "grabber," because it begins with a startling statement (few people would call warts wonderful) and because of the comparison between warts and mushrooms.

Or consider this lead from Joan Didion's "On Morality":

> As it happens I am in Death Valley, in a room at the Enterprise Motel and Trailer Park, and it is July, and it is hot. In fact, it is 119 degrees.

This is effective because her use of specific detail quickly pulls the reader into the writer's situation.

 Writing Activity 4.1

- ▢ Using the five-step method you've learned, write a paragraph describing a person or an experience.
- ▢ Write a lead that gives a startling fact about the person or experience you described.
- ▢ Write a lead in which you begin by quoting something that person often says, or write a lead by giving a quote of something you or someone else said in your experience.
- ▢ Write a lead in which you set a scene where that person is often found or where that event took place.
- ▢ Keep this paragraph handy for future reference.

Revising to Develop Ideas

English teachers often write "show, don't tell" on student papers. What they mean is that the student should add details, examples, and comparisons. These additions help your reader to see what you saw, hear what you heard, and so on. If a reader is not familiar with your subject, he should be able to say when he is finished reading, "Oh, so *that's* the way it is." If he is familiar with your subject, he should be able to say, "Yes, that's *just* the way it is."

Your early drafts of paragraphs will often be full of sentences that just tell, for you will be concentrating on getting ideas onto paper. When you revise, however, you will need to look specifically for places where you might add detail to show. To illustrate, we have rewritten a wonderful paragraph by Rachel Carson, a famous naturalist, and in our rewrite we have left out the details she put in. We have told while Rachel Carson has shown. Here's our telling version, followed by the paragraph as it originally appeared in the book *The Edge of the Sea*. (We have made notes on her original version to show some of the more effective uses of words and details that show the scene as the writer saw it.)

Our Version

One of my favorite paths to a rocky seacoast goes through an evergreen forest that I find enchanting. I usually go there in the early morning when it's barely light and slightly foggy. Many of the trees are dead—some standing and some fallen. All of them have moss and lichens growing on them. Moss also covers the ground. It's very quiet because the forest seems to muffle the sounds of nature.

Original Version

One of my own favorite approaches to a rocky seacoast is by a rough path through an evergreen forest that has its own peculiar enchantment. It is usually an early morning tide that takes me along that forest path, so that the light is still pale and fog drifts in from the sea beyond. It is almost a ghost forest, for among the living spruce and balsam are many dead trees—some sagging earthward, some lying on the floor of the forest. All the trees, the living and the dead, are clothed with green and silver crusts of lichens. Tufts of the bearded lichen or old man's beard hang from the branches like bits of sea mist tangled there. Green woodland mosses and a yielding carpet of reindeer moss cover the ground. In the quiet of that place even the voice of the

"pale" "drifts" "ghost forest" show enchantment and allow reader to sense mood

details help reader to see dead trees

comparisons help reader see moss

"yielding carpet" helps reader feel moss underfoot

surf is reduced to a whispered echo and the
sounds of the forest are but the ghosts of
sound—the faint sighing of evergreen needles
in the moving air; the creaks and heavier
groans of half-fallen trees resting against
their neighbors and rubbing bark against
bark; the light rattling fall of a dead branch
broken under the feet of a squirrel and sent
bouncing and ricocheting earthward.

"whispered echo,"
"ghosts of sound,"
and specific
examples help
reader hear

 **Writing
Activity
4.2**

- □ Using the paragraph you wrote for activity 4.1, find sentences that merely tell.

- □ As you read, make notes or marks in the margins to identify where you need to make changes or additions.

- □ Revise your paragraph so it includes the details, examples, and comparisons that show.

Revising for Effective Vocabulary

The words you choose as you write do a great deal to show not only what you are writing about but also your attitude toward your subject. For example, we might write, "The skinny girl walked in," or "The slender lady glided in," or "The lithe woman slinked in." Each of these sentences could describe the same event, but each shows a different attitude on the part of the writer.

Carefully chosen words can convey actions, ideas, and emotions in very powerful ways. To illustrate, we have again taken the liberty of changing a paragraph, this time one by the well-known author John Steinbeck. Again, we'll first look at our version; then we'll see what made the original more effective.

Our Version

The wind got there when they said it would, and blew hard across the water. It hit like a ton of bricks. The top of a tree blew off, almost hitting the place where we watched.

The next gust pushed one of the windows in. I pushed it back and put wedges in the top and bottom with a hand ax. . . . The trees waved and bent, and the water became foamy. A boat got loose and blew up on the shore, and then another.

Original Version

The wind struck on the moment we were told it would, and ripped the water like a black sheet. It hammered like a fist. The whole top of an oak tree crashed down, grazing the cottage where we watched. The next gust stove one of the big windows in. I forced it back and drove wedges in top and bottom with a hand ax. . . . The trees plunged and bent like grasses, and the whipped water raised a cream of foam. A boat broke loose and tobogganed up on the shore, and then another.

Words like "struck," "ripped," "hammered," "crashed," "stove," "forced," "drove," "plunged," "bent," and "tobogganed" certainly show the fury and activity Steinbeck wanted to portray.

As you experiment with words, use a **thesaurus**. A thesaurus is a dictionary-like book that lists words and gives other words with similar and opposite meanings. As a treasure-house of words, it can be an important tool for a writer, but we must offer a caution: be sure to use a dictionary with it. Sometimes the thesaurus will give you a word that means almost the same thing as another, but there may be enough of a difference in meaning to make it inappropriate for the way you want to use it.

 Writing Activity 4.3

- □ Once again look at your paragraph from activity 4.1.
- □ Underline words that you think could be made stronger.
- □ Using a thesaurus, find words to replace at least five of those you underlined.
- □ Be sure to use a dictionary for any word you are not certain about.

Revising for Clear Sentences

Sentences are the basic unit for expressing ideas in the English language. If you are a native speaker of English, you know a tremendous amount about sentences already, and you are often a good judge of whether a sentence is clear. When a sentence is not clear, however, analyzing why it isn't can be a complex task. Most of the sections of our appendix talk about ways of making your sentences clear, and much of your education as a writer will deal with this problem. Obviously, then, we cannot hope to do more than brush the surface of this important skill in this short section. We can, however, offer the following suggestions.

Sentence Checklist

1. Be sure each of your sentences expresses at least one complete thought. To check a paragraph, write your first sentence on a piece of paper, and read the sentence aloud. This allows your eye to see the sentence as a complete unit. It also converts the written language to the more familiar spoken language, thus allowing you to check the sentence for completeness by hearing it. If it is not a complete thought, revise the sentence until it is. Then skip a line, write the paragraph's next sentence, and read it aloud on its own, revising as necessary. Repeat this procedure for each sentence in your paragraph. For a more detailed discussion of checking your sentences, see the Appendix.
2. Try varying your **sentence structure**. Often an idea becomes clearer when it is paired with other ideas. Take, for example, the following sentences:

    My daughter Jennifer hates school. She loves to go downtown. She loves to hang out in the record stores.

    We can give the reader that same information more simply and clearly by combining those three sentences into one:

    My daughter Jennifer hates school, but she loves to hang out in the record stores downtown.

Often, however, an idea can become clearer when it is set off by itself as a separate sentence instead of included in another. Here's an example.

"All right, young man! If you think you're tougher than your dad, stand up!" shouted my father, so I stood up.

Look at the emphasis the last idea gains when it is set off by itself:

"All right, young man! If you think you're tougher than your dad, stand up!" shouted my father. I stood up.

3. Eliminate **wordiness** and stuffy or phony language. Many people seem to think that using long sentences and big words will make their writing sound good, but when the lengths of the sentences and words interfere with meaning, the writing is ineffective. It doesn't do what it is intended to do. Here is a student example from a recent paper:

It is my sincere hope that my college education will enable me to find employment in the area of education teaching at the fifth-grade level.

Revised, the sentence reads:

I hope that my education will help me find a job as a fifth-grade teacher.

As the next example shows, even professionals fall into the trap of thinking that longer is better. This is the first paragraph from an article in the *Journal of Higher Education.*

The term "computer literacy" has become <u>de rigueur</u> among <u>avant garde</u> educators and public officials. Despite its frequent use, however, computer literacy remains an amorphous concept. The purpose of this article is to postulate a plan-

ning framework which a college can use to decide what its students need to know about computers.

The notes below show some of the problems with this paragraph.

> The term "computer literacy" has become de rigueur among avant garde educators and public officials. Despite its frequent use, however, computer literacy remains an amorphous concept. The purpose of this article is to postulate a planning framework which a college can use to decide what its students need to know about computers.

not necessary; common English words are available

— inexact

— use familiar words; the reader should readily understand the intro

After careful revision, a simpler and more understandable introduction would look like this:

> Leading educators and public officials frequently use the term "computer literacy." Despite its frequent use, however, the term is not well-defined. The purpose of this article is to suggest a way in which a college can decide what its students need to know about computers.

4. Make sure the relationship of the ideas in your sentences is clear. The main reason for studying grammar and punctuation rules is to understand how these relationships are shown, and your skill in writing and revising sentences will grow as you learn and apply the rules. For now, we'll show you three sentences with unclear relationships and how they can be corrected.

> Swaying in the breeze, I saw the spider hanging by a thin web.

Cover up the words after "I saw." You will see that as the sentence reads, it says that the speaker ("I") was swaying in the breeze. The revision makes clear that the spider, not the speaker, was swaying.

I saw the spider swaying in the breeze, hanging by its thin web.

Here's another example.

My brother told his friend he had a flat tire.

We don't know who had the flat tire. Was it my brother or his friend? The revision makes it clear.

My brother told his friend, "I have a flat tire."

Here's a final example of faulty sentence relationships.

I don't know much about music. I enjoy going to concerts.

There seems to be a contradiction here, and the writer seems not to recognize it. The revision shows that the writer recognizes the apparent contradiction.

Although I don't know much about music, I enjoy going to concerts.

These examples illustrate just a few of the possible problems in showing relationships among ideas. You can learn more about such problems by studying the Appendix, but you'll find that you can spot many problems in your own writing simply by being aware that the relationships need to be clear. Ask yourself, "Just how are those ideas related?" Because you know English, you know a lot about how relationships are expressed. You know, for example, that "but" shows a different relationship between two ideas than does "so." Let your ear guide you.

 Writing Activity 4.4

- Refer again to the paragraph you wrote for activity 4.1.
- Write each sentence as described in Step 1 of the Sentence Checklist (page 57) and make any necessary changes.

□ Experiment with sentence variety.

□ Eliminate any wordiness or stuffy language.

□ Check the logical relationships of ideas and make any necessary changes.

Putting It All Together

Because revising is a continuous process, you rarely rewrite a paragraph and fix only one problem at a time. More often, you'll solve several problems at the same time: as you work to improve clarity, you will automatically change vocabulary and sentence structure along the way. Going step by step, however, gives you a definite place to start and helps make sure that you haven't overlooked something important.

As you revise each draft, think first about your opening. Will it grab your reader's interest? Next, look at your ideas. Are they adequately developed to show the reader what you're talking about? Third, check your vocabulary. Do the words accurately show the important points about your subject? Do they accurately reflect your attitude toward your subject? Finally, look at your sentence structures. Are they clear, varied, and appropriately worded?

To illustrate the process of revision, we'll close this chapter with three drafts of a student paragraph. As you look at each draft, remember that revising is a complex process and that all of the steps are related to each other. These revisions illustrate this complexity very nicely.

Three Drafts of a Student Paragraph

One of our students, Nelda, wrote the following three drafts of a paragraph. Notice how in each successive draft, she makes important changes until she feels she has created a paragraph that paints a clear picture of her experience. She's made some notes to herself in the margins.

Draft 1

The first time I went to an amusement park.(I won free rides for the day. It hap-) Save this until the end

pened on the merry-go-round. I got the
brass ring. Each time you went around the
circle you went by a ring dispensor and
took a ring. When it was my turn I put out
my hand to take a ring. I got the brass ring,
the merry-go-round stopped and the music got louder. A man came over and said
I had won free rides for the day. I was so
surprised all I could say was thank you.

don't switch from I to you

explain why I was so surprised

Nelda decided that she had not made it clear why she was surprised.
In her next draft notice all the details that she has added to show us why
getting the brass ring took her by surprise. Also, notice how the problem
with the first sentence (a fragment) is taken care of and how she has
corrected the problem of switching from first person "I" to second person
"you."

Draft 2

When I was in the fourth grade, my
teacher told us one day that we all were
going to go to an amusement park. I had
never been to an amusement park before,
but I didn't want them to know that. I tried
to picture one in my mind. I could see
grassy hills, maybe even a quiet lake, and
places to picnic and play. It seemed like
years but the day finally came when we
were to go. We rode on a big orange bus
and it was hot and crowded. Everyone was
yelling when we arrived. It looked like a
carnival to me. Everyone rushed to the
ticket line I could hear them talking about
the merry-go-round. They all wanted to go
on that ride first. So I did too. I followed
everyone to the merry-go-round and heard
them talking about a brass ring. What is a
brass ring I wondered. I just watched at
first so I would know what to do when it was
my time to ride. Each child picked out a
special horse. There were white ones,

do I need all of this?

vary sentence structure

Sounds choppy

too obvious

necessary?

black ones and brown ones. My favorite
was a black stallion. As (they) went around,
(they) reached out for a ring from a ring dispensor near the entrance of the big round
building. It was my turn to ride, I chose a   } *run on sentence*
big, black stallion. It was wonderful going
up and down to the loud music. I ap-   } *good — expand this*
proached the (entrance) and I reached out
and grabbed a ring. The music got louder
and (a man) came over to me and said I had
won free rides for the day. I had gotten the } *simple ending — I like it*
brass ring.

This draft shows many improvements over the first. Nelda has used
lots of specific details here which were lacking in the previous draft. Now
we really understand why she was so surprised to get the brass ring—she
had never been to an amusement park or ridden on a merry-go-round and
did not know about the brass ring or what it meant. Her vocabulary is
more varied, making the paragraph more interesting to read. She's used
more active verbs and specific adjectives and adverbs. In reading this
draft, however, Nelda felt she was now including too much at the beginning. She felt she needed to focus more on the actual experience at the
park. She circled words that could be more specific. When reading it aloud,
she felt that some of the sentences sounded choppy, so she decided to add
some introductory clauses to her sentences to make the ideas flow more
smoothly. Here is her final draft.

Final Draft

I first took a trip to an amusement park when I was
in the fourth grade. All that morning my classmates
buzzed with excitement. I had no idea what to expect,
but I didn't want anyone to know that. The ride on the
crowded orange bus seemed to take forever; when we
finally arrived, we all screamed and cheered. I was
amazed. It looked more like a carnival than a park. The
first thing everyone did was to rush to the ticket booth,
and I followed quickly. While waiting in line, I could
hear the kids yelling about the merry-go-round. I heard
the words "brass ring" and couldn't figure out what that
meant. We all ran to the merry-go-round; I watched as

favorite horses were spotted and claimed proudly by each child. I carefully chose the best, a black stallion, and when it was finally my turn to ride, I captured him quickly. I'd also seen how the kids grabbed for a ring, each time they went around, from a ring dispensor stationed near the entrance. I knew that I would do this too. The music started, and I began to feel the wonderful movement, up and down, around and around. As I approached the special spot, I reached out and seized my ring. All of a sudden the merry-go-round stopped and the music became louder. Much to my surprise a smiling man came over to me. He said I had won free rides for the day. I had caught the brass ring.

Nelda's final draft is a good one. It's clear from the beginning that her day would be filled with surprises. She has let the reader find out what she learned as she learned it—gradually and wonderingly. She's used an even more varied and specific vocabulary so we can see what she saw and feel what she felt. She's corrected her punctuation errors too, and as a result of all of her changes, the paragraph is one she's proud of.

As you have seen, revising is a complex activity, but it can be made less complex by dividing the process into steps. First, let your writing get cold. You'll do a better job of revision when you can see your writing more objectively. Next, do the three reading steps of listening to it, reading it with a different eye, and analyzing it. Finally, begin the actual revision of your paragraph by playing with it. First, experiment with different openings. Second, develop your ideas by showing, not telling. Third, experiment with different vocabulary to find the most effective words. And fourth, work carefully with your sentence structures. Refer back to this chapter as you work through this book. Revision is a skill that needs to be practiced continually.

Other Suggestions for Writing

1. Now that you have completed the various steps in the revision of your paragraph from activity 4.1, write a clean, final draft that includes your best revisions.

2. Write a narrative paragraph as you did for Chapter 3. Follow the steps in Chapter 4 and revise your paragraph.

Terms to Remember

lead   The opening of a piece of writing. Your lead should grab the reader's attention and make the reader want to go on reading.

sentence structure   The pattern in which ideas are stated in a sentence. A sentence can be structured to state a single idea, or it can be structured to combine two or more ideas in the same sentence. For more information, refer to the Appendix.

thesaurus   A dictionary-like book which lists words in alphabetical order showing words of similar and opposite meanings.

wordiness   The use of unnecessary words to express ideas. Unnecessary words do more to confuse the reader than to clarify ideas.

II

WORKING WITH PARAGRAPHS

Preview for Chapter 5

As you read Chapter 5, look for these words.

1. Description
2. Specific
3. Comparison
4. Noun
5. Adjective
6. General

In the preview to Chapter 1 we suggested that you skim through a new chapter and familiarize yourself with its headings to give yourself a general idea of what the chapter is about. One particularly useful preview technique is to turn the chapter title and these headings into questions and then to try to answer the questions as you read the new material. For example, for the Chapter 5 title you could ask, "What will I do when I write about an object and a place?" Keep this question in mind as you read this chapter, and look for answers to it.

Recall that main headings are usually in large type or dark print. As you read, turn each main heading into a question, and then try to answer that question. Turning main headings into questions gives you a purpose for reading the material and helps you focus your attention on the important ideas.

5

WRITING ABOUT AN OBJECT
AND A PLACE

In this chapter you will write about an object and a place, and we will show you some ways of describing them. We will show you two **descriptions**, one of an object (a coffee mug) and one of a place (a campsite). You will see the importance of using all of your senses when you write descriptions, and we will show you some ways of making sure that you do so. In Chapters 1 and 3, you were writing about what you remembered, but in this chapter you will write about what you directly observe, so Step 1, brainstorming, will be from a direct observation.

DESCRIBING AN OBJECT

STEP 1:
Brainstorming for Ideas

Once you've decided on an object to describe, you must brainstorm about the **specific** details of that object. Use all of your five senses. Look at the object; listen to it, smell it, taste it, touch it. What's it made of? What shape is it? What's its color, size, and texture? You won't always be able to use every sense to describe an object, but in any observation you do, try to use as many of your five senses as you can.

For our description, we elected to use the freewrite method of brainstorming, and since we had already chosen our subject—a mug—this is a focused freewriting. First we concentrated on the mug for a few minutes. With the coffee mug in front of us, we tried to note as many things as we could that have to do with our senses—seeing, touching, tasting, smelling, and hearing. Since the mug was empty, however, smell and taste were not significant. Here is a freewriting based on what we saw, heard, felt, and thought when we examined our particular mug.

> **mug isn't very tall—about 3 and a half inches. tapers to narrow base and holds about what any cup would hold. it's ugly—ugly mugly, pukey green, worst I've seen. dark brown inside like coffee, poor little animal struggling from inside. I'm thirsty, wish I had some hot coffee. poor little animal must get his bottom burned. handle keeps hand from getting burned—just stuck on—might fall off. Creature looks like a wombat— what's that? His head and shoulders and claws are over the side but the rest is inside wishing it was outside— back legs, tail, body down in the coffee. Beady eyes and sharp nose stare at me and its head hits mine when I drink. got this thing at a dog sale, and it's a real dog. gets a lot of attention, though. It feels heavy to me and clunks when I set it down. Thick sides, thick bottom thick, thick, thick, sick, sick, sick. bottom is rough, too, like fine sandpaper that might scratch the table. rest is smooth but colors are uneven, roughly vertical bands. I can feel the ridges as my fingers run down the cup, and when I hit it with my pen it goes clunk. why do I like this weird, sick, ugly mug?**

This freewrite gives us many clear, specific details about the mug. In addition, it has led us to record some of our thoughts about the mug. This combination of details and thoughts leads us directly to a dominant impression of the mug: it's ugly. The specific information about size (three and a half inches tall) and the **comparison** of the cup's creature to a wombat are good details that we will want to use in our paragraph. Such details enable us to convey a clear picture to our readers. The few minutes of concentration before we started writing helped us to see those specific details.

Writing Activity 5.1

- ☐ Choose an object that interests you.
- ☐ Examine it: touch it, smell it, listen to it, and so on.
- ☐ Concentrate on the object for a few minutes, and then freewrite about it.
- ☐ Give as many details and impressions of it as you can.

STEP 2:
Writing the Topic Sentence

The dominant impression that we discovered in our freewrite (ugly) becomes the controlling word of our topic sentence:

A good word to describe my coffee mug is "unusual," but "ugly" comes closer to the truth.

You may or may not have one dominant impression in your mind as you begin to brainstorm, but once you've completed this step, sit down for a moment and think about the one impression you get. Think about the one major idea that all the specific details seem to add up to. If you began with a clear impression and ended with the same impression, check your brainstorming work carefully. Are there details that might contradict your impression? Look back at the object itself. Can you find anything there that might contradict your impression? This double checking is important because we often overlook details that go against ideas we already hold about something. (Remember William Least Heat Moon's point about the desert on page 23.) Of course your original idea may also be correct, but you need to check. Our freewrite, for example, only confirmed our original idea, but the observation gave us details—such as the sound of the mug—that we hadn't noticed before.

Writing Activity 5.2

□ Reread your brainstorming from activity 5.1 and decide on one major or dominant impression you have about the object.

□ Write a topic sentence that contains that impression.

STEP 3:
Outlining the Paragraph

Now that you have a topic sentence, it's time to take the details from your freewrite and put them into an outline. This procedure will ensure that your paragraph will have good unity. Then you'll write your paragraph, developing the details even further and more specifically. It's a good idea to keep the object you describe close by while you outline, since you'll probably want to look at it again and again.

After reviewing our own freewrite and topic sentence and examining the mug again, we came up with the following outline (remember to turn your topic sentence into a question as you start your outline):

Topic sentence:

> **A good word to describe my coffee mug is "unusual," but "ugly" comes closer to the truth.**

Topic sentence question:

> **What is ugly about my coffee mug?**

Answers:

> 1. **Its colors are pukey green and ugly brown.**
>
> 2. **It has a figure of a creature crawling over the side.**
>
> 3. **It's heavy with thick, uneven sides.**
>
> 4. **It even sounds ugly.**

This outline gives us a good beginning for our paragraph and will guide us as we select details from our freewrite or from further observation.

 Writing Activity 5.3

□ Use your material from activities 5.1 and 5.2 to write an outline to help plan your paragraph.

□ Remember to make a question out of your topic sentence.

□ Refer back to pages 7–8 if you need a little more help on outlining.

Step 4:
Writing the First Draft

Now that we have brainstormed, written a topic sentence, and created an outline, it's time to write the first draft of our description. Take a look at our outline. Notice that the first and fourth answers to our topic sentence question contain the word "ugly," but that the second and third do not. There is a danger, then, that our paragraph can lose its unity as we begin to develop the ideas in the outline. We might lose our focus on the controlling word, ugly, by just describing the creature rather than by explaining how the creature helps make the cup ugly. Always keep your controlling idea in mind. It is the guide that gives your paragraph unity because it determines what can go into the paragraph and what must stay out of it. Here's our first draft.

Draft 1

A good word to describe my coffee mug would be "unusual," but "ugly" comes closer to the truth. When you first see it, you notice the mottled, pukey green color of its unevenly tapered body, or maybe you see the ugly brown stain about a third of the way around from the crooked handle. A little closer look shows you a wombat-looking creature that seems to be struggling up over the side after nearly drowning in hot coffee. The brown stain on the side extends to the inside of the cup, and the creature's body, back legs, and tail hang down in the center of the stain. Its sides seem unusually thick, and you can't set the heavy thing down anywhere without hearing a loud clunk. Usually if you tap one cup against another or tap a cup with a pencil or pen, you'll hear a musical clink. My cup responds with a dull thud. I'm not sure why I keep my ugly mug, but it certainly does have character.

Our first draft, like all first drafts, has some problems. We'll work on those problems in Step 5, Revising the Paragraph.

 Writing Activity 5.4

☐ Write a first draft of your description of an object.

☐ Set your rough draft aside for a while before you revise it.

STEP 5:
Revising the Paragraph

Though we won't spend much time in this text on the names of parts of speech, you'll need to know a few terms in order to evaluate and revise your writing. The first two of these are **noun** and **adjective**. We'll explain more terms as the need for them arises.

noun: A word that names a person, place, thing, or concept. Words like "a," "the," "some," and "those" are sometimes called *noun indicators* because they often precede a noun and indicate that the reader can expect to see a noun very soon. In the sentence, "The boy threw a frisbee to the white dog," for example, "boy," "frisbee," and "dog" are all nouns and are preceded by noun indicators.

adjective: A word that tells more about (*modifies* or *describes*) a noun. In the example sentence in the definition of noun, "white" is an adjective because it tells us more about the dog. We could add more adjectives to the sentence if we wished, and these adjectives might give the reader a clearer mental picture of what happened. Here's an example: "The handsome, young boy threw a large, plastic, red frisbee to the excited white dog."

When you describe objects or places, you'll find that nouns and adjectives play a large part in your descriptions. As you revise, look quite carefully at the nouns and adjectives you use. Make sure they are as specific as possible. If we were describing our computer, for example, we might say, "There are three little round things in the corner." A more specific description would be, "There are three round, black, half-inch diameter knobs in the lower right-hand corner of the monitor." In the second version, adjectives have been added to describe the color, the size, and the location, and we substituted the specific noun "knob" for the **general** noun "thing." We also added the noun "monitor" to give the reader a clearer picture of what part we're talking about.

As we revised our paragraph about the mug, we added specific nouns and adjectives. Here's our revision with notes and underlining to show some of the changes.

Draft 2 (with notes)

My pottery coffee mug is so ugly that it's almost (sickening.) When you first see it, you notice the mottled, (pukey) green color of its unevenly tapered body, or maybe you see the ugly brown stain about a third of the way around from the crudely attached, crooked handle. A closer look will show you a desperate, pathetic, wombat-like creature that seems to be struggling over the side after nearly drowning in hot coffee. The creature is in the center of the dark brown splotch that extends into the cup's inside; its thick body, stubby back legs, and scraggly tail seem to hang limply down inside. Although I have used

"sickening" sharpens the controlling idea

"pukey" relates to and reinforces the controlling idea

underlined words show a clearer picture of the cup and the little animal the cup for a year, I still can't pour coffee into it without a little feeling of pity for the poor beast and a sense that I ought to go scour the cup to get rid of the animal's (germs.)

last sentence changed to tie it in more closely with the topic sentence

"germs" relates to —— and reinforces the controlling idea

Draft 2 (without notes)

My pottery coffee mug is so ugly that it's almost sickening. When you first see it, you notice the mottled, pukey green color of its unevenly tapered body, or maybe you see the ugly brown stain about a third of the way around from the crudely attached, crooked handle. A closer look will show you a desperate, pathetic, wombat-like creature that seems to be struggling over the side after nearly drowning in hot coffee. The creature is in the center of the dark brown splotch that extends into the cup's inside; its thick body, stubby back legs, and scraggly tail seem to hang limply down inside. Although I have used the cup for a year, I still can't pour coffee into it without a little feeling of pity for the poor beast and a sense that I ought to go scour the cup to get rid of the animal's germs.

Notice how the addition of an adjective, "sickening," to the controlling word (ugly) focuses the paragraph more sharply on some particular characteristics of the mug. It led us to more adjectives like "desperate," "pathetic," and "scraggly." Note, also, how we've given the paragraph more variety by using different nouns to describe the same object: "mug" and "cup"; "stain and splotch"; and "creature," "beast," and "animal." Choosing strong and vivid nouns and adjectives is all part of the revising process we described in Chapter 4.

Writing Activity 5.5

□ Revise your paragraph from activity 5.4 that describes an object.

□ Pay particular attention to your choices of nouns and adjectives as you revise: make them as vivid as possible.

DESCRIBING A PLACE

In this chapter section, you will write a description of a place, but before you start writing we will show you an example of a problem that students often encounter. The problem is that of trying to write a description from memory rather than from direct observation. Descriptions from memory can be written, of course, but to write an effective description from memory, you must have done some careful observation at some time in the past. Most of us are not careful observers, however. Our memories are too vague and general to produce vivid descriptive writing. Here, for example, is the kind of brainstorming list that is often created when someone is trying to write about a place from memory.

1. **Sound of creek**
2. **Lots of trees**
3. **Rocks**
4. **Meadow**
5. **Tents**
6. **Beautiful**
7. **Peaceful**
8. **Away from hustle and bustle**
9. **Hot and sunny**
10. **Mosquitoes**
11. **Birds singing**
12. **Smell of trees and grass**

Now to see why that list won't work, let's try to make an outline from it. We feel that "peaceful" is the dominant impression or controlling idea. Here's our outline.

Topic sentence:

The campsite at Cedar Creek is a very peaceful place.

Topic sentence question:

What makes the campsite a peaceful place?

Answers:

1. **It is beautiful.**
2. **It is peaceful.**
3. **It is away from the hustle and bustle.**
4. **The sights are peaceful.**
5. **The sounds are peaceful.**

The problems with this outline come mainly from the fact that the details are too general. It would be difficult to write a paragraph that creates a specific picture in the reader's mind. For example, look at the word "beautiful." This word means many things to many people. What's beautiful to us may not be beautiful to anyone else, so if we used a word like beautiful in our paragraph, we'd have to develop it with specific information about why we think the place is beautiful.

Another problem is the answer, "It is peaceful." "Peaceful" has the same problem as "beautiful" (it is too vague), but it also repeats the controlling word of the topic sentence. In effect we're saying, "The campsite is peaceful because it's peaceful." People who study logic call this "circular reasoning," but it doesn't take a label for us to see that the idea isn't likely to lead us anywhere. The phrase "away from the hustle and bustle" is also too general, and it pulls our attention away from the campsite back to places that aren't peaceful. This idea certainly belongs in the list of details—since that's where we write down anything that comes to mind when we brainstorm about our subject—but it may cause the paragraph to lose its unity if added to the outline. "Sights" and "sounds," like the other words, have little specific information to suggest to us, the writers, what we must do in order to show you, the reader, what's peaceful about the campsite.

The trouble with our list, then, is that there is nothing in it that will help us to be specific. Before we can do an adequate job of developing the paragraph, we'll have to do a direct observation to decide what qualities the place has that make us say it's peaceful and to check whether our impression is accurate.

STEPS 1 AND 2:
Brainstorming for Ideas and Writing the Topic Sentence

In observing a place, we'll use a slight modification of the brainstorming method of focused listing to help us make sure that we are careful observers and that we use all of our senses. That modification is the Observation Chart on the next page.

Observation Chart			
Seeing	*Hearing*	*Smelling/ Tasting*	*Touching*
1. Trees: cedar, tamarack, firs, cottonwood, western hemlock, willow 2. Thick woods surround grassy meadow 3. Rocks in stream vary—small pebbles and large boulders 4. Colors—pale brown to reddish to white to black 5. Wet surfaces look smooth, shiny 6. Grass in meadow light green: contrasts with dark green of trees 7. Grass varies from ankle to knee high	1. Water splashes and gurgles over rocks and logs 2. Sounds like voices when you can't quite make out the words 3. Gets louder and softer as you move around the campsite 4. Never stops 5. Bird sounds: piercing squeaky brake sound of varied thrush, melodic song of redstart, hoarse croak of raven, light drumming of woodpecker	1. Meadow has sweet grassy smell, grass tastes sweet when you pick a piece and chew on it 2. Peppery smell in the air 3. Earthy earthworm smell of damp soil and resiny smell of trees are mingled in the breeze 4. Water tastes cold and fresh	1. Rocks feel smooth and round 2. Grass is prickly when you walk in it

Dominant Impression: Peaceful

Possible Topic Sentence: The campsite at Cedar Creek is one of the most peaceful places I know.

Writing Activity 5.6

- ☐ Choose a place to observe and write about.
- ☐ Make a chart like the one on page 79.
- ☐ Using your chart, list the details you observe. Put as much as you can into each column—observe carefully and fully.
- ☐ When your observation is complete, review your chart.
- ☐ Record your dominant impression.
- ☐ Write a possible topic sentence.

STEP 3:
Outlining the Paragraph

The Observation Chart (page 79) provides a solid base to work from for writing your descriptive paper. Often when you go through the observation process, you'll find that you want to change your controlling idea, and that's all right. Our observation, however, convinced us that we'd chosen the right impression from the beginning, so our more workable outline looks like this:

Topic sentence:

The campsite at Cedar Creek is peaceful.

Topic sentence question:

In what way is the campsite peaceful?

Answers:

1. **The continuous sounds of water splashing and gurgling over rocks and logs is soothing.**
2. **The thick woods shelter and protect the meadow, blocking out the sight and sounds of the dirt road that runs past.**

3. **The soft colors and smooth textures of the rocks in the stream have a calming effect on me.**

4. **The many smells in the meadow give me a feeling of harmony with nature.**

5. **The tranquil sounds of birds are pleasantly relaxing.**

This outline contains details that will help us *show* the reader why Cedar Creek is peaceful.

 Writing Activity 5.7   □ Outline your paragraph using details from the Observation Chart you created in activity 5.6.

STEP 4:
Writing the First Draft

Our more specific observations led to a more detailed outline, and that outline clearly identified for us the main ideas we would have to develop in our paragraph. The focus or controlling idea of our paragraph is "peaceful." Read over our first draft and see if the details convince you that Cedar Creek is indeed a peaceful place to be.

Draft 1

The campsite at Cedar Creek is one of the most peaceful places I know. It is a small meadow set in the thick woods of northeastern Washington. A narrow stream rushes along one edge, and the continuous gurgling and splashing of the water over rocks and logs is as soothing as the sound of my parents' voices in the next room was when I was a kid just falling asleep. The thick woods that surround and protect the meadow give me the same sense of security and peace that I had in my room then. When I'm down by the creek, even the soft

colors and textures of the rocks have a calming effect on me. The smooth surfaces, cool from the water and a little slick from mosses and algae, are a pleasure to touch, and the earthy colors seem to blend wonderfully with the surroundings. In the meadow, the earthwormy smells of the moist soil, the resiny smells of the trees, and the sweet, peppery smell of the grasses and flowers mix together on a light breeze, and I can hear many different birds. A sound like squeaky brakes tells me the varied thrush is nearby; a raven croaks hoarsely as it flaps overhead, and the musical song of the redstart doesn't quite drown out the distant tapping of a woodpecker.

We've made an effort to use a variety of words that will leave the reader with a sense of peace. Words like "soothing," "security," "soft," "calming," "smooth," and "musical" lend unity of impression to our first draft. We'll discuss these words further in Step 5, when we revise this paragraph.

 Writing Activity 5.8

□ Write your own paragraph about the place you outlined in activity 5.7.

□ After you've finished with your first draft, let it rest awhile before you go on to Step 5, Revising the Paragraph.

STEP 5: Revising the Paragraph

As you revise your description of a place, keep in mind that you can often make a description more vivid by comparing one thing to another. "What does it taste like? What does it look like?" People ask these questions about things they don't know, and our answers help them understand. By relating a familiar experience to one that is not familiar, you can help your readers understand the unfamiliar.

As we were observing and thinking about the details of the campsite, we were struck by the way running water can sometimes sound like distant voices, and as we were drafting, the idea of comparing the water's sound with the murmur of parents' voices came to mind. Notice how, in our revision, we've moved that comparison to the end of the paragraph in order to leave our readers with the image of the sense of peace and security it suggests. That comparison, it seems to us, does more than anything else to convey our controlling idea.

Draft 2

The campsite at Cedar Creek is one of the most peaceful places I know. It is a small meadow set in the thick woods of northeastern Washington; a narrow stream rushes along one edge. In the meadow, the sweet smell of grasses and flowers and a peppery smell blend with the resiny smell of the trees and the earthwormy smell of moist soil. It's a treasured, familiar smell. Down by the creek, the colors and textures of the rocks, cool and smooth to the touch and a little slick from mosses and algae, have a calming effect on me. The squeaky brake sound of the varied thrush, the musical song of the redstart, the distant drumming of a woodpecker, and even the hoarse croak of the raven give an air of calmness and tranquility. But my strongest sense of peace comes from the sound of the stream. As it gurgles and splashes over rocks and logs, it sounds like distant voices; it reminds me of when I would lie in bed as a child, hearing my parents' voices droning in the next room, feeling safe and secure just knowing they were there.

 Writing Activity 5.9

□ Revise your paragraph from activity 5.8 describing a place.

□ Pay special attention to your choices of nouns and adjectives.

   If there is one fact about description that needs to be stressed, it is the need for careful observation in the brainstorming step. Careful observation allows you to reach a dominant impression that will accurately reflect your experience of the subject in your topic sentence. The observed details will help you develop your paragraph as you write and revise. In other words, careful observation is the key that helps you to show rather than simply tell your reader what you are writing about.

Other Suggestions for Writing

1. Read pages 107–108 and do Writing Activity 7.2, page 108.
2. Write about an object that has great value to you.
3. Write about an object you'd like to get rid of because of the problems it causes you.
4. Write about an object you'd like to own.
5. Write about an interesting place in your home, your neighborhood, or your town.
6. Write about a place where you like to go to be alone.
7. Write about a photograph of a place. This is an especially challenging assignment, for your imagination will have to supply the details of sound, touch, smell, and taste.

Terms to Remember

adjective   A part of speech that modifies a noun by describing it or giving more information about it. In the phrase "blonde runner," "blonde" is an adjective.

comparison   The act of pointing out the similarities of two different things. Comparisons can be simple ("Mussels are a lot like oysters"), or they may take a paragraph or more to explain. A writer often uses comparison to help a reader understand the unknown by relating it to something the reader knows.

description   Giving a reader or a listener information about how something looks, sounds, feels, smells, or tastes in an effort to help the audience understand or picture in detail what is being described.

general   Calling to mind a large class or group of things. Lacking in detail or specific information.

noun   The name of a person, place, thing, or concept. In the phrase "blonde runner," "runner" is a noun.

specific   The opposite of general. Specific information is often definite or measurable. It creates a precise picture in the reader's mind.

Preview for Chapter 6

Be on the lookout for these important terms as you read Chapter 6:

1. Word choices
2. Verbs
3. Adverbs
4. Limiting or narrowing the focus

From each of the previous chapter previews, you've learned different techniques for previewing a chapter. Your chapter previews can help you anticipate or predict what will be discussed in the chapter. Making predictions about what ideas will appear in a chapter is a valuable aid to understanding, for as you make predictions, your interest is aroused, your mind begins to focus on the material, and your powers of concentration are sharpened. Before you read, then, let your chapter preview help you make predictions about what's to come.

You will learn from your preview of Chapter 6 that the chapter deals with writing about an activity. On the basis of your experience with this book, you can accurately predict that you will write a paragraph about an activity. You have read many descriptions of activities—newspaper reports of sporting events, bank robberies, high-speed chases, and so on. What makes these newspaper articles interesting or uninteresting? On the basis of what these descriptions usually include, what can you predict that Chapter 6 will tell you about describing an activity? On the basis of your chapter preview, what can you predict will be new to you in this chapter? On the basis of what you know about this book, what can you predict about the steps you'll take as you write your paragraph about an activity?

6

WRITING ABOUT AN ACTIVITY

In Chapter 3, you wrote about an experience of your own, and in doing so you probably described some action that happened. In Chapter 6, you will write about action that you observe rather than action you remember, and you will continue to sharpen the powers of observation that you worked on in Chapter 5.

A major purpose of writing is to share with other people your impression of the world around you, so the purpose of your paragraph describing an activity will be to convey to a reader *your* dominant impression of the actions that you observe. Because you are a unique individual, you see any activity from your own unique point of view. Your impression is determined by who you are and what you've experienced. How well you describe that impression will be determined by how well you observe.

When you describe a place or an object, many of the important details are simply there, and you can go back and observe them again and again. You can be slow and deliberate about choosing words to describe them. But if you are observing, say, children at play in a park, you won't see or hear the same things twice. The details of the place—trees, buildings, and so on—will be stable, but the details of the activity itself will be constantly changing, so you will have to record your observations quickly and accurately if you are to remember them in the detail necessary to write well about them. An interesting fact is that the more conscious you are of your **word choices** in the brainstorming or observing step, the more carefully and accurately you will observe.

In the revising step of Chapter 5, you paid careful attention to the nouns and adjectives you used in your description, and your choices of such words will continue to be important as you describe an activity. Because you are describing an *activity*, however, the most important 87 words you use will be those that show action. There are two kinds of words that are especially important: **verbs** and **adverbs**.

> **verb:**   A word that shows action or state of being. In the sentence, "The girl danced," "danced" is a verb that shows action. In the sentence, "The girl was tired," "was" is a verb that shows state of being. [Verbs are discussed more fully in the Appendix. In this chapter, we will focus only on verbs that show action.]

> **adverb:**   A word that tells more about (*modifies* or *describes*) a verb, adjective, adverb, or even a whole sentence. In the sentence, "The boy shouted happily," "happily" is an adverb that modifies the verb "shouted." An adverb usually answers the question "how?"

You can see the importance of verbs and adverbs by comparing the following descriptions of the same action:

(verb)
The dancer raised her leg off the floor. At the same time,
(verb)
her arm rose over her head.   (adverbs show *how*
                                          action happened)
(more exact verb)
The dancer stretched her leg <u>slowly</u>, almost <u>painfully</u>,
                                              (adverb)
off the floor. At the same time, her arm <u>weightlessly</u>
(more exact verb)
drifted over her head.

Our notes show why the second description is more effective than the first: it shows a clearer picture of the action.

Now let's go to Step 1 and see how your knowledge of adverbs and adjectives can help make you a better observer as well as a better writer.

STEP 1:
Brainstorming for Ideas

In this section, we have chosen to list details rather than to cluster or freewrite, since our goal is to gather information while an activity occurs. Because listing is a fast way of brainstorming, it works well as a way of recording events while you observe them, particularly if the action is happening quickly.

As you brainstorm, try for the right word the first time. You might, for example, make a note that says,

boy runs from first to second

But you might also record,

boy trots confidently from first to second

Note how the second version captures the specific action. If you begin your observations by planning to use the best words to describe what happens and how it happens, you will find yourself watching the action and the actors more closely. Of course your first task is simply to observe and record the action, so you can't spend too much time searching for just the right word. Get in the habit, though, of asking, "What, exactly, did he do?" "How, exactly, did she do that?" "What word can best show that action and attitude to a reader?" The more you practice looking for the right words, the more quickly the right words will come to you, so practice looking at any action through the eyes of a writer, a person who paints pictures with words.

Finally, as you brainstorm the details of the activity you observe, remember to use all of your senses. Record not only what you see, but also what you hear, taste, smell, and touch, as well.

As our example for this chapter, we observed Marcia's two small children eating some sweet rolls. We made separate lists of details, and then we each wrote about the activity without comparing notes. Even though we watched the same activity, each of us brought a different personality and set of experiences to the observation. The difference in point of view is evident even in our lists.

Marcia's List of Details

1. **Stacey pokes finger inside of roll, licks sticky finger loudly**
2. **Says, "Good, isn't it?"**
3. **Jeff and Stacey share bites**
4. **Jeff yells, "There's frosting inside mine!"**
5. **Licks his fingers, wipes them on pants**
6. **Both rub hands in hair absentmindedly**
7. **Spill sugar on table, globs of chocolate**

8. Giggle, make strange gurgling noises
9. Stacey opens mouth very wide, tries to stuff all in
10. Both talk with mouths full of food
11. Stacey says over and over, "mmmmmmmmmm"
12. Jeff falls off chair
13. Sugar and crumbs fall on carpet
14. Stacey stands on chair, waves arms up and down jerkily
15. Hangs over table smearing sugar on face and clothes
16. Sits up again, food all over shirt
17. Holds hands up in air, away from clothes and table, being careful while alternately rubbing fingers on chair, arms, clothes, table, hair
18. Stacey makes designs—lines and circles, in sugar on table
19. Stacey climbs off chair, walks in sugar on floor

Ed's List of Details

1. Stacey growls and giggles
2. Leans over table—on knees on high chair
3. Holds hands apart and in front, giggles
4. Jeff picks chocolate off, throws back head, comments to Stacey
5. Stacey brushes hair back, takes another bite, licks fingers
6. "There's frosting inside mine"—walks around table, extending finger—Jeff smacks sugar off her finger
7. "I got salt on mine"—leans across table, extending finger—Jeff smacks sugar off her finger
8. Jeff moves to stool so he can share with Stacey
9. Jeff's eating slows to tasting custard from his, sugar from Stacey's

10. Jeff chatters, Stacey eats, blows a "razzberry" on palm of hand

11. Stacey smears powdered sugar on table, blows another razzberry, looks around to see if she can get a laugh—no laugh

12. Jeff blows razzberry and giggles, Stacey does too

13. Jeff reaches inside and takes custard out with fingers, picks up roll and takes a big bite, roll wraps halfway around his head

14. S. does a little dance in her chair, leans on one elbow on table, licks fingers and giggles

15. J. runs to kitchen, asks for milk

16. Sits on stool, goes over top and falls to floor, bumps head, goes for a kiss, returns, drapes self on stool, takes fingerful of custard, cocks head, puts finger in mouth, rocks on stool

17. Each has roll about half gone, Stacey licks finger, then waves hand

18. Stacey blows a razzberry on hand

19. Stacey settles back, eats meditatively, drinks milk, puts cup down, looks over her shoulder and says, "No monsters behind me." Plays with her shoe.

Even from our lists you can see that our viewpoints differ greatly: Marcia sees the mess, while Ed, who doesn't have to clean up afterward, sees the fun. No two people see quite the same thing or interpret what they see in quite the same way.

 Writing Activity 6.1

- ☐ Choose an activity you find interesting.
- ☐ Carefully observe it, recording the events as you see them happen.
- ☐ Use strong verbs and adverbs.
- ☐ Use as many of your senses as you can.

STEP 2:
Writing the Topic Sentence

Looking back at our lists of details, you can see that Marcia watches the activity from the perspective of a mother and chief cleaner-upper. Her focus, then, is on the mess and the work it creates for her. Her point of view helps shape her topic sentence:

I watched, dismayed, as my two children ate their rolls.

Ed, on the other hand, is a little more neutral or impartial in his observation. It's not his house, he likes the children, and he enjoys watching them have fun. His topic sentence is:

The kids were delighted with their treat.

Sometimes you will quickly form a dominant impression of an event, but sometimes it can be hard to state your dominant impression. If you're having trouble, ask yourself what one word you would use if, at gunpoint, you were forced to describe the activity with just one word.

 Writing Activity 6.2

□ Look back at your own list of details from activity 6.1.

□ Write a word that captures the dominant impression of the event you observed.

□ Using that word, write a possible topic sentence for your paragraph.

STEP 3:
Outlining the Paragraph

In the outline step of writing, our individual viewpoints continue to influence which details are included and which are excluded as we plan our respective paragraphs. Each of us focuses only on those points that will convey our unique impression of the activity. Our differences in perspective and focus, therefore, become even more evident in our outlines.

Marcia's Outline

Topic sentence:

I watched, dismayed, as my two children ate their rolls.

Topic sentence question:

Why was I dismayed as I watched my two children eat their rolls?

Answers:

1. **I saw the mess on Jeff and Stacey's faces.**
2. **I saw the mess on Jeff and Stacey's hands.**
3. **I saw the mess in Stacey's hair.**
4. **I saw the mess on Jeff and Stacey's clothes.**
5. **I saw the mess on the table.**
6. **I saw the mess on the chair.**
7. **I saw the mess on the floor.**

Ed's Outline

Topic sentence:

The kids were delighted with their treat.

Topic sentence question:

What did the kids do to show they were delighted with their treat?

Answers:

1. **They laughed and chattered as they ate.**
2. **They stayed close to the table instead of running around.**
3. **They shared various tastes.**
4. **They sometimes took big bites and sometimes savored the good parts.**

At this point in the writing process, it's important to stop, take a good look at the outline, and determine whether it will be a good framework for a paragraph. Do the answers really answer the question? Is there too much in it? Is something missing from it?

Looking at her outline, Marcia decided there is too much information in it. The problem lies in the topic sentence: it is too broad. If she were to fully develop the topic sentence, she would need to write much more than one paragraph. Even before beginning her first draft, then, she **limited** her subject and revised her topic sentence to focus just on Stacey:

I watched, dismayed, as Stacey ate her roll.

By **narrowing the focus** from both of the children to just one of them, Marcia narrowed her paragraph to a manageable size. Also, she shifted her point of view from the entire scene to a specific part of it, much like a movie camera pans in for a close-up. This shift will allow her to supply enough specific details about Stacey for the reader to gain a clear picture of at least part of the event. Obviously, this new topic sentence requires a change in both the question and the answers of Marcia's outline. Here's her new one.

Topic sentence:

> **I watched, dismayed, as Stacey attacked the huge, gooey roll.**

Topic sentence question:

> **Why was I dismayed as I watched Stacey attack the huge, gooey roll?**

Answers:

1. **She smeared custard and powdered sugar on her hands, face, and hair.**
2. **Powdered sugar fell to the table top and then to the floor.**
3. **She lay in the sugar and jelly, making her shirt filthy.**
4. **She ground the mess into the carpet when she was finished.**

Writing Activity 6.3

□ Outline your materials from activities 6.1 and 6.2.

□ Decide whether or not your outline will work as a framework for a paragraph.

□ If your outline seems too broad, narrow your topic sentence and write a new outline.

STEP 4: Writing the First Draft

As you learn to be thorough and careful on the first three steps, the actual writing step will gradually become easier to manage. Writing well will always be hard work, but you're mastering a writing system that you can apply to any kind of writing you may need to do.

After reviewing our outlines, we struggled with our paragraphs about the kids and their rolls and came up with the following rough drafts. As before, we let our outlines guide our selection of details and their order in the paragraphs.

Marcia's First Draft

I watched, dismayed, as Stacey attacked the huge, gooey roll. It was covered with a fine, white powdered sugar and filled with thick, yellow lemon custard, offering her a variety of activities. She began by opening her mouth wide and stuffing in as much as she could, leaving a ring of white paste around her lips and up one cheek. Next she poked a stubby index finger into the jelly and licked her finger; she continued scooping until the center was empty and her hand was covered with goo. She then wiped a stray strand of hair off her face, and the hair stuck to her forehead. Meanwhile, the powdered sugar fell from the roll and covered the table top, and Stacey began to draw designs in it. She stood up and rubbed her hands, arms, and elbows in the sugar, knocking it to the floor. Soon Stacey lay over the table and rested her chest in the sugar and jelly and then stood up to reveal a shirt ready for the laundry. Having eaten enough, Stacey climbed down, walked over the mess, and ground it into the carpet. I moaned as she skipped by, grinning at me, satisfied.

Ed's First Draft

Stacey picked up her powdered-sugar-covered roll, bit down on it, and growled and giggled while Jeff delightedly picked a large chunk of the chocolate frosting off his roll. They were obviously delighted with their treat. After his first large bite, Jeff shouted, "There's frosting in mine!" and he slowly began taking the custard filling on his fingertip and licking it off. After a couple of tastes, he walked around the table to offer Stacey a taste. She, meanwhile, was standing on her knees in the high chair, leaning over the table, weight on her elbows and forearms, alternately rocking back to take a bite, smear powdered sugar around the table, brush her hair back, blow a razzberry, giggle, or lick her fingers. When Jeff returned, Stacey leaned across the table, and Jeff loudly kissed the powdered sugar from her extended finger. Picking up his roll, Jeff again bit into the custard-filled center. The sides of the roll wrapped nearly halfway around his small head. Stacey, too, again took a big bite, smearing powdered sugar on the lower half of her face. By this time, their chewing had slowed—they were awfully big rolls for small children—but there was no move by either to leave the table. Stacey licked her finger, then blew another razzberry on her palm. Taking a drink of milk, she looked over her shoulder down the hall. "No monsters behind me," she mused, and quietly began playing with her shoe. The half-eaten roll lay safely within reach.

In looking over his paragraph, Ed felt that the paragraph was focused on something other than his topic sentence, but he couldn't say exactly what was wrong. He decided to let it sit for a day before he tried to revise.

It's normal and common for writers to have vague feelings of discomfort about what they have written, and it's important for a writer to learn to pay attention to those feelings. Often those vague feelings are signals that your mind is at work on the problem and that, given time, your mind will probably identify and maybe solve the problem.

Writing Activity 6.4

- ☐ Write a first draft of your description of an activity.
- ☐ Circle the verbs and adverbs.
- ☐ Let your paragraph sit for awhile before you begin to revise.

STEP 5:
Revising the Paragraph

When she was ready to begin her revision, Marcia reviewed her paragraph. She had circled the verbs but didn't notice any adverbs, and as she reread, she made notes to herself about changes she wanted to make. Here's her first draft with her notes added.

Marcia's First Draft

I watched, dismayed, as Stacey attacked the huge, gooey roll. It was covered with a fine, white powdered sugar and filled with thick, yellow lemon custard, offering her a variety of activities. She began by opening her mouth wide and stuffing in as much as she could, leaving a ring of white paste around her lips and up one cheek. Next she poked a stubby index finger into the jelly and licked her finger; she continued scooping until the center was empty and her hand was covered with goo. She then wiped a stray strand of hair off her face, and the hair stuck to her forehead. Meanwhile, the powdered sugar fell from the roll and covered the table top,

— focus on action

Show action more clearly

and Stacey (began) to draw designs in it.
She (stood) up and (rubbed) her hands, arms,
and elbows in the sugar, knocking it to the
floor. Soon Stacey (lay) over the table and
(rested) her chest in the sugar and jelly and
then (stood) up to reveal a shirt ready for the
laundry. Having eaten enough, Stacey
(climbed) down, (walked) over the mess, and
(ground) it into the carpet. I (moaned) as she
(skipped) by, grinning at me, satisfied.

show action more clearly

only sound given

Marcia rewrote her paragraph, improving the problems she had found in her review. We have circled verbs and adverbs on her rewrite, and we've made some notes to point out some of the changes that make Marcia's revision a much stronger paragraph than her first draft.

Marcia's Revision

V   ADV
I (watched) dismayed, as Stacey (glee-
V
fully) (attacked) the large, gooey roll. Open-
V
ing her mouth wide, she (stuffed) in a huge
bite of the powdered-sugar-covered treat
V
and (smiled) up at me with a clown face—
lips and cheeks smeared with white pow-
V
der. The bite had (revealed) a lemon cus-
V   ADV
tard filling, and Stacey (cheered) (loudly)
V
when she discovered it. She (poked) a
stubby index finger into the jelly and
V   ADV
(scooped) out the filling, (noisily) licking her
V
finger. More earnest now, she (jammed) in
her whole hand for the yellow treasure,
V
then (paused) to wipe a stray strand of hair

more specific verbs show action more clearly

adverbs show how action was completed

sound

focuses on Stacey's action and shows mess more clearly

from her face, glueing the lock firmly to her forehead. As the powdered sugar fell from her roll and covered the tabletop, Stacey began to trace lines and circles with her finger. Pulling herself to her feet, she left sticky lumps of custard on the arms of the chair. Leaning over the table, she used her hands, elbows and arms to draw more elaborate designs and in the process knocked white sugar to the floor. I watched it snow quietly on the carpet. Oblivious, Stacey now slowly rested the entire top half of her body on the table, rubbing her hair, face, and chest in the mess. She rose proudly to reveal the disastrous results on her head and shirt. Finally, having had enough, she climbed down, walked over the food-covered carpet, and ground the mess expertly into every fiber. I moaned softly as she grinned a satisfied grin and left to discover a new adventure.

> focuses on Stacey's action and shows mess more clearly

Obviously, Marcia has made major changes and additions to her paragraph, and that's what often happens as writers revise. A third draft would probably lead to still more changes, and you will often be asked to do three or more drafts of what you write. You can, however, make each revision more effective by carefully studying the draft you plan to revise. The techniques we have shown you—circling verbs and adverbs and making notes to yourself—can help you do that studying. Here's Marcia's same draft without notes. Read it for pleasure.

Marcia's Revision

I watched, dismayed, as Stacey gleefully attacked the large, gooey roll. Opening her mouth wide, she stuffed in a huge bite of the powdered-sugar-covered treat and smiled up at me with a clown face—lips and cheeks smeared with white powder. The bite had revealed a lemon custard filling, and Stacey cheered loudly when she discovered it. She poked a stubby index finger into the jelly and scooped out the filling, noisily licking her finger. More earnest now, she jammed in her whole hand for the yellow treasure, then paused to wipe a stray strand of hair from her face, glueing the lock firmly to her forehead. As the powdered sugar fell from her roll and covered the tabletop, Stacey began to trace lines and circles with her finger. Pulling herself to her feet, she left sticky lumps of custard on the arms of the chair. Leaning over the table, she used her hands, elbows and arms to draw more elaborate designs and in the process knocked white sugar to the floor. I watched it snow quietly on the carpet. Oblivious, Stacey now slowly rested the entire top half of her body on the table, rubbing her hair, face, and chest in the mess. She rose proudly to reveal the disastrous results on her head and shirt. Finally, having had enough, she climbed down, walked over the food-covered carpet, and ground the mess expertly into every fiber. I moaned softly as she grinned a satisfied grin and left to discover a new adventure.

Recall that when Ed wrote his first draft, he had a vague feeling that something wasn't quite right about it, so he decided to let the work sit before he began to revise. As Ed reviewed his rough draft later, he realized the problem: he wanted to talk about the children's discoveries rather than their delight. He changed his topic sentence so it would speak only of the discoveries the kids had made, and that change gave the paragraph the sharp focus that it had lacked in the first draft.

Ed's Revision

It was wonderful watching Stacey and Jeff discover the marvels of their pastries. Stacey picked up hers, bit down on it, and growled and giggled, scattering powdered sugar on the table. Jeff deliberately scooped up a glob of chocolate frosting and grinned as he popped the finger into his mouth. Satisfied that the roll was going to be as good as he'd hoped, he slowly took a large bite. "There's frosting inside!" he shouted as soon as he could talk. Stacey licked the sugar from her fingers as Jeff scooped custard filling into his mouth, then walked around the table to offer a fingerful to his sister. "There's salt on mine," she observed, and offered a finger to Jeff who loudly kissed off the powdered sugar coating. Completely absorbed in the tastes, the activities, and the pure pleasure of the treat, Stacey knelt on her high chair, sometimes leaning most of her body on the table, sometimes drawing back to take a bite, scoop out some filling, smear powdered sugar around on the table, or giggle and blow a razzberry. Jeff, having eaten his roll into a crescent, was hard at work on the center, the outer edges wrapping nearly halfway around his small head. As their stomachs filled and they realized there would be no new tastes or textures, their chewing slowed, but they made no move to leave their precious goodies. Stacey licked her fingers, then her whole hand, then contentedly blew a razzberry on her palm. She finished her milk and looked back over her shoulder into the hall. "No monsters behind me," she mused and quietly began playing with her shoe. Jeff chewed slowly and quietly. The discovery was complete.

In revising, Marcia narrowed her paragraph at the outline stage by focusing just on Stacey rather than on both of the children. Ed narrowed his paragraph in the second draft to focus on the discoveries the children made rather than on their general delight. In each case, the changes made the details sharper and clearer. This sharper focus almost forces the writer to discuss the subject in more detail, and that detail gives life to a piece of writing.

But the focus isn't the only thing that clarifies our picture of the action in these paragraphs. Look again at these two sentences from Marcia's drafts:

First draft

Stacey ... stood up to reveal a shirt ready for the laundry.

Second draft

She rose proudly to reveal the disastrous results on her head and shirt.

Both sentences show what Stacey did, but the second sentence shows us how Stacey felt about what she had done and how Marcia felt about what Stacey had done. Four words, the verb "rose," the adverb "proudly," the adjective "disastrous," and the noun "results," bring the actions and reactions dramatically to life.

As you revise your description of an activity, be sure that you focus your reader's attention where you want it and that you look for words that will show not only a clear picture of the action but also people's attitudes toward the action.

 Writing Activity 6.5

- □ Revise your paragraph from activity 6.4 using the categories for judging paragraphs from Chapter 1 (pages 11–12).
- □ Choose precise nouns and adjectives.
- □ Pay particular attention to your choices of verbs and adverbs.

Other Suggestions for Writing

1. Carefully observe a sporting event, either live or on television. Make notes as you observe, and then write a paragraph about a particularly exciting part of the event.
2. Watch children doing something. Write about their activity.
3. Watch people working. Write about what they do in the process of getting a task done.
4. Observe people in a meeting—in a classroom or a church, for example. Write about what people do during the meeting.
5. Write about the backstage activity during a play, concert, or other performance.

Terms to Remember

adverb   A part of speech used to modify or describe a verb, adjective, adverb, or even a whole sentence. Here we focus on its use to modify a verb. In the sentence "He ran quickly," "quickly" is an adverb.

limiting or narrowing the focus   Centering the reader's attention on a single aspect of the subject being written about.

verb   A part of speech that expresses action or state of being. In the sentence "The dog barked," "barked" is a verb that expresses action. In the sentence "The girl was tired," "was" is a verb that expresses a state of being.

word choice   A term used to describe the particular words used by a writer. The English language has many words that mean the same or nearly the same thing, and a writer selects or chooses the most specific or effective words to convey an idea.

Preview for Chapter 7

In Chapter 7, look for these words and phrases that might be new to you:

1. Purpose
2. Comparison paragraph
3. Example paragraph
4. Process paragraph
5. Cause–effect paragraph
6. Transition
7. Point-by-point style
8. Block style
9. Definition paragraph
10. Opinion paragraph

Let's take a minute here to review all of the preview techniques we've mentioned so far. Before reading a textbook, look at the table of contents and see what information the book contains and how it is organized. Before reading any textbook chapter, read the chapter title, count the number of pages, and look at each main heading to see what the chapter is about and how long it will take you to read it. Finally, look at the end of the chapter and quickly read any summary information, review questions, or, as is the case in this text, definitions of words. All of this preview activity should take about five minutes and is well worth the time it takes because, having become somewhat familiar with the material, you will better understand what you read. In turn, increased understanding will give you more confidence and more success in any course you take.

7

MORE PARAGRAPH PRACTICE

You can probably remember times when you learned a new skill—how to drive a car, or how to ice-skate, or play tennis, or whatever. Most likely, learning the basic steps was the hardest part, sometimes even the most frustrating and discouraging. But once you got the basics down and continued to practice, you probably found that using your new skill became much easier and actually fun. The same is true of writing. In earlier chapters you learned a step-by-step process of writing paragraphs. Now that you know basically how to proceed, this chapter gives you a chance to practice those steps and to experience the rewards that come as you watch yourself improve. Just as with tennis or driving, writing will become much more enjoyable as you become more comfortable with it.

In the previous chapters, you have read and written descriptive and narrative paragraphs. You have written about a person, an object, a place, an activity, and an experience you remember. In the first part of this chapter, we show you some descriptive and narrative paragraphs that our students have written in response to a variety of assignments, and we give you a chance to practice your skills on those assignments. You or your instructor can choose the assignments that are most appropriate.

In the second part of the chapter, we introduce some other kinds of writing that are commonly used in college assignments. Again, we show you student models and offer you a chance to practice on the assignments that you or your instructor think will help you most as you develop your writing skills.

The process of writing any of these paragraphs does not change; you will still go through the same five steps. The student paragraphs we have chosen are pieces that we have particularly enjoyed reading and our students have enjoyed writing.

PRACTICE ON THE DESCRIPTIVE PARAGRAPH

Remember that to write an effective description you must be thorough in your brainstorming, whether you are writing from memory or from direct observation. Next, you must identify your dominant impression of your subject and state it in your topic sentence. Then as you write and revise, be sure to include details that involve your reader's senses—sight, smell, touch, and so on. Finally, remember that using comparisons is an excellent way to help your reader understand what you are describing.

Writing about an Unusual Person

When you write about an unusual person, be particularly careful as you brainstorm, draft, and revise to identify the characteristics that set that person apart from most others. What, exactly, makes your subject unusual?

As you read Gregg's paragraph, notice the detail in his description of his subject's looks and actions. He states his dominant impression in his last sentence.

Gregg's Paragraph

I heard her before I saw her. Leaning heavily on a battered shopping cart, she pushed it down the broken and cracked sidewalk, creating a loud clacking sound. I could tell from a distance that she was quite old by the way she walked and held her short, stocky body. Her head was covered by a greasy, wet, wool cap. A dirty, frayed overcoat covered her bent, dumpy body. A pair of unmatched green and gray socks were draped over her worn, muddy, oversized walking shoes. As she approached the bus stop bench where I sat, I could see her cracked, white lips moving constantly in her own private conversation. She glowered at me as if I were an intruder in her world. Her rheumy gray and red eyes were framed by greasy, gray locks that hung limply down around her torn collar. An alcohol-reddened nose protruded from underneath bushy gray eyebrows. She ambled past me and purposefully approached the garbage can at the end of my bench. With surprising quickness, she nimbly sifted through the garbage. Suddenly she pulled back her coat sleeve from her dirty wrist and plunged after an aluminum can; she quickly shoved it into one of her many brightly-colored shopping bags. She looked suspiciously at me as if I were going to steal her newfound prize. I looked quickly away. When I looked back, she had replaced the lid of the trash can and continued on her search for treasure from trash. As I watched her walk away, I was struck by the contrast between her independence and her pitiful condition.

 Writing Activity 7.1

- Write a paragraph describing an unusual or out-of-the-ordinary person. The person does not need to be someone you know. If you wish, base your description on a photograph or a drawing of a person.

- Complete each of the five steps of the writing process.

Writing about the Room You're In

When you describe a place, observe it carefully. Study the notes you make, and state your dominant impression. Be sure that the details you choose and the words you select to describe those details are all focused on the dominant impression.

As you read Larry's paragraph printed here, notice especially how his details and vocabulary develop and reinforce the idea that the room he describes is dull.

Larry's Paragraph

This classroom is too dull to do anything in except study. All that seems to be going on around here is that the cement blocks of the walls are cracking. The drapes are drab; they must match the personality of the person who picked them out. The plants don't help either, for their dying leaves almost match the off-white walls. The windows are small and set so high on the wall that I can't see anything but gray, cloudy sky out of them, and the two boring rows of neon lights don't do anything to brighten the picture. The monotonous droning of the ventilator is just about enough to put someone in the grave. The clock doesn't make any noise at all, but its hands seem to move at about half the speed they should. If I were to wish to be somewhere else in the world, I'd wish to be anywhere else!

 Writing Activity 7.2

- Write a paragraph describing the room you are in.
- Observe it carefully, using any of the three brainstorming techniques discussed in Chapter 2.
- Form your dominant impression.
- Complete the other steps of the writing process.

Writing about Your Pet or Another Animal

When you describe an animal, observe its looks and actions in much the same way you would observe a person. Notice what human qualities it seems to have, for comparisons of animals with people can be effective. Notice, too, what animal qualities it has that your reader might expect to find, and what qualities it has that make this individual animal unique.

In her paragraph, Deborah focuses on the qualities of her cat that make it unique. The details about the cat's nose, ears, and actions all support her topic sentence. Also, the paragraph shows the warm relationship between Deborah and her cat; it's clear that she is writing about something that she knows and cares about.

Deborah's Paragraph

My cat "Bunny" looks like her name. She has snow-white fur with brownish-red spots and weighs 12 pounds.

Her moist pink nose and long flat ears are constantly twitching and moving in a nervous, approval-seeking way. Loud noises and sudden movements startle her, and discipline for wrongdoing sends her scurrying for unknown hideaways in my big closet. At night when I retire, she is there nestled securely on my bed. In the morning as I busily prepare for my day, she hops around under my feet making sure that I don't forget to feed her. Her appearance and manner are so rabbit-like that sometimes I forget that she is a cat.

 Writing Activity 7.3

- □ Write a paragraph describing a pet you own. If you do not own a pet, write about a friend's pet or go to a pet store or the zoo and write about an animal you see there.
- □ As you observe, be sure to record details about the animal's habits, personality, and appearance.
- □ Be sure the details and vocabulary choices in your paragraph focus on and support your dominant impression.

PRACTICE ON THE NARRATIVE PARAGRAPH

Remember that to write an effective narrative, you must brainstorm thoroughly, recalling as many details as you can about the event you want to describe. You will be writing from memory, and you often won't remember specific details unless you force yourself to. Remember that the reader wasn't at the scene of your experience, so your reader can understand that experience only from the words you put on paper. The words you choose must vividly convey the details. The order in which you present the details will also affect your reader's understanding of the experience. Finally, your controlling idea, stated or unstated, will be your dominant impression of the event.

Writing about an Unforgettable Experience

Writing about an unforgettable experience requires that you know what makes the experience unforgettable and that you share the experience with the reader in such a way that the reader, too, will know. Manuel writes about a surfing experience. His paragraph does a good job of sharing the sights, sounds, and smells of being inside a wave, but unless the reader has experienced such things as pulling himself into a wave or "kicking through," the reader may not understand what is unforgettable about Manuel's experience. There is a problem in Manuel's paragraph, then, with audience awareness, but the specific sensory details are very effective.

Manuel's Paragraph

One of the world's truly unique experiences is riding inside a large wave, better known as "getting tubed." One typical hot summer day in July, I grabbed my board and headed down to the beach. I paddled out to the first reef, waited until a good wave came by, and then paddled hard to catch it. Then I stood up, dropped down to the bottom, reached back, and pulled myself into the wave. Being inside that wave was the essence of tranquility, knowing that I had so much power behind me, yet feeling the calm. I could see out through the water, and everything was blurry but strangely bright. The smell of salt was everywhere. I heard the whirling sound of the wind blowing through the tunnel formed by the falling crest. It was peaceful; I didn't have a care in the world; I started to lose myself. Suddenly, though, I knew it was time to kick through, and I paddled back out, hoping to find another "perfect wave."

 Writing Activity 7.4

- Write a paragraph about an experience you will never forget.
- Show not only what happened, but also why you find the experience unforgettable.

□ Be sure to include all the details necessary for your reading audience to understand the experience.

Writing about a Day's Events

When you write about the events of a day—just as when you tell someone about the events of a day—you leave out most of what happened. Those details you choose to include in your writing must therefore be clearly related to the controlling idea of your paragraph.

As you read Tracy's paragraph about her friend Rose, notice how her choices of words and details show the loneliness and monotony of her friend's life. Although Rose surely must work with other people and have some contact with friends or family, Tracy has chosen not to include these details in her paragraph, thus reinforcing the idea that Rose's life is lonely.

Tracy's Paragraph

Rose seems to be a lonely person. The main reason is the fact that her husband is incarcerated. She lives the life of a prison wife. Her days are routine: she gets up and gets ready for work, which takes an hour, drives an hour to work, works eight hours, drives an hour home. Rose walks into her small apartment and automatically goes to her closet for a change of clothes. There isn't time to water the plants; she has a visit to make. This is the one part of her day she looks forward to. The time spent with her husband is her time for sharing and relaxation. Upon arriving at the reformatory, she knows she has a long hour and a half wait before she sees her husband. She reads to pass this time away. The three hours with her husband go by too quickly. Rose knows she must say good-night again and go home alone. At home again, Rose takes her bath, watches an occasional television program, and drifts off to sleep with thoughts of problems she has talked over with her husband on her mind.

Writing Activity 7.5

- Write a paragraph about a day in your life or the life of a friend. The day may be typical or unusual.

- Brainstorm thoroughly to discover your controlling idea.

- In your paragraph, include only those details that support your controlling idea.

Writing about a Learning Experience

When you write about an experience from which you learned something—whether it is a fact or an idea you learned in school or something you learned about yourself—the details of your paragraph must clearly show what you learned and how you learned it. Tammy's paragraph begins with a clear statement about what she learned. Then it gives some necessary background to help the reader understand the situation. Finally, it shows what she did and how she learned from it.

Tammy's Paragraph

Yesterday I learned that I should never wait to ask my teachers for help. As I sat in my math lecture class, I felt hopeless, lost, and worried. I was worried because I had gotten four chapters behind in my homework, and even though I had studied long and hard the day before, trying to make them up, I was more lost than ever. I simply couldn't grasp the work in the first chapter that I was behind in, so there was no way I could finish or even understand the next three chapters. While the teacher was lecturing, I couldn't understand or participate. In fact, my situation seemed so hopeless that I didn't even hear half of what the teacher said. After class, embarrassed about being so far behind but knowing I had no other choice, I asked the teacher for help. I'll never put off asking for help again. The teacher explained the material that was so important to me, and he made sure I understood it. I learned one more thing, too. I'm not the only person who gets confused and falls behind; there were two other girls also in to see him.

 Writing Activity 7.6

- Write about an experience from which you learned something.
- State clearly what you learned.
- Show how you felt during the experience.

PRACTICE ON OTHER TYPES OF PARAGRAPHS

So far in this book you have been practicing your skills on descriptive and narrative paragraphs, but there are other kinds of paragraphs that you will be expected to write in many of the courses you take. The basic principles and the process of writing do not change for these paragraphs. In fact, you have already been using many of the specialized techniques you will learn in this section.

This section will discuss, show, and give you practice in writing paragraphs in specific patterns for specific purposes. For example, a writer's **purpose** might be to show the similarities of two teachers that she once had, and thus she would choose to write a **comparison paragraph**. If she wanted to write about the several different kinds of teachers she's had, she might choose to write an **example paragraph**. She could choose to write a **process paragraph** to show how a person might become a teacher, or she could write a **cause–effect paragraph** to show how one of her teachers made her want to become a teacher herself.

Sometimes, of course, a writer will start writing about a subject with no particular pattern in mind and decide in a second, third, or later draft that the paragraph should be presented in a specific pattern. Knowing what patterns are available and how those patterns work can help any writer.

Writing the Example Paragraph

Sometimes an idea can be best explained by using examples, and in such cases the writer must be sure that the examples do, in fact, illustrate the controlling idea. If, say, you want to show a reader that your Aunt Elizabeth is stingy, you might write something like this: "Last night at the restaurant, my Aunt Elizabeth left a twenty-five cent tip for a ten-dollar meal." If you were writing a paragraph about Aunt Elizabeth, you would develop your controlling idea with several such examples.

In Ben's paragraph, the controlling idea is that his good luck charm brings him luck only after he's used it for something. He uses examples to convince his reader that the charm really does seem to bring him luck.

Ben's Paragraph

Not many people have army can openers, especially one as beat up as mine, and not many can openers are good luck charms. The really strange thing about my good luck charm, though, is that it only works after I've used it for something. For example, one time my truck wouldn't start in front of Safeway, so I pulled out my good luck charm and used it to scrape and tighten the battery cables. Sure enough, the truck started. Satisfied that I could get home, I went into the store, did my grocery shopping, and bought a couple of lottery tickets. When I was back outside, I looked at my numbers and saw I had won 2,000 dollars! Another time, when I was in the army, I did not receive an expected promotion. After using my can opener to open a lot of beer cans that night, I was promoted to corporal the next day by some special orders from our headquarters. I never did find out why those orders were issued. I think that if I use my can opener a lot more, good luck will just follow me around.

 Writing Activity 7.7   □ Write a paragraph that states an idea and explains it with the use of examples.

Writing the Process Paragraph

When you want to explain to a reader how to do something, a process paragraph is your only choice. There are two chief things to keep in mind as you write a process paragraph: first, tell your reader what process you are describing, and, second, give every necessary step in the order in which it occurs. Use clear **transitions** (first, second, third, next, finally, and so on) to let your reader know when you are moving from one step to another.

Vic lets the reader know immediately that he will show the process of making a baby laugh. Then he shows the steps to take, starting with the simplest cases and moving to the most extreme. Vic uses clear transitions such as "after that," "at this point," and "with this maneuver" to keep us moving through the process. Also, he consistently uses the second person "you" throughout the paragraph because he is giving directions specifically to the reader.

Vic's Paragraph

A most rewarding experience is making a baby laugh. The process involves a small amount of mental preparation. You must understand that it is okay to act goofy in front of a baby. After that knowledge is firm in your head, you should mold a grand ear-to-ear smile. The smile should be accompanied by a vast variation of facial contortions. A few examples are lifted eyebrows, wiggling ears, and a great look of surprise. If baby has not yet laughed, you can quickly develop a repertoire of strange but lively sounds. Hoots, beeps, barks, shrieks, and squeaks all work rather well. You must experiment with the particular pitch and tone which may tickle the individual baby's fancy. At this point the baby should be laughing. If so, keep up the good work; however, in some extreme cases all of the above might not affect that unresponsive child. These cases will require physical action because there are areas on everyone that react to the tickle of a finger. Some of these key locations are under the arms, on the tiny tummy, or on the bottoms of the feet. They may vary with different models. With this maneuver the baby will be laughing gleefully, and everybody's happy with a joyful baby. This is the true reward for your efforts.

**Writing
Activity
7.8**

□ Write a paragraph explaining how to do something. Think of something that not many people know how to do; avoid the obvious, such as how to bake a cake or how to change your oil.

□ Write in complete sentences rather than in recipe-like shorthand.

□ Use clear transitions like "first," "second," "next," and "finally."

Writing the Comparison Paragraph

Sometimes when we write, we find ourselves focusing on how things are alike, and in cases like that, we might choose to develop the entire paragraph in the comparison pattern. The comparison paragraph shows similarities, and the contrast paragraph shows differences, but "comparison" is often used to refer to paragraphs that show either similarities or differences. In writing comparison (or contrast), you must first state what two things are being compared. You must know which specific points you plan to compare, and you must arrange the details in a logical order.

Details in a comparison paragraph may be arranged either in **point-by-point** or in **block style**, and the two paragraphs that follow show those two styles. The first example, David's paragraph, is point-by-point; it compares a jet mechanic and a surgeon on six points, and it completes its discussion of one point before it goes to the next. The second example, Frank's paragraph, uses the block style; it compares people who climb Mount Everest with people who eat in the school cafeteria, and it discusses the climbers completely before it discusses the eaters. In something as short as a paragraph, the block style is often smoother and more effective than is the point-by-point.

As you read David's paragraph, notice that the comparison is well-balanced. Each point he makes about the mechanic he also makes about the surgeon. Words like "just as" and "both" help to keep the reader's mind sharply focused on the comparison.

David's Paragraph

Being a jet mechanic is a lot like being a surgeon. First, the jet mechanic has to examine an engine just as

carefully as a surgeon examines a person when something is wrong. After diagnosing the problem, both the surgeon and the mechanic have to take on the intricate and complicated job of fixing it. Jet mechanics use expensive instruments and tools, just as surgeons do, and both are required to know everything about their profession or the operation could be a failure. The work is difficult, hard, and time-consuming in both jobs; however, the mechanic and the surgeon both feel a certain satisfaction when the job is completed, when the jet engine works properly, or when the cured patient walks out the hospital doors.

As you read Frank's paragraph, notice that both parts are about equal in length and that the second part deals with each point that is brought up in the first part. The discussion, then, is balanced. The phrase "like the climbers" is an effective transition between the two parts because it clearly lets us know that the first part has ended and the comparison has begun.

Frank's Paragraph

Eating lunch in the school cafeteria is a lot like climbing Mount Everest. To get to the mountain, climbers have to travel a long way through the foothills. When they arrive at the mountain, they start up a route they've decided on ahead of time, but they'll usually find some problem that makes them change their plans. As they get closer to the top, the climbers face great hardship and danger, but the few who reach the top experience a thrill that can't be matched. Like the climbers, cafeteria diners begin with a long trip since lines are always long and slow. Once they get to the steam tables, diners' plans, like those of the climbers, usually change because of unexpected problems. Maybe the cooks have run out of a main dish, or maybe the food just doesn't look good. As the diners near their goal, they too face hardship and danger. First they must somehow find the money to pay for what they've chosen, then comes the death-defying act of eating the food. The comparison ends there, though, because the only thrill in finishing a cafeteria lunch is knowing that you won't have to go back again until the next day.

Writing Activity 7.9

- ☐ Write a paragraph comparing two things that at first seem to be very different from each other.
- ☐ Choose the specific points on which you will compare your subjects.
- ☐ Arrange those specific points in a logical order.

Writing the Cause–Effect Paragraph

Sometimes it is useful to explain why things happen; the cause–effect paragraph does just that. If you don't study for a test and you fail the test, your failure is the effect, and your lack of study is the cause. If you burn your hand on your coffee cup and then drop and break it, the burn is the cause, and the broken cup is the effect. Of course it wouldn't take a paragraph to explain either of these two incidents, but explaining something like why the sky appears blue or why you have certain feelings can require a paragraph or much more.

When you write a cause–effect paragraph, you must analyze your subject very carefully. Be sure that what you identify as a cause is, in fact, a cause. Ask, "Does that really cause this? Is this really an effect of that?" Be careful not to jump to conclusions.

In Paige's paragraph, she explains that dandelions make her happy because they remind her of her grandmother. Dandelions are the cause; happy thoughts of her grandmother are the effect.

Paige's Paragraph

On my way home from school yesterday, I saw a yard full of dandelions, and suddenly I felt very happy. As I thought about that, I realized that I felt happy because dandelions always remind me of my grandmother. Gram used to tell me that dandelions were her favorite flower, even though the rest of the neighborhood folks spent time and money trying to rid their lawns of the hated weed. When I see them, I can hear her voice saying, "I sure despise that old, cold winter more than these pretty, bright yellow flowers. I'm glad they're finally here." Also, they make me remember the warmth of her hugs when I'd pick a large bunch and run into the house with them. She'd find a vase to hold them and give them a place of honor on the mantle, and that made me feel special, for I felt that I'd given her something special. The joy that was always on her face is the thing I remember best about Gram, and dandelions always bring back the vision of that face. It's no wonder that dandelions make me happy.

 Writing Activity 7.10

□ Write a paragraph that shows how something causes an effect or effects.

□ Be sure you distinguish clearly between the cause and the effects.

Writing the Definition Paragraph

We often use words such as "freedom," "success," "pleasure," or "love," but these words usually require some definition because they mean different things to different people. They are highly abstract. Also, common, apparently simple words can have unusual meanings for some people, and these unusual meanings need to be explained or defined. When you write a **definition paragraph** to define an abstract term or give a special definition to an ordinary term, you must show your reader, as exactly as you can, what that term means to you. Both of our sample paragraphs do this well.

As you read Maryanne's paragraph, notice that she begins with a general definition of "success." She follows that general definition with specific examples. The examples help us to understand exactly what she means by "success." We can look at a person in a certain situation and say, "Maryanne would (or would not) call that person a success."

Maryanne's Paragraph

To some people, success can be measured in dollars, but to me success is the feeling that I've done the best job I can do at something I enjoy doing. Last fall, for example, I had decided that my effort at raising sheep would be successful if I could win a ribbon at the county fair, but even though I didn't win a ribbon, I still call the experience a success. I know I did the best I could, I made some new friends, I learned from the winners how to do better next time, and I returned home feeling successful. I'm not the only person who defines success this way, either. My friend Fred was what most people would call a successful businessman, but he never woke up feeling happy. Two years ago, he quit his job and is now making a lot less money, but he is enjoying his new job. Both of us would call him a success because he enjoys what he is doing, and he feels he does it well.

As you read Tammera's paragraph, you will see that she begins with a specific definition of "fad" and goes on to explain what, in her experience, has led her to define "fad" as she does. There is no doubt in our minds about what Tammera means by the word "fad." The paragraph is also wonderfully humorous, largely because Tammera is able to laugh at herself.

Tammera's Paragraph

To me, the word "fad" means almost the same thing as "fade" because fads fade away. It always seems that by the time I've caught on to a fad, it's dissolved. The fashion fads have fooled me most often. Last spring when mid-calf pants were in, I too, wanted to be in. Therefore, I proceeded to cut the bottom six inches off every pair of pants that I owned. They all still fit half a year later, but not one pair was in style. You'd think I would have learned. A few months later, I saw the trendy movie *Flashdance*. The clothing styles in the film were uniquely different. Once again, I cut the arms and collars off every sweatshirt and T-shirt in my closet. When

the movie dropped from the top ten, so did the fad, and
I was foiled again. Now I have learned my lesson. I won't
be fooled again by these spurious, fleeting fads. I just
purchased a pair of pink, plastic shoes. . . .

 **Writing
Activity
7.11**

□ Explain or define what a specific word or phrase
  means to you.

□ Give examples from your own experience.

Writing the Opinion Paragraph

Everyone has opinions, and most of us don't hesitate to express them,
at least to our friends. Opinions, though, vary from person to person, and
some opinions deserve more consideration than do others. The opinion of
an expert mechanic about what caused an airplane crash is more likely to
be accurate than is the opinion of an untrained eyewitness. In events that
directly concern us, though, we are all experts in some way or another,
and our opinions are important.

When you write an **opinion paragraph**, write about something that
is important to you and that you know about from your direct, personal
experience. State clearly what your opinion is, and be sure you explain
why you hold that opinion.

Kirsten wrote her opinion paragraph as one of her assignments, but
she later rewrote it as a letter to the editor of the local newspaper, where
it was published. The letters to the editor column is one of the most widely
read sections of any newspaper, and it is an important place for citizens to
share their opinions about matters that concern them.

Kirsten's Paragraph

On March 3, the Spokane Falls Community College
girls' basketball team won the state championship for
the second year in a row. Since that was our second

consecutive state title, one would think that <u>The Spokes-man—Review</u> would print a large article announcing this achievement. Turning to the sports section of Sunday's paper, I noticed large pictures and lengthy articles on the girls' state "B" basketball championship game and another article announcing that the Spokane Community College men's team had finished fifth in its state tournament. Mention of the Spokane Falls girls' team championship didn't appear until three pages into the sports section. This article had no pictures. Being a member of this talented team, I am disappointed to find so little mention of our successful team.

Here is Kirsten's letter as it was published in the Spokane, Washington, *Spokesman—Review*. The editor has made some changes because editorial-page editors like letters to be brief, to the point, and about one specific issue. They may sometimes edit letters by omitting sections or by correcting spelling and punctuation, and they will almost always make the paragraphs shorter.

Kirsten's Letter

"Your Views"
The Spokesman—Review
Spokane, WA 99210

Dear Editor:
    On March 3, the Spokane Falls Community College girls' basketball team won the state championship for the second year in a row.
    Since that was our second consecutive state title, one would think that *The Spokesman—Review* would print a large article announcing this achievement.
    Turning to the sports section of Sunday's paper, I noticed large pictures and lengthy articles on the girls' state "B" basketball championship game and another long article announcing that the Spokane Community College men's team had finished fifth in its state tournament.
    Mention of the Spokane Falls girls' team championship didn't appear until three pages into the sports sec-

tion, and this article had no pictures. Being a member of this talented team, I am disappointed to find so little mention of our successful team.

Kirsten Riegel

 Writing Activity 7.12

☐ Write a paragraph expressing your opinion about something that is important to you and that you know about from personal experience.

☐ Be sure you have one clear controlling idea.

☐ Be sure you support your ideas clearly.

☐ Be sure your facts are correct.

☐ If you wish, write your paragraph as a letter to the editor.

This chapter marks the end of our discussion of general paragraph writing skills. The rest of this book discusses the kinds of writing you're likely to have to do for other college courses and how you can apply the principles of good writing you've learned so far. As you may have already discovered, the more you write and practice these skills, the more confident you become each time you write.

Terms to Remember

block style   The style used in a comparison paragraph when the writer discusses all points about the first subject of the comparison, then goes on to discuss those same points about the subject being compared.

cause–effect paragraph   A paragraph developed in a pattern that shows why things happen. A cause–effect paragraph shows the results (effects) of some action (cause).

comparison paragraph   A paragraph developed in a pattern that shows how two or more things are similar or what they have in common. A comparison paragraph may also show differences; this pattern is also referred to as comparison–contrast. Showing only differences is using the contrast paragraph pattern.

definition paragraph   A paragraph that explains what a word or phrase means.

example paragraph   A paragraph that is developed by the use of examples that support, clarify, or explain the controlling idea.

opinion paragraph   A paragraph that states an opinion and explains why the writer holds that opinion.

point-by-point style   The style used in a comparison paragraph when the writer compares both subjects on one point, then both subjects on another point, and so on.

process paragraph   A paragraph that explains how something is done. A process paragraph shows, in order, the steps that are taken to accomplish something.

purpose   What the writer hopes to accomplish with a piece of writing. A writer whose purpose is to explain how to do something would write a process paragraph, but a writer whose purpose is to explain the meaning of a term would write a definition paragraph.

transition   A word, phrase, or sentence that moves the reader's attention from one idea to another. Words like "and" or "plus" show that you are adding information; words like "but" or "however" show that you are contrasting ideas. Effective use of transitions is an important aid to readers, particularly if the ideas being discussed are difficult to understand.

III

WRITING THE SUMMARY PARAGRAPH

Preview for Chapter 8

The list of new terms for Chapter 8 is long, but the ideas are important.

1. Summary
2. Skim
3. Implied topic sentences
4. Major supporting details
5. Minor supporting details
6. Block diagram
7. Paraphrase
8. Quote
9. Generalizing

Authors use a variety of ways to highlight important ideas or concepts in the chapters of a textbook. They may put a word in italics, number a list of ideas, or use a different color of type to make sure you see the information. In this text, we have also used a variety of ways to highlight important ideas. As you preview this chapter, look for boldface (darkened) print, large print, numbered lists, and lists marked by large, black squares. Become familiar with and be conscious of any signs and symbols which are included in the chapter to help you identify and remember the key points.

8

WRITING A SUMMARY

In this chapter, we will shift gears and begin work on a different kind of writing. Instead of discovering, creating, and writing about your own ideas, you will be identifying and writing down the ideas of others. You'll be writing **summary** paragraphs.

A summary condenses information. It makes a little out of a lot. You summarize when you take notes at a lecture or meeting, or when you tell someone about your vacation. News articles or letters home are summaries of events; a topic sentence is a summary of a paragraph. For this chapter, you'll summarize, or retell, what other people have written. When you write a summary, you look for the main points that the original writer makes and then state them in your own words. You shorten the original without changing its meaning.

Knowing how to write effective summaries is a skill useful in and out of college. Writing a summary of a textbook chapter will help you to review before an exam. An instructor may ask for a summary to see that you have read and understood an article, story, or textbook chapter. Sometimes you will have to summarize someone else's ideas for a longer paper you're writing. And, as in a book or movie review, your summary might encourage someone to read the original piece, or it might let someone know that the piece will not be useful. Finally, writing summaries can improve your own writing by making you more conscious of how other writers put ideas together. Summaries thus help you discover new ways of combining ideas in your own writing. For all of these reasons, summary writing skills are important skills to know.

MAJOR STEPS IN SUMMARIZING

There are five basic steps to summarizing another piece of writing. These steps differ a little from the steps in the writing you have done so far, but you may notice a few similarities. The steps are as follows:

1. Understanding the original
2. Stating the controlling idea
3. Identifying supporting details
4. Writing the first draft
5. Revising the summary

In this chapter, you'll first practice summary writing on some short pieces; then you'll practice on longer pieces, which, of course, are what you will usually summarize. In summarizing a single paragraph, you will see that Steps 4 and 5—drafting and revising—are shortened and combined because your summary will be only a single sentence. When you summarize longer pieces, however, you'll write a complete paragraph, so you'll need to do Steps 4 and 5 separately. But no matter what length the piece is, the first thing you must do is understand what the author is saying.

STEP 1:
Understanding the Original

Good summary writers are, above all, careful readers. To be a careful reader, you must first preview the writing to see what it will offer you. Then you must thoroughly read it—sometimes several times—to get a good handle on what the author says. This process of preview and careful reading leads to a complete understanding of the original that will prepare you for writing a good summary.

In the chapter previews of this book, we have already explored how to preview a textbook chapter. Previewing something you plan to summarize requires much the same techniques. Namely, follow these guidelines:

Preview Checklist

- Look at the title of the work and try to predict what you'll read about. Turn the title into a question and try to answer it as you read.

- Flip through the article to see how long it is, whether it's divided with headings and subheadings, and whether it has pictures, charts, graphs, or other aids to understanding.
- **Skim** the entire article (read it once through *quickly*) to get a general idea of its meaning and organization. Read the first and last paragraphs completely since these often contain important clues to meaning and purpose.

When you've finished your preview, read the article carefully, several times if necessary, until you understand it thoroughly. Here are a few guidelines to help you in this step.

Reading Checklist

- On your first careful reading, underline any important ideas you see. If you find yourself underlining most of the sentences, you're underlining too much. At this point, you should simply be trying to see the big picture.
- Circle any words whose meanings you are not sure of. Look up the words in a dictionary. Write the meanings of those words in the margins.
- On your next careful reading, make notes in the margins or on a separate piece of paper. Pretend you're talking to the author. Write down questions you have or any other observations.
- Carefully read the article as often as necessary until you understand the author's meaning.
- Close the book, and then, in your own words, write a short statement of what the article says. If you feel comfortable with this one-sentence comment, you're probably ready to go to Step 2.

STEP 2:
Stating the Controlling Idea

You're used to stating the controlling idea—the topic sentence—in your own writing, but now you'll need to find and state the controlling idea of someone else's writing. Because the topic sentence guides both the writer and the reader, when you read something to summarize, you must identify the author's controlling idea and let it guide your understanding.

In turn, when you write your summary, you must clearly state the author's controlling idea so that it can guide your reader's understanding of your summary. There are three things you can do to help you identify and state the controlling idea:

Controlling Idea Checklist

- Ask yourself what the subject of the article is. Be as specific as you can. Is the article about cars, or is it specifically about Mustangs? Is it about Mustangs, or is it specifically about body designs in Mustangs?
- Ask yourself what the article says about the subject. What point is the author making? Is the author saying that body designs in Mustangs have improved over time?
- Write a complete sentence that contains the subject of the article and states the author's point. This is the author's controlling idea. It will also become the controlling idea of your summary.

We examine the following example in light of this checklist.

Example 1

Although an egg appears fragile, its shell is remarkably strong. This is because its oval shape embodies the same principle as an arched bridge. Eggs will bear extremely heavy weights on their rounded sides before breaking. Scientists have found that the average weight needed to crush a fowl's egg is 9 pounds. They had to pile 13 pounds on a turkey's egg before it gave way, 26 pounds on a swan's egg, and 120 pounds on an ostrich egg before it broke.

The subject of this paragraph is eggs or, more specifically, the shells of eggs. (We could be more specific still and say it is the shapes of eggshells.)

What the author says about eggshells is that their shape makes them remarkably strong.

The controlling idea, then, can be stated like this:

The shape of eggshells makes eggs remarkably strong.

Let's find the controlling idea of one more example.

Example 2

> Eggs are not all shaped alike. Birds that lay their eggs in sheltered places (in nests or hollow trees or underground burrows) usually lay oval or spherical eggs. But many sea-birds, which nest on rocky ledges, lay pear- or cone-shaped eggs that taper sharply from the broad end. The guillemot, an arctic bird, makes no nest and often lays its single egg on the flat ledge of a cliff. If the egg were spherical, it might be knocked over by the birds or blown off by the wind. Because the egg is pear-shaped, it does not roll when bumped but swings around in circles. Birds that lay many large pear-shaped eggs arrange them with the narrow pointed ends inwards and almost touching, so as to pack as many as possible under the mother's breast.

The subject of this paragraph is eggs or, more specifically, the shapes of eggs.

What the author says about the shapes of eggs is that they vary according to where the birds nest.

The controlling idea for this paragraph, then, might be stated as follows:

The shapes of birds' eggs vary according to where the birds nest.

Note that the controlling idea was stated clearly in the first example but implied, or suggested, in the second. **Implied topic sentences** are more difficult to find than are stated topic sentences, but they are equally important because they guide what the paragraph or article is about.

In the upcoming writing activity, you will state the controlling idea of this next paragraph:

Example 3

> There is another big difference in the eggs laid by various birds. The quarter-inch-long eggs of hummingbirds go sixty to the ounce; a single ostrich egg may weigh three pounds. Between these extremes is the domestic hen's egg of 2 to $2\frac{1}{2}$ ounces. A naturalist once found that an empty ostrich egg shell would hold up to 18 hens' eggs. Ostrich eggs are small stuff, however, compared with the eggs of the now extinct

elephant bird. Some eggs of this huge, flightless bird discovered in Madagascar are 13 inches long. You could break 6 ostrich eggs or 150 hens' eggs into one of them.

 Writing Activity 8.1

☐ Write the subject of the Example 3 paragraph.

☐ Write what the author says about the subject.

☐ Write your statement of the controlling idea.

☐ Check your work against our sample printed at the end of this chapter (page 154). Are you close? There are, of course, many ways of saying any one idea, so don't be concerned if your words differ somewhat from our answer.

STEP 3:
Identifying Supporting Details

When you outlined your own paragraphs in previous chapters, the answers to your topic sentence question were the supporting details. They supported and clarified your controlling idea. When you write a summary, you'll identify the supporting details in the material you are reading; as you write those details down, you'll actually be outlining your summary.

Let's look at how Steps 1–3 can be applied to a short paragraph.

Example 4

Suspect silver coins can be tested in four ways. First, the ridges, or "reeding," on the edges of bad coins are usually uneven or missing in places. Second, the bright ringing sound is absent when the fake is dropped on a hard surface. Third, a bad coin almost always feels greasy to the touch. Finally, there is an "acid test" in which a drop of acid solution blackens any coin without a rich silver content.

The subject is testing suspect (that is, possibly counterfeit) silver coins.

The author says they can be tested in four ways.

The controlling idea is directly stated in the first sentence:

Suspect silver coins can be tested in four ways.

The supporting details are clearly identified by the words "first," "second," "third," and "finally." As we discussed in Chapter 7, authors commonly use transitions, or signal words, like these to identify main points. Having identified the controlling idea and supporting details, we are ready to outline our summary. We'll start by turning our statement of the controlling idea into a question.

Controlling idea:

Suspect silver coins can be tested in four ways.

Controlling idea question:

What are the four ways to test suspect silver coins?

Answers:

1. **check the edges**
2. **drop them on a hard surface**
3. **feel them**
4. **drop acid on them**

The answers to the question are the **major supporting details** for the paragraph you have read.

Steps 4 and 5:
Writing the Summary

When you write a summary of something as short as a paragraph, you need only state the controlling idea and the major details in a single sentence.

A summary of the Example 4 paragraph, then, could be:

> **Suspect silver coins can be tested by checking their edges, dropping them on a hard surface, feeling them, and dropping acid on them.**

Further Practice

Our next example paragraph is a little more complex, for it has both major and **minor supporting details**. Just as major details support and clarify the controlling idea, minor details support and clarify major details. We include the major details in a summary, but not the minor details. Let's first identify the subject and controlling idea of the following paragraph, and then we'll look more closely at the major and minor details.

Example 5

The theater audience in a horror movie can be divided into three groups. First of all, there are the gigglers. Members of this group may giggle out of nervousness, or they may find the scenes really funny. Then there are the hand grabbers. This group seems to think it can get through anything as long as there is something to hold. The last group contains the talkers. They always have a comment to make. For example, when the horrible-looking monster comes into view, they turn to a neighbor and say something clever like, "He's certainly attractive, isn't he?"

The subject is the theater audience in a horror movie.
The author says the audience can be divided into three groups.
Our statement of the controlling idea:

> **The theater audience in a horror movie can be divided into three groups.**

Again, the controlling idea we identified is identical to the author's topic sentence.

The clues to finding the major supporting details are the transitional words, "first of all," "then," and "the last group." While the Example 4 paragraph simply stated each major detail in a single sentence, this paragraph explains each of its major details with at least one additional sentence. These explanatory sentences contain minor supporting details that are not needed in a one-sentence summary. Our summary outline will therefore look like this:

Controlling idea:

The theater audience in a horror movie can be divided into three groups.

Controlling idea question:

Into what three groups can a horror movie audience be divided?

Answers:

1. **gigglers**
2. **hand grabbers**
3. **talkers**

Again, we can write a one-sentence summary of the paragraph by stating the controlling idea and the major details. Using our outline of the supporting details, we summarize Example 5 as follows:

The theater audience in a horror movie can be divided into the gigglers, the hand grabbers, and the talkers.

In Writing Activity 8.2 you will practice identifying the details in the following paragraph.

Example 6

Good preparation for a speech is essential, and there are several things you can do to prepare. First, you must select an appropriate topic. The best topic is one that will interest both you and your audience. Next, you need enough good material to present. It would be embarrassing to run out of things to say in just a short time, and being overprepared can prevent this. Another idea is to plan the order in which you will present your material. Last, practice your speech. The more you practice, the less nervous you will be on your big day.

Writing Activity 8.2

- □ Write the subject, what the author says about the subject, and your statement of the controlling idea of the paragraph in Example 6.
- □ Turn your statement into a question.
- □ Using the outline format, answer the question with the major supporting details of the paragraph.
- □ Write a one-sentence summary of the paragraph.
- □ Check your answers against our sample at the end of this chapter (page 154).

PRACTICING ON LONGER PIECES

Now that you've prepared a one-sentence summary of a paragraph and have learned the general techniques, it's time to summarize longer, more complex material.

Step 1:
Understanding the Original

The following article is from *Reader's Digest.* Before you read it, remember to preview the article by following the Preview Checklist on page 130. When you preview this article for a summary, turn the title into a question: "How can TV be hazardous to children?" After you preview the article, we'll talk more about what a first look reveals about the work.

WARNING: TV CAN BE HAZARDOUS TO CHILDREN

By Vance Packard

In recent years, television has made it a lot more difficult to be a good parent. While the evidence grows that heavy, indiscriminate TV watching can damage a child's development, television is more pervasive than ever before.

If I were raising a child today I would be a lot tougher about what he or she watched than 90 percent of today's parents are. I say this because I spent five years studying the changing world of children.

Television is a major part of that world. I think the sheer amount of time children now consume watching TV is a national scandal. They spend about as many hours a year in front of the tube as they spend in front of teachers. Nielsen surveys show that nearly 3 million children ages 6 to 11 are still watching TV between 10 and 11 p.m. About 380,000 of these watch past midnight. If the home has cable, they could be catching R-rated shows.

If I were a parent of young children today, I wouldn't allow any of my kids under 15 to have a television set in his or her room. Having a set so readily available simply puts too much pressure on children to watch excessively.

Don't get me wrong. I wouldn't put the TV set in the attic. Much of what's on TV can delight young viewers, provided they are given proper guidance. But I would be very uneasy if my children had unsupervised access to television, for the following reasons:

1) I would be concerned that TV was turning my children into materialistic cynics, distrustful of adults.

The typical youngster finishing high school has been the target of several thousand *hours* of commercials on TV. This selling barrage does more than influence children's brand preferences. It helps shape their concept of life.

Much of the advertising aimed at children is designed to make them effective naggers. One children's programming director was quoted in *Advertising Age*: "If you truly want big sales, use the child as your assistant salesman. He sells, he nags, until he breaks down the resistance of his mother or father."

Close to total believers in what adults tell them, very young children are uniquely vulnerable to the verbal curves tossed at them by TV pitchmen. By age seven to ten, according to a report in the *Harvard Business Review*, children are bothered by misleading or exaggerated ad messages. And by the time youngsters reach 11 or 12, they have become cool cynics.

Some studies also indicate that frequent exposure to the plotting, hoodwinking and manhandling depicted on TV may be eroding the very important sense of trust a child learns from loving parents.

2) I would wonder whether heavy viewing was making my children passive and less imaginative.

An essay called "The Electronic Fix" in the U.S. government publication *Children Today* cited two similarities between drug-taking and heavy TV viewing: both blot out the real world and promote passive states.

In general, studies show that children whose TV viewing is heavy score much lower than light viewers do on national reading tests. Does their viewing cause them to go easy on homework? Does it limit their reading for pleasure and thus their literacy? TV viewing over long stretches is not nearly as challenging mentally as reading is.

Preschool kids play less if they are heavy viewers—and that is bad. Play is important for growing children. It helps stretch their imaginations and ease anxieties. Interacting with playmates not only improves verbal skills but also teaches children how to have arguments and still be friends. I'd hate to have kids without those talents.

3) If my children showed frequent signs of being restless or tired, I would wonder whether heavy TV viewing was responsible.

The flickering screen gives a swirling view of the world. On commercial TV, most sales pitches come in 30-second bursts, many even shorter. Evening-news segments average only about two minutes. Some experts worry that a heavy-viewing child is more prone to have a short attention span. The whirl of scenes can also tire the mind. T. Berry Brazelton, the noted Harvard pediatrician, has observed that children under five are likely to show signs of exhaustion if exposed to more than one hour of TV a day.

If television became a strong influence in my children's lives, I would make sure their viewing was a life-enhancing force, not an insidious one. How would I do this? As much as possible I would guide my youngsters away from shows likely to generate distrustfulness or emotional upset, shows that make buffoons of law officers, and programs larded with ads specifically geared to seduce kids. Every week I'd go through a program guide with my children and we would look for shows that might prove interesting and rewarding:

—Shows involving exploration or experiments. It was good news when Mr. Wizard, who uses every-day objects to help youngsters understand science, was brought back by Nickelodeon.

—Shows that stimulate the imagination. Charlie Brown specials, Jim Henson's Muppet characters and the Disney Channel often do this.

—Shows in which adults and kids are shown doing things together. A disturbing trend of our times has been the growing isolation of youngsters from adults.

—Shows that promote thought about the special problems of growing up or about conditions in the world. For example, I have been much impressed with "CBS News Sunday Morning." In general, today's news programs give young viewers a better understanding of the world than I ever had at their age.

After reviewing the week's possibilities with my children, I'd help them draw up a viewing schedule. If they were of school age and under 14, I would let them choose up to ten hours of programming from the list—an hour a day Monday to Thursday, two hours a day on Friday, Saturday and Sunday. Preschoolers would be limited to seven hours—one hour a day. If my youngster wanted to watch a two-hour show on a school night, he'd have to skip TV the next night.

At an early age, say by four, my kids would know that commercials are different from regular programming. I would explain the purpose of ads. We'd talk about any overstatement or slickness.

Children are tremendously influenced by the way their own folks behave, so I would try to be a model for them. If I had young ones today, I wouldn't slouch hour after hour in front of the tube. I would spend my spare time reading, helping in some way to make my community a better place—and most of all, playing with my kids.

In our preview, we saw that the article covered about two and a half pages in the magazine. We saw three numbered statements of concern written in italics, and we noticed that the last section was set off with extra space between paragraphs.

After skimming it for meaning and organization, we decided the article had an introductory section, a section that lists and discusses the author's concerns, and a section that lists and discusses what the author would do to reduce television's ill effects on his children. The preview done, we were ready to read the piece carefully, looking for important ideas and referring to the Reading Checklist on page 131 as necessary. In our first reading, we underlined the major details, and we circled unfamiliar words and looked up their definitions, writing the meanings in the margins. In our second reading we made notes in the margins in the form of a **block diagram**. A block diagram sections off the article into chunks of material to reveal its organization, which is, of course, more complex than that of the sample paragraphs we reviewed earlier. Diagramming this way helps you to see an article's organization more clearly.

WARNING: TV CAN BE HAZARDOUS TO CHILDREN

By Vance Packard

In recent years, television has made it a lot more difficult to be a good parent. While the evidence grows that heavy, indiscriminate TV watching can damage a child's development, television is more pervasive than ever before.

indiscriminate = not controlled

pervasive = present everywhere

If I were raising a child today I would be a lot tougher about what he or she watched than 90 percent of today's parents are. I say this because I spent five years studying the changing world of children.

Television is a major part of that world. I think the sheer amount of time children now consume watching TV is a national scandal. They spend about as many hours a year in front of the tube as they spend in front of teachers. Nielsen surveys show that nearly 3 million children ages 6 to 11 are still watching TV between 10 and 11 p.m. About 380,000 of these watch past midnight. If the home has cable, they could be catching R-rated shows.

If I were a parent of young children today I wouldn't allow any of my kids under 15 to have a television set in his or her room. Hav-

— introduction

ing a set so readily available simply puts too much pressure on children to watch excessively.

    Don't get me wrong. I wouldn't put the TV set in the attic. Much of what's on TV can delight young viewers, provided they are given proper guidance. But <u>I would be very uneasy if my children had unsupervised access to television, for the following reasons</u>:

    1) I would be concerned that TV was turning my children into materialistic cynics, *distrustful of adults.*

    The typical youngster finishing high school has been the target of several thousand *hours* of commercials on TV. This <u>selling</u> bar-rage does more than influence children's brand preferences. It <u>helps shape their concept of life</u>.

    Much of the advertising aimed at children is designed to make them effective naggers. One children's programming director was quoted in *Advertising Age*: "If you truly want big sales, use the child as your assistant salesman. He sells, he nags, until he breaks down the resistance of his mother or father."

    Close to total believers in what adults tell them, <u>very young children are uniquely</u> vul-nerable to the verbal curves tossed at them by TV pitchmen. By age <u>seven to ten</u>, according to a report in the *Harvard Business Review*, children are <u>bothered by misleading or exaggerated ad messages</u>. And <u>by the time youngsters reach 11 or 12, they have become cool cynics</u>.

    Some studies also indicate that frequent exposure to the plotting, hoodwinking and manhandling depicted on TV <u>may be eroding the very important sense of trust a child learns from loving parents</u>.

    2) I would wonder whether heavy viewing was making my children passive and less imaginative.

Margin annotations:

— introduction

controlling idea for this section

author's first concern

cynics = scornful, distrustful people

barrage = outpouring or bombardment

— makes children nag

vulnerable = likely to be hurt

— children become cynical

— may destroy trust

— author's second concern

An essay called "The Electronic Fix" in the U.S. government publication *Children Today* cited <u>two similarities between drug-taking and heavy TV viewing</u>: both blot out the real world and promote passive states.

makes children passive

In general, <u>studies show that children whose TV viewing is heavy score much lower than light viewers do on national reading tests</u>. Does their viewing cause them to go easy on homework? Does it limit their reading for pleasure and thus their literacy? TV viewing over long stretches is not nearly as challenging mentally as reading is.

heavy viewers score lower in reading

<u>Preschool kids play less if they are heavy viewers</u>—and that is bad. Play is important for growing children. It <u>helps stretch their imaginations and ease anxieties</u>. Interacting with playmates not only <u>improves verbal skills</u> but also <u>teaches children how to have arguments and still be friends</u>. I'd hate to have kids without those talents.

children play less

3) If my children showed frequent signs of being restless or tired, I would wonder whether heavy TV viewing was responsible.

author's third concern

The flickering screen gives a swirling view of the world. On commercial TV, most sales pitches come in 30-second bursts, many even shorter. Evening-news segments average only about two minutes. Some experts worry that a <u>heavy-viewing child is more prone to have a short attention span</u>. The <u>whirl of scenes can also tire the mind</u>. T. Berry Brazelton, the noted Harvard pediatrician, has observed that children under five are likely to show signs of exhaustion if exposed to more than one hour of TV a day.

short attention span

tired minds

If television became a strong influence in my children's lives, <u>I would make sure their viewing was a life-enhancing force, not an insidious one</u>. How would I do this? As much as

controlling idea for this section

insidious = harmful, evil

possible I would guide my youngsters away from shows likely to generate distrustfulness or emotional upset, shows that make buffoons of law officers, and programs larded with ads specifically geared to seduce kids. Every week <u>I'd go through a program guide with my children and we would look for shows that might prove interesting and rewarding</u>:

— <u>Shows involving exploration or experiments</u>. It was good news when Mr. Wizard, who uses every-day objects to help youngsters understand science, was brought back by Nickelodeon.

— <u>Shows that stimulate the imagination</u>. Charlie Brown specials, Jim Henson's Muppet characters and the Disney Channel often do this.

— <u>Shows in which adults and kids are shown doing things together</u>. A disturbing trend of our times has been the growing isolation of youngsters from adults.

— <u>Shows that promote thought about the special problems of growing up or about conditions in the world</u>. For example, I have been much impressed with "CBS News Sunday Morning." In general, today's news programs give young viewers a better understanding of the world than I ever had at their age.

After reviewing the week's possibilities with my children, <u>I'd help them draw up a viewing schedule</u>. If they were of school age and under 14, I would let them choose up to ten hours of programming from the list—an hour a day Monday to Thursday, two hours a day on Friday, Saturday and Sunday. Preschoolers would be limited to seven hours—one hour a day. If my youngster wanted to watch a two-hour show on a school night, he'd have to skip TV the next night.

At an early age, say by four, my kids

Margin notes:
- guide children to good viewing
- exploration and experiments
- imagination
- children and adults together
- think about self and world
- make a viewing schedule

would know that commercials are different from regular programming. <u>I would explain the purpose of ads</u>. We'd talk about any over-statement or slickness.

— teach them about ads

Children are tremendously influenced by the way their own folks behave, so <u>I would try to be a model for them</u>. If I had young ones today, I wouldn't slouch hour after hour in front of the tube. I would spend my spare time reading, helping in some way to make my community a better place—and most of all, <u>playing with my kids</u>.

— set a good example

— play with them

The last thing you must do at the reading stage is to try to write a short statement of what the article says. After diagramming the article, we tested our understanding of it by writing the following short statement without looking back at the article.

> **If I were raising children today, I would worry about television's effects on them, and I would try to prevent the ill effects of TV.**

Notice that the statement goes a little beyond what the title of the article suggests. That is, instead of talking just about the hazards of tele-vision, the author also talks about what might be done to prevent those hazards. The article has two main ideas, and our statement includes both of them.

STEP 2:
Stating the Controlling Idea

The next step on the way to summarizing is to state the controlling idea of the article. Remember that the controlling idea should contain the subject of the article and the author's main point or, as in this article, main points. This article has only one subject: the hazards of television to children. The author tells us two things about that subject: what hazards concern him and what he would do about those hazards if he were raising children today. Our statement of the controlling idea is this:

> **Unsupervised television watching can harm children, but parents can take actions to prevent this harm.**

Having stated the controlling idea, we are ready for the next step.

STEP 3:
Identifying Supporting Details

In longer pieces it is, of course, more difficult to identify major details, but turning our statement of the controlling idea into a question and answering it can still help us:

Controlling idea:

> **Unsupervised television watching can harm children, but parents can take actions to prevent this harm.**

Controlling idea question:

> **How can unsupervised television watching harm children, and what actions can parents take to prevent the harm?**

Answers:

1. **It can make children materialistic, cynical, and distrustful.**
2. **It can limit their activities and their imaginations.**
3. **It can make them restless or tired.**
4. **Parents can control and limit children's television watching.**
5. **Parents can explain advertising to children.**
6. **Parents can set a good example.**

Since there are two parts to the controlling idea, we needed to write two parts to the question, each with its own question word. The "how" part asks about harm and the "what" part asks about actions. Answers 1–3 relate to the first part of the question while answers 4–6 relate to the second.

STEP 4:
Writing the First Draft

In summarizing single paragraphs, we wrote one-sentence summaries. Most extensive articles, however, require at least a paragraph. There are several important rules to keep in mind as you write your summary paragraph.

1. As you summarize, keep the ideas in about the same proportions and order as those in the original. In the TV article, for example, the author devotes more space to his concerns about the harm of television than to his suggestions for prevention. In our summary, then, we'll discuss the harms more fully than the prevention, and we will discuss the harms first since that is the order of the original article.

2. Identify the author and source in the opening sentence. Note how we do that in our first draft.

3. **Paraphrase**, or put things in your own words. This not only helps you to be sure you understand the piece you are summarizing, but it also reminds you that you're shortening or condensing the ideas, not just choosing a few to quote. Try not to **quote** unless the author has used a word or phrase that is particularly effective. If you do quote, use quotation marks any time you use more than three of the author's exact words. (See Section 20.1 of the Appendix for a discussion of quotation marks.)

4. Make every effort to give your readers no more information than they need to understand the author's original message.

5. Include only what the author says. Do not add your own opinions or interpretations.

Here's the first draft of our summary.

Draft 1

In his <u>Reader's Digest</u> article, "Warning: TV Can Be Hazardous to Children," Vance Packard says that unsupervised television watching can harm children, but that parents can take actions to prevent this harm. Much TV is good, but children spend as many hours a year watching TV as they spend in school, and many of them watch late-night shows. Children need to have their TV watching supervised. First, television can turn children into materialistic cynics who distrust adults. TV advertising encourages children to nag their parents for advertised products. Young children are especially vulnerable because they believe what they see in the advertisements, but children from seven to ten are bothered by misleading ads. By the time they are eleven or twelve, children are cynical about the ads, and they may be losing the important sense of trust learned from their parents. Second, television watching can make children less active and imaginative. Children who watch a lot of television don't read as well as those who watch little, and they also play less. Play helps children develop their imaginations, improves their verbal skills, and teaches them "how to have arguments and still be friends." Third, because television segments are short, children who watch TV can have short attention spans. They can also become tired from the rapid changing of scenes. To prevent the damage that television can cause, parents can make sure that their children watch shows like Mr. Wizard that involve experiments, shows like the Charlie Brown specials that help the imagination, shows that show children and adults together, and shows that make them think about problems in their lives or the world. Parents can limit children under fourteen to ten hours of TV watching a week and preschoolers to seven hours. They can also talk to their children about advertising. Finally, parents can set a good example for their children and can play with them.

STEP 5:
Revising the Summary

As usual, we didn't attempt a revision until the day after we did our first draft. The time away from it helped us to see some problems with it that we hadn't noticed before. Our first step was to reread the article and then to reread our summary.

We saw that we had included some details from the introduction and some other minor details that are not necessary. Two sentences summarize part of the introduction but do not support the controlling idea of our summary: "Much TV is good, but children spend as many hours a year watching TV as they spend in school, and many of them watch late-night shows. Children need to have their TV watching supervised." Also, our discussion of the kinds of shows children should watch goes into too much detail. The shows which we have named can be lumped together as "educational or imaginative shows," and this technique of lumping or gathering several small ideas into one general term is called **generalizing**. Generalizing is an important way of condensing.

Mainly, our revision leaves out detail that is not necessary in a summary, and it does more paraphrasing—we use more of our own words. Finally, because we want to show the author's scornful attitude toward people who watch too much TV, we include a particularly telling quotation.

Here, then, is our revised summary paragraph.

Final Draft

In his <u>Reader's Digest</u> article, "Warning: TV Can Be Hazardous to Children," Vance Packard says that unsupervised television watching can harm children, but that parents can take actions to prevent this harm. First, TV advertising can make children materialistic and distrustful. Young children believe what they see in the advertisements, but as they get older, children become cynical and may lose the important sense of trust learned from their parents. Second, television watching can make children read less and play less. Third, because television segments are short, children who watch TV can have short attention spans. They can also become tired from the rapid changing of scenes. To prevent the damage that television can cause, parents can do several things. They can make sure that their children watch educational or imaginative shows. They can limit children's TV watching. They can also talk to their children about advertising. Parents can set a good example for their children, rather than "slouch hour after hour in front of the tube." Finally, they can play with their children.

Our revision is more effective because it gives only the information necessary for the reader to understand the author's original message. It paraphrases rather than quotes, and it combines specific ideas into general terms. Finally, it shows the author's attitude toward his subject.

You probably have noticed that our revision is shorter than our first draft, and that's exactly what you need to work for when you revise your summary paragraph.

Now it's time for you to practice summarizing an article. Preview and read the following article, "Battling the Blahs When a Job Seems Routine," by following the checklists on pages 130 and 131. You'll find that the controlling idea is clearly stated and that major details are fairly easy to identify. You might find the last part a bit difficult, though, for instead of directly stating things you can do, it talks about reasons for the blahs and asks some questions. One of your jobs will be to state the suggestions implied in this last part and to decide on how many of the minor details you need to include. You will write a summary in Writing Activity 8.3. This article is from *Family Weekly Magazine.*

BATTLING THE BLAHS WHEN A JOB SEEMS ROUTINE

By Peggy Schmidt

Every so often, perhaps during a tedious staff meeting, a trying commute to work, or a seemingly endless afternoon in the office, that feeling of "Why am I doing this?" occurs. It's natural to get down in the dumps about your job from time to time. When the doldrums strike, there are several things you can do to fight them before your ho-hum attitude affects your work.

Boredom is one of the most common causes of feeling blue about your job. "Every job has a lot of repetitive tasks from which you need to take not just a coffee break, but a mental break," says Richard Irish, an executive search expert and author of *Go Hire Yourself an Employer.* He suggests switching gears: if you have a job that involves a lot of paperwork or thinking, consider throwing darts at a board in your office as a diversion, as Irish does himself. For those whose business keeps them on the phone, a crossword puzzle can be refreshing. People whose hands are on a computer keyboard a good part of the day may find a balance in doodling. If your company provides exercise equipment or space (as an increasing number do), use it.

Altering the routine of your job itself is another possibility, says Irish. Rearrange the times when you normally schedule meetings. Or you might initiate a project that is outside of but consistent with your responsibilities. You can also get out of your rut by having lunch with people who work outside your department or company, even people you don't know well, but would enjoy knowing better. Don't feel hesitant about inviting someone new to lunch; most people are flattered that you're interested in learning more about them and what they do.

Another reason for slipping into the job doldrums is not getting positive feedback from your employer. "Each one of us has a recognition quotient that we need filled if we're going to continue turning in good work," says Irish. "Pats on the back are not given out nearly as frequently as they should be."

Rather than feel resentful that you're not appreciated, the next time you turn in an assignment, tell your boss that while you put your best effort into it, you would like to know if there is anything that could be improved upon. If he says yes, you stand to benefit from constructive criticisms. Or you may simply hear what you've been wanting to—that you're doing a great job.

The most serious reason for getting caught in the job doldrums is the frustration that comes with feeling that you're not getting anywhere in your job—or deciding that there is no future for you with your employer. "Plenty of people in that situation slack off because they lose their motivation, but a failure to take positive steps only makes the problem worse," says Irish. Before you take the drastic step of looking for a new job, ask yourself:

—Are you being too impatient? Talk to others with your level of experience and education. If you work for a small company, compare your situation with people who work in other companies.

—What's standing in your way? Often it's the person who

has the job you want. Is it worth it to wait for him to retire, move up or on? A personality conflict with a supervisor can also be an impediment. If that's the case, you'll have to win his respect or consider a job move outside his realm of influence. Finally, company policy or precedent may be holding you up, even if you have proven you can handle more responsibility. The challenge is to figure how management can make an exception without risking complaints.

—Do the people in power share your view of your accomplishments? Be aware of what criteria management uses to make judgments. Then ask yourself whether you meet them or want to meet them. Lastly, make sure that management is aware of your desire to take on more responsibility.

If you decide that there isn't much you can do to improve your situation, scouting out new job possibilities will bring renewed enthusiasm. You may even discover that your current position isn't as bad as you had thought.

 Writing Activity 8.3

□ Write the subject of the article, what the author says about the subject, and your statement of the article's controlling idea.

□ Turn your statement into a question and answer the question to form an outline of your summary paragraph.

□ Check your work against our suggestions on page 155 and make any revisions you think are necessary.

□ Write your rough draft.

□ Revise it at least once.

Suggested Responses

Writing Activity 8.1, page 134
Subject: **A difference in birds' eggs**
What the author says: **The eggs differ in size**.

Statement of controlling idea:

> **The eggs of various birds differ greatly in size.**

Writing Activity 8.2, page 138
Subject: **Good preparation for a speech**
What the author says: **There are things you can do to prepare.**

Statement of controlling idea:

> **There are several things you can do to prepare well for a speech.**

Controlling idea question:

> **What can one do to prepare well for a speech?**

Answers:

> 1. **choose an appropriate topic**
> 2. **find plenty of good material**
> 3. **plan the order**
> 4. **practice**

One-sentence summary:

> **To prepare for a speech, choose an appropriate topic, find plenty of good material, plan the order of your presentation, and practice.**

Writing Activity 8.3, page 153
Subject: **Feeling tired of your job**
What the author says: **There are things you can do if you're tired of your job.**

Statement of controlling idea:

> **When the doldrums strike, there are several things you can do to fight them before your ho-hum attitude affects your work.**

Controlling idea question:

> **What can you do to fight the doldrums?**

Answers:

> 1. **If you're bored, take a mental break.**
> 2. **Alter the routine of your job.**
> 3. **Ask your boss for comments on your work.**
> 4. **Take positive steps before looking for a new job.**

Our summary:

> **Peggy Schmidt, author of "Battling the Blahs When a Job Seems Routine," in the <u>Family Weekly Magazine</u>, says there are several things you can do to fight the blahs. If boredom makes your job seem dull, take a mental break by doing something different for a while. If your routine makes the job dull, change the routine. If you're not getting enough positive feedback, ask your boss for comments on your work. Finally, if you feel that there's no future in your job, take positive steps. Test whether you're being too impatient by comparing your job with those of others. Figure out why you're not advancing, and then find a way to advance. Make sure your accomplishments are noted. If none of these work, looking for a new job might show you that the old one isn't that bad.**

Other Suggestions for Writing

1. Turn to Chapter 9 and practice your summary skills on the articles there.
2. Summarize a paragraph, a portion of a chapter, or a whole chapter from one of your other textbooks.
3. Summarize an editorial from your local newspaper.

Terms to Remember

block diagram   Identifies and shows the sections of the major parts of a piece of writing.

generalizing   Taking specific items and grouping them together with a single term. We might generalize about bread, milk, eggs, and butter by referring to them as groceries.

implied topic sentence   Something that is implied is suggested or hinted at rather than directly stated. Often the details of a paragraph add up to a single idea, but that idea is not directly stated in the paragraph. In these situations, we say the topic sentence is implied.

major supporting detail   An idea or piece of information that directly supports the controlling idea and is, therefore, important in explaining or otherwise clarifying the controlling idea.

minor supporting detail   An idea or piece of information that supports or clarifies a major detail. In your paragraph outlines, the answers to your topic sentence question are major details. The ideas you include in your paragraph to develop those major details are minor details.

paraphrase   To restate someone else's ideas in your own words.

quote   To restate someone else's ideas in the exact words the person used.

skim   To read quickly, looking for overall meaning. You will usually skip some phrases and sentences as you skim.

summary   A shortened version of what someone has done, said, or written. A summary of written material contains only the essential ideas of the original; it leaves out many minor details.

Preview for Chapter 9

New terms to look for in Chapter 9 are

1. Patterns of organization
2. Division and Classification
3. Time Sequence

Before reading a textbook chapter, it's sometimes a good idea to go back to the table of contents of the book and read just that section dealing with the chapter you plan to read. Chapter 9 is long because it contains several articles for summarizing, so looking at the outline of this chapter in the table of contents will help you to see quickly how the chapter is organized. This quick overview will then make your preview easier because you'll know more about what you are looking for.

9

READINGS FOR MORE
SUMMARY PRACTICE

This chapter offers several readings on which you can practice your skills as a summary writer. Some essays are organized quite simply, while others have more complex **patterns of organization**. We have already discussed several of these patterns of organization in Chapter 7, and we also introduce some new ones here. Recognizing common patterns of organization can help you in both your reading and your writing. You will find elements of one or more of these common patterns in almost anything you read, and you will find yourself using these same patterns as you write. We introduce each reading with a brief description of its pattern of organization and of any special problems you might find in summarizing the piece.

READING 1:
"To Have and to Hold"

The first piece in this chapter is organized in the pattern called **Division and Classification**. In this pattern, an author breaks a single subject into smaller units so that each of the units can be discussed separately. This pattern is often used when a writer wants to show how one set of ideas fits into a larger pattern or to show relationships among ideas. In "To Have and to Hold," the piece which follows, the author takes one large topic, divides it into four separate categories, and discusses each category.

To summarize a Division and Classification paper, you must decide what topic is being divided and into what categories it is being divided.   159

Your statement of the controlling idea should include that information. Your major details will be the individual categories themselves. Transitions that can guide you to those categories are words like "first," "second," "third," "one," "another," "the most important," and "finally."

This first piece has an introductory paragraph, four supporting paragraphs, and a concluding paragraph. Its controlling idea is clearly stated in the introduction; it identifies the topic and tells you into what categories the topic will be divided. This piece was adapted by Alan Meyers from *The People's Almanac.*

TO HAVE AND TO HOLD

By Alan Meyers

Today, most men and women still honor the traditional marriage contract with its pledges of love, honor, and respect, and with its legal obligations of alimony and child support if the marriage later dissolves. However, high divorce rates and our changing times have caused many men and women to try alternative forms of marriage. Here are four of the most common forms.

The first, which dates back to the 1700s in England, is the *common-law marriage.* In it, a man and a woman do not undergo a wedding ceremony but they agree to live together as husband and wife. After seven years, they are considered legally married. This practice originated because at one time getting married (or divorced) was a complicated procedure. Now, however, only fourteen states and the District of Columbia recognize common-law marriages, and most people choose either to live together without claiming to be married, or they go through the official wedding ceremony.

The second alternative marriage form is the *trial marriage,* which is very popular today. Many people are reluctant to commit themselves to a marriage contract before they are sure that their partner is really the one for them. Therefore, they agree to live together (and later, perhaps, separately) without marrying. This arrangement is especially popular with young people or with older people who have divorced and do not want to make another mistake.

A third, but far less common, form of alternative marriage is the *group marriage.* It gained some popularity in the flower-child protest days of the late 1960s but seems to be dying out now. In this arrangement, the members of a group share several (but not necessarily all) the partners in the household, and any number of people can join the fun. While such groups may be liberating and exciting as long as they last, they almost always break up for non-sexual reasons, usually personality conflicts.

Finally, there is a form of legal marriage that has gained in popularity over the last several years: the *contract marriage*. In it, couples attempt to make a formal civil agreement tailored to their individual needs and situations. Such contracts can run on for pages and deal with such items as sexual expectations, employment, and money (how much each partner has in a checking account). Reading them, you begin to think that what the partners gain in legal guarantees they lose in trust and love. Here, for example, are a few clauses in marriage contracts as reported by *Time* magazine:

1. Wife will not say she does not believe her husband loves her.

2. Ralph agrees not to pick at, nag, or comment about Wanda's skin blemishes.

3. Wanda will refrain from yelling about undone household chores until Sunday afternoon.

Of course, in addition to the four alternative forms of marriage first described, there are other forms. These include the homosexual marriage, the "open" marriage (with husband and wife free to experiment with different partners), and the renewable contract marriage (that must be renegotiated every few years). They're all a sign of our ever-changing and complex life today.

Writing Activity 9.1

□ Write a summary of "To Have and to Hold."

□ Be sure your first sentence states the controlling idea and includes the author and source information.

□ Since the author divides the common forms of marriage into four categories, these will form the major supporting details.

□ Carefully examine your work for Steps 1–3 of writing a summary paragraph before beginning your first draft.

□ Let your first draft get cold before you revise it.

READING 2:
"Leaving the Office Behind"

This next piece is an example of **Time Sequence** because it presents its information in order of time. It starts on the job, takes us through the trip home, and ends at home. Specifically, it is a subdivision of Time Sequence called *Process*, because its purpose is to tell readers how to do something. However, since the author cannot prescribe a single sequence of steps for everyone in her reading audience, she also uses *Example* as a method of development, so the organizational pattern is a combination of Process and Example. We discussed both these patterns of organization in Chapter 7.

The divisions of this piece are clearly identified, but rather than use words like "first" and "second," this one uses headings in boldface print. The introduction takes several paragraphs. The controlling idea, while not directly stated, is a direct answer to a question that the author asks. You'll have to make some decisions about which minor details you should include in your summary. This article is from *View* magazine, March 1985.

LEAVING THE OFFICE BEHIND

By Dr. Barbara Mackoff

When Dorothy clicked the heels of her ruby slippers in "The Wizard of Oz," she made the most magical transition between work and home in the history of film. As team manager, she had accomplished all of her objectives in the Emerald City: a heart for the tin man, a brain for the scarecrow, and courage for the cowardly lion.

All she had to do to get from Oz to Kansas was to click her heels and murmur, "There's no place like home." But for most of us—whether we have been off to see the wizard or to *be* the wizard—our transition from work is something less than magical. It takes much more than a click of our heels to ensure a smooth voyage home.

Ninety-nine million of us do it five times each week. We leave work to come home. Traveling home in cars, on buses and trains, we all struggle to unwind. We may be tired, preoccupied with unfinished business or tense from battles with supervisors and co-workers. We may be elated and absorbed in our successes and career plans. Many—if not most—of us have difficulty shifting gears at the end of the workday and too often we pass on the tension of our jobs to the people we love.

Are you having trouble leaving your job behind each day? Do you:

—Think of evenings and weekends as a time to get "caught up" with work?

—Have difficulty turning off your thoughts about a demanding new project or client?

—Argue with your partner, roommate, or children after a frustrating day at work?

—Often feel too tired or preoccupied with the office to enjoy making love?

—Spend entire dinner hours complaining about your boss and co-workers?

How can you shift gears after a busy, pressured day at work?

Begin your transition on the job

At 4:30 you may find yourself doing the most demanding work of the day. When your day ends with a feverish finale, you will carry that intensity all the way home with you. Plan to schedule the least demanding tasks for your last half hour on the job. Use the time to return phone calls, use the copy machine, clear off your desk. Diana Morrison, a city planner, stays an extra half hour after work to unwind. She listens to soothing music on her radio and previews the next day's schedule. In this way, she is able to shift from the fast pace of her job to the more relaxed rhythms she hopes to enjoy with her family at home.

Postpone unfinished business

As you leave your job, you may feel pursued by thoughts of the work you left behind: phone calls to return, paperwork, deadlines, quotas.

"Work always sits on one side of my brain," is the way David Hanson, an insurance broker, describes being haunted by thoughts about work. Yet most unfinished business can't be completed at home; so why deny yourself an evening of rest and recuperation?

Try to end your day with a mental picture of yourself completing every item on tomorrow's agenda. Carla Randall lists her sales calls and assigns a time to meet with each client. She walks away from her desk saying, "I'll deal with those on Wednesday; tonight, I'm going to relax."

When work thoughts intrude at home, borrow a line from Scarlett O'Hara and tell yourself "I'll think about it tomorrow." But unlike Scarlett—who expected Rhett Butler to take care of her business—you will be back on the job the next day.

Identify your feelings

Each work day moves so swiftly that you may be unaware of the intense feelings evoked during your encounters at work. When you can identify and connect with your feelings on the way home from work, you can prevent yourself from passing on the tension from your job to your family and friends.

When Sharon Mackay, a teacher, came home feeling angry and disappointed about budget cuts in her program, she decided to warn her husband: "I had a horrible day and anything you say will make me furious." Because of her warning, her husband responded generously—by bringing her dinner in bed.

Take time on your way home to name the people who played a starring role in your day and to identify the feelings you experienced in your contacts with them. One businessman types a sarcastic memo to his boss and discards it on his way home. While others sing along with their car radios, you might consider talking back to your supervisor, customers or associates. These imaginary conversations can free you to make plans for the evening that do not include these difficult people.

Start laughing

Laughter is the four-star technique for recovering from work. To lighten your thoughts about the day, rethink stressful events in a humorous vein. For example, review your

workday as a movie or television show that needs a musical
score. If someone went over your head to make a decision,
review that tense moment, but this time, add a tune to ac-
company your thoughts—Frank Sinatra singing "I Did It My
Way."

Consider how you might feel if the most stressful moments on your job had been set-ups for "Candid Camera."
Imagine that millions of television viewers had witnessed
your boss's temper tantrum or your ordeal with payroll's
computer; enjoy the giddy relief you would feel when Allen
Funt jumped out of the closet. When you begin to see your
work in comic terms, you'll find yourself laughing at your
mistakes and creating the prospect of a happier evening at
home.

Re-charge energy

David Stein, a social services director, has incorporated
running into his transition after work. "Running is my cock-
tail, my punching bag," he says. "It's the way I release all of
my tensions from the day; I don't seem to be able to run hard
and hold on to angry feelings." He has discovered exercise is
an ideal way to dissolve the tensions of the day and to ener-
gize himself for the evening.

Many of us excuse ourselves from exercise saying we are
"too tired," yet all of the evidence points to the fact that
moderate exercise will make you feel energized rather than
exhausted. The trick is to remember the way you felt after
the last time you exercised: Try to get a mental image of
yourself after your last swim, run or tennis game. Picture
yourself after your shower, feeling relaxed and renewed,
happily on your way home.

If your excuse is a time shortage consider other alternatives: walking home, parking in a distant lot, ten minutes of
jumping rope on your living room floor, combining social
time by exercising with a friend, involving your family in an
exercise program, or preparing simple dinners to allow for
extra time to exercise.

Enlarge your perspective

As we travel home from work, most of us are preoccupied
with the small, maddening details that soap opera writers
adore. Our world shrinks each day as we focus exclusively on
the people and events in our workplace. To change the sub-

ject and quickly enlarge your perspective, try reading the headlines, watching the news, listening to National Public Radio, eavesdropping in elevators—anything that will allow you to shift your attention away from the problems and personalities on your job.

Kathleen Nelson, a public relations specialist, has a favorite technique for creating perspective. She looks into the future and asks herself: "In 1995, how important will it be that my slides jammed in the projector and I had to reschedule my presentation?"

Re-connect with loving feelings

John Ellsworth, a newly married musician, was disappointed to learn that it took more than a hug from his wife to erase the tensions of his day. "I always thought that when I got married, I could easily leave thoughts about my music behind. Do I really have to make an effort to respond to her?"

Don't assume that it is natural or easy to turn away from thoughts about work and focus on the people you love. Instead, plan to make a deliberate effort to shift from the task oriented focus of your day to the warm, playful or sexy feelings you want to express with the people you love.

As you prepare to greet family or friends, take a moment to picture each person's face. Mentally count your son's freckles, capture your wife's smile. If you have trouble creating a mental image, peek at the family photo in your wallet. Then, switch your thoughts to that person's day: did your son have an English exam? Did your wife have an important meeting? What frustrations might your husband be bringing home?

Remember that you can ruin an entire evening, just by saying hello the wrong way. You can survive the first three minutes at home by greeting family and friends warmly and postponing a discussion of the day's horrors. Mention the good news first: "I'm glad to see you."

Turn in your suit

Carol Jacobs, an accountant, changes her clothes immediately when she comes home from work. "When I change," she explains, "I feel like I am shedding the day, getting back to basics." And although leaving behind the pressures of work is not as simple as a change of clothes, it can help most of us—whether we work in a lab coat or a tweed jacket.

You can go home again. Help yourself to the techniques that allow you to unwind from work—to leave the office behind—and enjoy the comforts of home and love.

Writing Activity 9.2

- □ Write your summary of "Leaving the Office Behind."
- □ State the controlling idea and the source information in your first sentence.
- □ Be sure to include information about each of the three main time periods.
- □ Give only as many examples as are necessary to help your reader understand the author's main points.

READING 3: "Climbing Kilimanjaro"

The organizational pattern of this next piece is also Time Sequence, but it is a subdivision known as *narrative*. You have studied and written narrative paragraphs, so you know that a narrative tells a story, usually in chronological order. Transitional words and phrases that guide you to major details in the narrative pattern are time words such as "first," "second," "finally," "the next morning," "later," and "soon after that."

Because this next piece tells a story, the controlling idea is not stated; the reader is expected to understand it simply by understanding the author's attitude toward the main event of the story. His dominant impression of the event seems to be that it was miserable. Your task in summarizing is to show, in chronological order, how the details illustrate the controlling idea.

CLIMBING KILIMANJARO

By Charles Bracelen Flood

I once enlisted in an army, and after that experience I vowed that I would never voluntarily expose myself to discomfort again. That was still my point of view when I arrived at the Kibo Hotel in Marangu, Tanganyika, Africa. I was traveling with two friends of mine from New York, Deirdre and Elizabeth Ahearn, and the three of us were thoroughly enjoying our trip through Africa. We had been told that the Kibo Hotel was a lovely place high in the hills, far off the beaten track, and with excellent food.

It was all of that, but there was more. The first evening, as we sat before a fireplace in an informal living room whose walls were covered with Masai spears and the mounted heads of gazelles, we became aware of Kilimanjaro.

"Are you young people here to climb the mountain?" an old Englishman with white hair and a red face asked, and then took a swallow of the gin and tonic in his hand.

I answered "no" immediately, since I was determined that I was not going to climb any mountains ever, but the girls were more curious, and politely asked which mountain.

"Kilimanjaro, of course," the old boy replied, pulling his chair up closer. "You're in the foothills right now. All the parties leave from here. You should try it. It's just a walk, really." He smiled at Elizabeth, and then his expression hardened as he looked at me. "It only takes five days," he said. "You really *should* do it."

By late the next afternoon I had assumed that the crisis had passed, that the girls had forgotten about mountain climbing, and that we would be checking out of the hotel and on our way the following morning. We were sitting in the lovely garden of the hotel, having tea and gazing out over the green hills to the dusty African plains in the distance. A couple of monkeys were playing in a cage on the lawn, the sun was shining, and the only sound was that of the teacups.

Suddenly a line of men came into view, around the edge of a brilliant flowered hedge, and came up the walk to the hotel. In the lead was a tall young man with a khaki sun helmet, khaki shirt, khaki shorts, khaki knee socks, and formidable hobnailed boots. His face was dirty and cruelly sunburned, and there was a dazed expression on his face. Behind him came seven Africans, all carrying big olive-colored duffel bags on their heads. Their legs were covered with wet red mud, and they all looked as if they were about to drop from exhaustion.

"Hello," the young man said, stopping at our table as the rest of his party went past onto the terrace of the hotel. He took off his sun helmet and leaned on his alpenstock. "I did not get to the top," he said in a strong German accent. He looked like a young golden-haired god, but he was a tired young god. He grinned ruefully at his sun helmet. "If you get to the top the porters put flowers on your hat. I could not get up. When I wake up this morning my head was sick. Kaput." He bowed to the girls and walked into the hotel.

I looked at the girls, and knew I was in for it. This last · encounter had been the acme of romance. It was as if drums and bugles were resounding in the silent garden. Strangely enough, I began to feel better about the situation: If that perfect Alpine specimen had failed, there was no particular disgrace in my failing.

By late the next afternoon we were emerging from the rain forest after several hours of climbing. The hotel had equipped us from head to toe, and behind us came Thomas, our ancient Chaga guide; Sambwe, our cook; and seven porters. These porters were possessed of superhuman strength. At a rest stop I had hefted one of the duffel bags that they carried on their heads, and estimated it to weigh substantially more than an army full-field pack. I knew that in my duffel bag there were five blankets, several sweaters, shoes, and pieces of high altitude gear, plus a camera and other equipment. It was with no little surprise that I watched this duffel bag go hurtling by me balanced on the head of one of the Chaga porters, whose pink-soled black feet would literally sprint through the cold red mud of the steep trail. These men would run a mile or so ahead of us and then sit waiting for us to catch up. Then they would get up, politely follow us for about a hundred yards, and then, incapable of going as slow as our maximum speed, pass us again, muttering apologies in Swahili as they tore through the thick undergrowth at the side of the path. Only Thomas, our sad-eyed old guide, stayed with us at all times.

The first night was spent in Bismarck hut, where a stove helped to keep us warm in the foggy mountain night. It was at Bismarck that we began to comprehend, for the first time in a day of slippery, exhausting, jungle climbing, what a broad and high language barrier stood between the nine Africans and ourselves. We asked for water and were given tea. We asked for coffee and got fruit juice. We asked what time we would start off again the next morning and received polite indications that we were not understood.

By the next day, moving up through steep Alpine meadows, the porters had begun to move somewhat more slowly, and I occasionally forced myself to stay up with them. Thus I moved along for a mile at a time in a cloud of Swahili, and although I may delude myself, I think I began to get some idea of the conventions of that tongue, but I never had the faintest idea of the subject of conversation.

The morning of the third day life became earnest. The porters put sandals on their feet. Thomas took the girls and me aside after breakfast, and by repeating place names accompanied by many gestures, he conveyed the plan of battle. We were to make the final hut, Kibo, by evening. We had to carry with us all the food and water we would need for the next thirty-six hours. We would eat dinner tonight at Kibo hut, sleep until the middle of the night, and then start up to the summit in darkness. Whatever the outcome of our assault on the mountain, we must get back down that last sheer slope, out of Kibo during the afternoon, and be back here at Peter's hut that evening.

Finally understanding each other for the first time in the trip, Thomas and I set off at the head of our column, followed by the girls, who looked very fetching in shapeless high-altitude clothes and wide-brimmed men's hats, with Band-aids across their noses to protect them from sunburn and windburn. Soon we moved into a strange world. We left behind some trees which looked like huge pineapples supported by stems eight feet high, and entered an altitude where bushes became shrubs and shrubs became moss. After a sandwich lunch, we hiked up onto the Saddle, and from there on we were no longer on earth.

The Saddle is a deceptively vast shallow bowl located at fifteen thousand feet. At one side of it the jagged snowy spires of Mawenzi thrust two thousand feet up out of the volcanic plain. On the other side of it stands its immeasurably bigger brother, Kibo, the great classic peak of Kilimanjaro. Seen suddenly as one comes up onto the Saddle, Kibo possesses both remarkable beauty and a certain stark and massive ugliness. The far side of the mountain has symmetry and the Fujiyama-like snows, but here, at the back door, the snow merely trims the edge of the crater, and the shape is that of Gibraltar. It rises out of the lifeless stratospheric plain like what it is: an enormous mountain. It is just that one has already been climbing Kilimanjaro for three days, and the sight of an enormous mountain on top of the mountain is both terrifying and awe-inspiring.

After a few minutes of staring, one settles down to the immediate problem, which is this desert of volcanic dust, so high up that even the moss has stopped growing on the boulders which the old volcano has thrown across the plain. We moved toward Kibo, but we no longer had a conventional frame of reference. The mountain and the Saddle were so huge that all the ordinary sense of space fled. Our porters went ahead of us and to our amazement disappeared into the distance, a distance which we thought was no more than half a mile between the mountain and ourselves. Hours later we were still walking toward that mountain, walking slowly through the gray-brown pebbles and stones and dust. The mountain obligingly became larger and larger, until it filled half the sky. The sun went down behind its crest, and a viciously cold wind started whipping across the Saddle. The altitude was at last taking a toll. We could move forward no more than forty or fifty yards at a time. The simplest movements became an effort, and twenty yards of walking would bring about a severe beating of the heart.

That night was one long shudder. We lay in our bunks, fully dressed and staring into the darkness as we shivered. Every breath we took was a deep search for oxygen, and all three of us suffered from a combination of stabbing headache and nausea. At one o'clock in the morning there was a loud and authoritative banging at the door of the cabin, and I staggered out of my bunk and let in Thomas and Sambwe, who had been spending the night in the cooking shed. We drank some tea, retied our bootlaces, adjusted our gloves and hoods and scarves, and stepped out into the night.

It was an eerie scene. Thomas stood in front of the hut, a small, stooped black man wearing a brown wool cap and an old khaki army coat. He had woolen puttees on above his climbing boots, and he was carrying a cane in one hand and a lantern in the other. We all nodded, and started up the final trail.

The next eleven hours were, and still are, a long and painful blur. Out of it a few things remain clear. I remember the girls falling down repeatedly and gamely getting up again to stagger forward in the darkness on the bare, slippery, pebbly slope. Finally, at about seventeen thousand feet, when Elizabeth said that she could no longer feel her feet, I told the girls to go down. I remember waiting on the slope at three o'clock in the morning for Thomas to come back up after leading the girls down to the hut, and realizing that up here there is no such thing as a horizon. The earth dropped away so steeply that there were stars not only above me, but stars twinkling slightly below, out beyond the edge of the Saddle. It was as if I were in an airplane, and the curvature of the earth no longer applied to me.

Sunrise came, and after breakfasting on water and part of a chocolate bar, I settled down to the hardest morning of my life. Thomas always seemed to be a mile ahead of me, sitting somewhere in this forty-five-degree sea of pebbles, staring down at me impassively. I would manage to go forward five steps, and then the lack of oxygen would catch up with me in a great rush and I would fall onto the pebbles, turning so that I would land on my back. I would jam my alpenstock into the pebble surface, so that I would not slide down the mountain. The toughest part of this climbing and falling was the effort it cost to put one foot in front of the other, but there were some appalling psychological factors as well.

The principal difficulty was the loss of any normal sense of balance or perspective. I felt the way one does when an airplane banks at an angle to the earth. I would look up the sheer slope and see the big solid yellow-brown rocks at the crest of the mountain, thousands of feet above me. Staring up at those rocks, I became convinced that they were hanging over me at such an angle that I would have to be like a spider traversing a ceiling to get to a point where I could move up them vertically. Again, when I looked down into the vast brown bowl of the Saddle, there was no relation to normal balance. On all sides of the brown plain there was nothing but clouds, and one had the feeling that it would be possible to dive off the slope, execute a simple jackknife, easily clear the edge of the Saddle, and fall forever through masses of soft white clouds. Every half hour I would notice that the peaks of Mawenzi, across the way, had become smaller. By ten o'clock I could see over the jagged peaks eight miles away, and by eleven o'clock Mawenzi seemed to be a minor mountain, hopelessly chained to the brown plain from which it sprang.

By eleven-thirty I was suffering. Thomas had occasionally pointed to the rocks at the top and said, "Gilman." Gilman's Point was the place, at approximately nineteen thousand feet, where climbers could stop and officially claim to have climbed Kilimanjaro. There were slightly higher points along the edge of the crater, but if you got to Gilman's the porters would crown you with mountain flowers when you re-entered the altitudes where things could grow. I had long since decided that if I could get to Gilman's I would not worry about anything higher. The question now was whether I could even do that. My heart was going like a trip hammer, and I remember wondering if it would give one particularly loud bang and stop beating. The lava dust on the windy, sunny slope had turned my mouth into a piece of rubber. Every time I tried to swallow, I choked. Up ahead on the slope Thomas sat and watched me struggle.

At twelve-thirty I pulled myself up out of three thousand feet of gravel and lay down beside Thomas on the yellow rock. Mawenzi seemed like a hillock across the cloudy Saddle, and Kibo hut was indistinguishable in the distance below. I had been climbing for eleven hours.

Two days later we came into the garden of the Kibo Hotel. Thomas was limping badly, the girls had blisters on their feet, and my unshaven face was so sunburned it was bloody. The only person in the garden was the old Englishman, who was sipping his tea as he read a book. He looked up and regarded me with a vague smile.

"Got to the top, I take it," he said, looking at the circle of flowers around my sun helmet.

"Yes," I said out of a dry throat, as the porters passed by under their loads.

"Not too bad, was it?"

"Not too," I said, and followed the girls into the hotel.

Writing Activity 9.3

- □ Write your summary of "Climbing Kilimanjaro."
- □ State the dominant impression in your first sentence, and give the author and title.
- □ Your summary of the introduction can be short, but be sure that the body of your summary includes the major details that illustrate the controlling idea.

READING 4:
"What Is Language?"

The article which follows is an example of *Definition*, and it follows the classical pattern of a definition. First it places the term being defined into a large group, and then it explains what separates or distinguishes that term from the other things in that group, giving further explanation and examples where necessary.

To illustrate the pattern, let's try to define the term *apple*. First we'd place the term into a large, general category: *an apple is a fruit*. Next, we'd distinguish it from other terms such as *grape* or *orange* or *banana* that belong to that same general category. We'd specify that the apple grows on trees, is firm-fleshed and usually red, yellow, or green, and is round. Then we might go on to name some specific examples with which our readers might be familiar.

As you read the following definition of "language," be careful to identify the large classification into which the author fits language and to distinguish between main points, subpoints, and examples or illustrations. Guide words in definitions are words like "consists of," "defined as," "is," and "means." This piece was adapted from *Introduction to Linguistic Structures*, a book by Archibald A. Hill.

WHAT IS LANGUAGE?
By Archibald Hill

According to linguists, language is a purely human activity, but while we all use language, we seldom think about what language is. In its broadest definition, language is a form of symbolic behavior. It has, however, five defining characteristics that set it off from other forms of symbolic behavior.

First, language is a set of sounds. That is also true of the communications of mammals and birds, but bees, whose system of communication is very much like a language, use body movements rather than sounds. Still, no human language is based on anything except sound. Even our written and sign languages have grown out of the spoken language.

Second, there is no necessary connection between the sounds of a language and the objects in the outside world. A visitor from Mars could not predict that the animal called *dog* in English will be called *chien* in French and *perro* in

Spanish. There is no good reason why a particular collection of sounds identifies a particular animal. That's just the way it is in that language. We learn how to make meaningful sounds and we learn the meanings of the sounds we make by living in a society; in other words, the speakers of a language pass that language on to any new members of their language community. By contrast, many animal sounds are instinctive. All cats mew and purr, for example.

A third defining characteristic of language is that it is systematic, and one important feature of a language system is that it, like any other system, is predictable. Because a system consists of recurring patterns, people who are familiar with a system and who then see only a part of any pattern within that system can make predictions about the rest of that pattern. Speakers of English who see a partial sentence like "John _____s Mary an _____" can predict that the first blank must be filled with a verb and the second with a noun. They will also know that the verb can't be a word like *looks* or *sees*, and they will know that the noun has to begin with a vowel sound. The sentence can be "John gives Mary an apple" or "John hands Mary an onion," but it can't be "John *gaves* Mary an *book*."

A second feature of a language system is that many substitutions can be made within a given pattern without changing that pattern. If, for example, we say, "John gives Mary an apple," we can replace *John* with words like *he, Jack, William, the man, her husband,* or many others. Words like *buys, takes, offers* can be used to replace *gives*. The meaning may or may not change, but the pattern remains the same. A parakeet may say the sentence "Birds can't talk!" with human pitch, voice tones, and nearly perfect sounds. But the bird never says "Dogs can't talk!" or "Birds can't write!" Because he is not using a pattern in which he can make substitutions, he cannot be said to be using language. He is simply uttering a collection of sounds.

A third feature of a language system is that it groups or classifies the units of language into classes that are simpler, more predictable, and more sharply separated than are objects in the world. For instance, a whole series of objects is grouped under the single word *chair*, and *chair* is grouped with those words we call *nouns*. In our daily lives we may have trouble deciding whether something is a chair, a stool, or a tree stump, but if someone says "Have a chair," we'll sit on the very thing we've been trying to name. In language, we think of nouns and verbs as separate things; we might say that nouns represent things and verbs represent events. But the physicists, and indeed our own experiences, tell us that it is sometimes hard to decide whether an object is best described as a thing or an event. What, for example, is that sudden, bright glow in the sky from a Fourth-of-July rocket? Is it a thing? Or is it an event?

To return once more to the defining characteristics of language, the fourth characteristic is that language is a set of symbols. There are many non-language sets of symbols, but language is different from them. The simplest example of a non-language symbol is the sound of the bell that made Pavlov's famous dogs salivate. Those dogs were fed at the sound of a bell, and after a time they began to drool when the bell was sounded even when no food was present. For them, the sound of the bell had become a symbol for food. The dogs responded to a substitute stimulus. A response can also be a symbol. The dog who has learned to "speak" at the sight of food is using a substitute response; his bark is a symbol. In each case, the symbol is something that is present in the dog's physical environment. In human speech, however, we can talk of things that are not present, of things that took place in the distant past, or of things we have only imagined. And our talk can stimulate responses in our fellow human beings. The difference between the dogs' use of symbols, then, and man's use of language is that the dogs' use of symbols is directly connected with experience while man's use of symbols, on the other hand, is connected not only with experience but with all parts of the symbol system itself.

To illustrate, let us suppose that two speakers of English are in a room, and one of them is cold. A direct response would be for the person who is cold to close the window. Instead, he might use a substitute response which would also be a substitute stimulus: "John, please close the window for me." John might respond directly by closing the window, or he might use a substitute: "Wait until I finish this page." This response might lead to remarks about John's manners, and those remarks might lead John to explain his response, to apologize for it, to comment on the laziness of the original speaker, or to begin a discussion of solar energy for heating houses. The stimuli can all be symbols, and the responses can all be symbols. Each speaker reacts to the other's language as well as to his own, and the conversation might end up so far from where it started that both speakers will have forgotten how it began. It is man's ability to deal with symbols in this way that enables him to talk and think about things like theoretical mathematics. Dogs can't do that.

The last defining characteristic of language is that it is complete yet open. Its completeness allows speakers of a language to make a linguistic response to any experience they have. Obviously the ancient Greeks had no words for automobiles or atom bombs, but a speaker of ancient Greek would have been perfectly able to describe an automobile had he seen one. Likewise, the openness of language would have allowed speakers of ancient Greek to coin a word for automobiles had such things become part of the Greek culture.

Language, then, is a form of symbolic behavior in which sounds are used in an arbitrary and symbolic way within a system that gives a speaker the ability to respond to, classify, and communicate with others about anything he experiences.

 Writing Activity 9.4

□ Write your summary of "What Is Language?" When you place language in its general category, you will have stated the controlling idea.

□ Be sure to include all the characteristics that distinguish language from the other members of its class.

READING 5: "How Pro Football Was Ruined"

The major pattern of organization in the article which follows is *Cause–Effect*. As we discussed in Chapter 7, the Cause–Effect pattern is used to show why and how things occur as they do. An author might attempt to show a single cause with a single effect, a single cause with multiple effects, multiple causes with a single effect, or multiple causes with multiple effects. Your first job in summarizing a Cause–Effect article is to identify the cause or causes and then to identify the effect or effects. Key transitions in this pattern are "as a result," "because," "consequently," "due to," "for," "hence," and "therefore."

This next piece also includes *Comparison–Contrast*, another pattern we discussed in Chapter 7. The author considers the way in which pro football is televised and then compares that with an imaginary broadcast of quite a different activity in order to illustrate his point. His comparison provides convincing evidence that a piece of writing is made effective by much more than its major and minor details. He closes with a brief summary.

In summarizing Comparison–Contrast, you must know what things are being compared and what points of similarity or difference the author is considering. Transitions are "alternatively," "on the other hand," "however," "in contrast," "likewise," and "similarly."

In the article reprinted here, Merullo argues that television broadcasting of football has changed his Sunday afternoons. You'll need to identify the controlling idea more precisely than that by stating both the cause and the effect. You'll also need to decide how to deal with the comparison he uses to illustrate his controlling idea. This article appeared in *Newsweek*, January 23, 1984.

HOW PRO FOOTBALL WAS RUINED

By Roland Merullo

In the old days—about 15 years ago—I could sit down in front of my television on a Sunday afternoon in the fall and spend a few relaxing hours watching a professional football game. But those days are gone.

The pros still play on Sundays and their games continue to be televised: that part is reassuringly the same. What has changed is that watching football is no longer relaxing. I make all the same preparations I used to make: something to drink and invitations perhaps to a friend or two with whom to share the pleasure. But then the game begins, and, instead of relaxing, I feel only a subtle dulling of the senses, a kind of electronic Novocain that numbs the brain.

I watched a close game recently, the kind of seesaw battle that, 15 years ago, would have had me clutching the arms of my chair until the final seconds. But I could barely sit through it. Every play, no matter how mundane, was shown two or three times, accompanied by volumes of analysis. By the start of the fourth quarter I felt as if I had watched three games and been through two years of coaching school.

Fourth Down: Now I have nothing against the instant replay. Besides ensuring us that we will never miss a big play, it has helped reduce domestic violence. Arguments over a referee's call can now be settled the second time the play is shown—or the third or the fourth. The instant replay is a good thing. But too much of anything good becomes bad. There is only a handful of crucial plays in even the most important games; replaying three out of every four downs only dilutes the action and renders this fan impassive.

To make matters worse, we are continually being tuned in—for four or five seconds—to other games all over the country. More big plays, more analysis, more chatter and more confusion.

Years ago one announcer and one game sufficed. The video presentation was not as polished: occasionally an ad would run beyond the allotted time and we'd miss part of a play. Still I felt like I was watching a *football game* and not a colorful antic concocted in a TV studio. My train of thought wasn't constantly interrupted by people screaming at me or removing half their clothes to try to get me to buy something. What expert commentary I had came from a friend in the next chair who had played three years of high-school ball. Things may have been slow at times, but that fit the mood of a Sunday and made me appreciate and remember, for years, in some cases, the really great plays.

It would be bad enough if only the regular-season games were being spoiled this way. But Super Sunday has also gone to the dogs. I am told to tune in at 1 o'clock, which I do. But the game doesn't start at 1; it starts at 4. Meanwhile I am treated to the expert prognostications of everyone from former stars to the local bookmaker. By game time my mind is saturated: the real action seems like an afterthought.

I make my living as a carpenter and sometimes, after a weekend of trying to watch football, I imagine what it would be like if my work were televised and the same standard of broadcasting overkill applied. The action goes like this:

"Merullo's about to put that two-by-six in place now, Vic. It's a tricky one."

"It's in, Ric."

"I'm not sure."

"Yes, the referee on the far side of the house just gave the signal. It's in."

"Right, let's see that one again."

"OK, Ric. At six feet, 165 pounds, Merullo is one of the smallest framers in the league, but he gets that nail out of the apron as fast as anyone. Still holds the record at Iowa State, I believe."

"We can watch that now on STOP-AC-INSTA-DIAGRAM. This line marks Merullo's left index finger. Notice how he slips his hand into the apron here, at X, grasps the head of the nail—looks like a tenpenny common nail."

"It is, Ric."

"Then he'll put it in place here—at Y, and drive it home. You'll notice that his right wrist is heavily taped. The trainers were working on that last night. He's playing in pain today."

"One of the toughest old boys in the league, Ric."

"Right, Vic. Now let's go to Burnt Michalson who'll give us some of the action in Missoula."

"Thank you, Ric. This is Burnt Michalson. It's 25 above zero today in Missoula, Mont., and at lunchtime the roof the Bedard brothers are working on is two-thirds complete. Here's some of the action from earlier in the day when Jason Bedard slipped and nearly fell from the staging. You can see the expression of alarm on his brother's face. Again, at lunchtime in Missoula, it's the Bedard brothers' roof two-thirds complete."

Carpentry, it's fair to say, is not much of a spectator sport—no contact, no cheerleaders, no high salaries. Football, on the other hand, is something millions of people enjoy watching. Unfortunately, what we are shown these days is not football, but a collage of bits of football-like activities, each surrounded by several more bits of information. The old simple beauty is gone, and Sunday afternoons will never be the same.

Writing Activity 9.5

- Write your summary of "How Pro Football Was Ruined."

- Identify the cause (what ruined pro football?) and the effects (in what ways was it ruined?).

- Decide whether to include a summary of the comparison.

READING 6:
"The Bad News Grizzlies"

In this final selection, the author begins with some narrative to lead up to his statement of a problem. He then relies heavily on the Cause–Effect pattern. Authors frequently rely on such a mixture of patterns, but recognizing the patterns when you encounter them will help you identify the main points of anything you read. In addition, being conscious of how other writers use these patterns can make you more conscious of how you can use them in your own writing.

To find the controlling idea in this piece, you'll need to look carefully. The author states a problem, discusses its causes, talks about attempts at solutions, and then, in his conclusion, restates the problem in a slightly different way. This selection is from *Family Weekly Magazine*, June 10, 1984.

THE BAD NEWS GRIZZLIES

By Jon R. Luoma

This is a story about bears. Like some of the oldest and best stories about bears, this one begins with the words: "Once upon a time."

Once upon a time, there were at least 100,000 grizzly bears ranging across almost all of the western half of the United States. A huge and powerful animal with no natural enemies, the grizzly held a position of absolute dominance in the wilderness forests of the West. The grizzly in America was a king of beasts.

The early nineteenth century explorers Lewis and Clark encountered droves of grizzlies on the banks of the Missouri River, and some early frontiersmen told of seeing the great bears on the Pacific coast, eating the carcasses of beached whales. But as the nation was settled, these great, hulking beasts began to vanish.

By the 1960s there were only two regions south of the Canadian border where the grizzly thrived. One of these was the nation's most famous "bear country"—Yellowstone National Park on the Wyoming–Montana border.

Much of Yellowstone's 2-million-acre "park" is rugged, isolated wilderness; just what grizzlies need to survive. Because the park is protected from heavy development, logging and mining, there once was every reason to believe that the grizzly would endure.

Yet today it is clear that the grizzlies of Yellowstone could become a "once-upon-a-time" story too: Only about 200 grizzlies now inhabit Yellowstone. They are listed as a "threatened" species, though that word may not reflect the seriousness of their plight. As Gary Brown, assistant chief ranger for resources management at Yellowstone puts it: "It isn't the number of grizzlies that concerns us, it's the population trend. And the most recent data we have shows a downward spiral."

Naturalist John Muir once said of the grizzly: "To him everything is food except granite." Indeed, grizzlies are huge creatures, typically ranging from 300 pounds up to, in rare instances, half a ton, and they have voracious appetites. That's part of the problem.

A natural diet of berries, nuts, roots, insects, fish, and even deer and elk is not the only one that appeals to a bear. Grizzlies by nature are wary of humans, but potential bear-food abounds near people. If a bear is rewarded once by an easy meal, it will almost inevitably return to the same spot. Eventually the bear comes to associate the proximity of people with a first-rate meal. And for the bears, contact with humans often means bad news.

Bears that stray outside of the park in search of an easy meal are still shot by ranchers who fear for their livestock, and by poachers who kill for profit.

And occasionally even those who want to save grizzlies

have been responsible for killing them—not for profit, but of an ironic, bitter sort of necessity born of the bears' run-ins with humans.

Dr. Chris Servheen, grizzly bear recovery coordinator for the U.S. Fish and Wildlife Service, is a man committed both professionally and personally to saving the animal. Yet he was forced to put a 435-pound grizzly to death last year. In the early morning hours of June 25, the bear had entered a campsite in the Gallatin National Forest, just outside of Yellowstone park, and without warning, dragged a camper out of his tent and ripped him apart for no apparent reason.

Such attacks are exceedingly rare in grizzly country. There have only been four in the entire Yellowstone ecosystem since the turn of the century, two of them before 1920, and two in the last 12 years (six fatal attacks have occurred at Glacier National Park in Montana since 1967). Yet wildlife managers say they must operate on the assumption that some bears are a threat. An unarmed human is no match for a grizzly that can break a cow's neck with a swat of its paw and rip open the tough hide of an elk with one swipe of its knife-like claws.

Unless a problem bear has actually attacked someone, wildlife managers usually trap it in a cylinder and fly it by helicopter to the park's deep backcountry, hoping that it will stay out of contact with humans. It seldom works, however, and those bears that seem incurably habituated to humans must eventually be removed from the ecosystem. Some are flown to remote wilderness areas in northern Canada; others are shipped to zoos.

Unfortunately, removing a bear from the region accelerates the population problem in that it is a blow to future breeding success. "It would be great if a bear we ship to Canada could beat the odds and establish itself in unfamiliar territory," says Yellowstone's Brown. "But it doesn't do a thing for the future of the Yellowstone ecosystem."

At the core of the grizzly's clouded future is the fact that as few as 32 breeding-age females are left in the park. Grizzly sows normally breed only once every three years, giving birth to an average of two cubs. Thus, further declines seem inevitable.

"We can't do much about the birthrate problem,"

Servheen admits, "so we have to do something about the man-caused mortalities. If we can stop the destruction of grizzly bear habitats and if we can limit mortality, the bear might still recover."

The various state and federal agencies that administer the park are now working together to limit deaths.

Vigorous efforts are being made to stop poaching, and the enforcement program has been enhanced by a National Audubon Society reward program that offers up to $10,000 for information leading to the arrest of poachers. Furthermore, last year the park agencies instituted new policies designed to minimize conflicts between bears and humans. Part of the effort focuses on educating campers. But more important, when there is potential for conflict, trails or campsites or even whole tracts of the park may now be temporarily placed off-limits in deference to the needs of the bears.

By the time the bears of Yellowstone went into hibernation last winter, these measures appeared to be succeeding; there were only six documented cases of grizzlies killed by humans in 1983, a decrease from 14 the previous year.

There's no certainty that the success will continue. But researchers agree that unless it does, the Yellowstone grizzly is almost certainly doomed.

There has not always been such unanimity among those studying the problem. In fact, a disagreement in 1968 dealt the grizzly a costly blow.

In that year, a program that Ranger Brown now calls "natural regulation" was begun, the intent of which was to encourage entirely wild populations of animals within the park, independent of human support. In the case of the grizzlies, that meant closing the park's open-pit dumps where they regularly congregated for an easy meal.

But twin brothers John and Frank Craighead, at the time the only wildlife biologists to have intensively studied Yellowstone's grizzlies, raised the argument that the bears had become dependent on the dumps as a highly stable source of protein.

Despite the Craigheads' recommendation for a gradual phasing out, all the dumps were closed by the early 1970s. The Craigheads warned that it would force some bears into settled areas in search of food, and inevitably raise bear mortality at the hands of humans. Indeed, known grizzly mortality in the region roughly doubled during the first five years that bears were making the transition from dumps to natural sources of food.

Today, it is generally accepted that the Craigheads were right all along about the grizzly bear's decline. And if the bears are to be saved, it will take a concentrated long-term effort on the part of all the park's agencies.

Brown acknowledges that there are difficult times ahead, and that the park's various functions often conflict. "We want to provide as much of the park as possible for the people," he says. "At the same time, we want to make sure that the bear survives. But the two interests are often in conflict."

Still, there will be grizzlies in Yellowstone this summer. Hikers into the park's backcountry will, quite rightly, feel a twinge of awe at one of the few animals on earth that humans must fear—a creature that, like Yellowstone itself, is a spectacular piece of raw nature preserved. And just maybe the story of the grizzlies of Yellowstone will never have to begin with: "Once upon a time. . . ."

 Writing Activity 9.6

☐ Summarize "The Bad News Grizzlies."

☐ Because this piece is difficult to read, your work in Steps 1–3 is particularly important. Check it carefully before you begin your rough draft.

Other Writing Activities

1. Summarize a textbook chapter that you must read this week for another class.

2. Choose a magazine article that interests you and summarize it.

3. Summarize a chapter from a novel you are reading.

Terms to Remember

Division and Classification A pattern of organization that arranges ideas to show how they fit into a pattern of similar ideas or how they can be broken down into smaller units.

patterns of organization Ways in which ideas can be arranged or organized in a piece of writing. Writers organize the ideas in their writing in different ways to accomplish different purposes. For example, a writer might organize ideas about marriage in the Division and Classification pattern in order to show the various forms marriage can take. She might arrange ideas about marriage in a chronological pattern in order to show how her ideas changed over time. Or she might pattern her ideas as a list of examples to show that marriages can be successful and happy.

Time Sequence A pattern of organization that arranges ideas to show how they occur in time. Narrative is one subdivision of Time Sequence. Process, wherein a reader is told what steps to take and in what order, is another.

IV

WRITING LONGER PAPERS

Preview for Chapter 10

Here are the new words for Chapter 10.

1. Essay
2. Thesis statement
3. Introductory paragraph
4. Concluding paragraph
5. Body paragraphs

We've discussed what to do in a chapter preview, but what comes after the preview? The obvious answer is reading, but our answer is *active* reading. To read actively, read with a pencil in your hand and use it. Underline important ideas as you come to them. For example, we've told you that "essay" is an important word in this chapter, and the first sentence of the chapter defines that word. It is a good idea to underline that definition. Besides underlining, mark in the margins anything you don't understand or agree with so that you can discuss it with your teacher.

10

INTRODUCTION TO THE ESSAY

An **essay** is a collection of paragraphs that focus on and develop a single idea. The essay gives you an opportunity to explore more complex topics or to discuss a subject in more depth than you can in a paragraph. Like a paragraph, the essay has a controlling idea; for an essay, we call this controlling idea the **thesis statement**. The type of essay we will discuss usually has five or six paragraphs. The **introductory paragraph** is the first one, and it introduces the essay and states the thesis. The **concluding paragraph** is the last paragraph, and it completes the essay by bringing it smoothly to an end. The three or four **body paragraphs** in between the introduction and conclusion develop or explain the main points of the paper. The introductory and concluding paragraphs are slightly different from the kinds of paragraphs you've been studying, but the main or body paragraphs are identical to the ones you've been writing for this course. A diagram of an essay looks like Figure 10.1.

The process of writing an essay is very similar to the process of writing a paragraph. It's just a little more complex because the end result is longer.

STEP 1:
Brainstorming for Ideas

The techniques for brainstorming don't change at all from those discussed in Chapter 2. You're just looking for a main idea that is broader or larger than the controlling idea of a paragraph. For the essay that we use   191

INTRODUCTION
(contains thesis)

BODY PARAGRAPH
(states and develops first main point)

BODY PARAGRAPH
(states and develops second main point)

BODY PARAGRAPH
(states and develops third main point)

CONCLUSION
(brings essay smoothly to close)

Figure 10.1

as our example, student Rod Foster used listing to explore possible topics for an essay; then he used clustering to brainstorm about his chosen topic. Here is his list from his first brainstorming.

fishing

school

working on the farm

motorcycles

driving a combine

my home town

high school graduation day

Susan

swimming

the creek

The list is short because when Rod got to the last item he knew that the creek was what he wanted to write about; it had meant a lot to him in his lifetime. Choosing a topic that you know and care about will ensure that you have enough information to develop your paragraph or essay. It will also ensure that your writing will be honest and in your own voice. Sometimes student papers leave the reader asking, "So what?" When you write about things you care about, your excitement will almost always come through, and the result will be a paper that is both interesting to write and interesting to read.

When Rod chose his topic, he knew he could write a lot about the creek, and he then spent some time clustering in order to explore, narrow, and focus his ideas. His cluster is shown in Figure 10.2, page 194.

 Writing Activity 10.1

   □ Explore possible subjects for an essay by listing.

   □ Choose a subject, then explore it thoroughly by using one of the brainstorming methods you have learned. If you need to, review Chapter 2 for brainstorming methods.

Figure 10.2

STEP 2:
Writing the Thesis Statement

Like the topic sentence of the paragraph, the thesis statement of the essay states the controlling idea. As Rod looked at his cluster and thought about why he wanted to write about the creek in the first place, he developed this thesis:

Harrington Creek is one of my favorite places to go.

Just as the topic sentence is a one-sentence summary of the paragraph, the thesis is a one-sentence summary of the essay. The thesis will usually be included in the introductory paragraph of the essay, often as the last sentence of that paragraph. As we plan and develop the essay, the thesis needs to control what details go in and what details stay out, and Rod's thesis controls the essay by restricting it only to reasons why Harrington Creek is one of his favorite places to go.

As you outline, draft, and revise your essay, your thesis will probably become more and more specific because your ideas will become clearer and more sharply focused as you explore them in writing. As you read Steps 3–5, notice how Rod's thesis changes to control his essay even more tightly.

 Writing Activity 10.2

□ Write a thesis statement that you think will work as the controlling idea for an essay about the topic you chose in activity 10.1.

□ This is an important step, so share your thesis with your instructor before going on to Step 3.

□ Revise your thesis as necessary.

STEP 3:
Outlining the Essay

Outlining an essay is similar to outlining a paragraph in that you write your thesis statement, turn it into a question, and answer the question. When you write your essay, the thesis will be one of the sentences in your introductory paragraph, and your answers to the thesis question will be the topic sentences of your body paragraphs. Let's look at Rod's outline.

Thesis:

Harrington Creek is one of my favorite places to go.

Thesis question:

Why is Harrington Creek one of my favorite places to go?

Answers:

1. **It has an excellent view.**
   Examples: **It's on a hill, flows into a valley, mountains in background, rock formations, golden wheat fields are all around, water falls to a deep hole**

2. **The creek has an excellent swimming hole.**
   Examples: **30' diameter, 8' deep in the shallow end, 15' deep in the deep end, a 20' cliff on the deep end for diving**

3. **Harrington Creek has the most and the biggest fish that I have seen in a creek.**
   Examples: **There are at least 100 fish in the swimming hole alone, the creek runs for miles and in some places can be reached only by air, the average sized fish is 10", there is a story that an old man pulled a 5 pound fish out.**

4. **The fishing hole is an excellent spot to skin dive.**
   Examples: **Water is 8' to 15' deep, under rocks and in little crevices are crayfish that are fun to catch, the fish are so overpopulated that they swarm around you when you go down to the bottom.**

Note that as he wrote each answer to his thesis question, Rod jotted down some ideas and details he might use in developing his paragraphs. You should also do this because each of the answers to the thesis question in your outline will become the topic sentence of a body paragraph. You will find the details that develop your body paragraphs in your brainstorming, but if some come readily to mind as you outline your essay, list them in your outline, too.

Of course you may, if you wish, outline each body paragraph; if your examples are as detailed as Rod's, however, you may not wish or need to do so. You probably know enough about your own writing ability by now to know whether you should do paragraph outlines.

Writing Activity 10.3

☐ Outline your essay.

☐ Be sure your question contains the important words from your thesis.

☐ Be sure your answers do, in fact, answer the thesis question and can work as topic sentences for the body paragraphs they will control.

☐ Jot down details to use in developing your body paragraphs.

STEP 4:
Writing the First Draft

Some people like to begin the first draft by starting with the introduction, and some people like to use the thesis all by itself as the introduction while writing the first draft. Our usual advice is to begin with the paragraph that seems easiest to write, which is usually one of the body paragraphs. Rod chose to expand his thesis statement so that it would show the organizational pattern of his essay. His expanded thesis shows the subject of each paragraph and the order in which Rod plans to discuss his main supporting points. Rod drafted his body paragraphs in the order predicted by his thesis.

ROD'S FIRST DRAFT

Harrington Creek is one of my favorite places to go because it has an excellent view, a perfect swimming hole, good fishing everywhere, and it is deep enough in spots to skin dive.

The creek is on a hill, and it flows down into a valley. Rock formations are scattered all around and down the hill and into the valley. The rocks are surrounded by rolling golden wheat fields that ripple in the wind. The background is surrounded by mountains that are miles away. The Creek falls ten feet into a deep hole.

This hole is a perfect swimming hole, thirty feet in diameter, eight feet in the shallow end, and is fifteen feet in the deep end. Directly above the deep end is a twenty foot cliff that is a great diving platform. If you swim under the waterfall and sit, the pounding water will massage your back. This comes in handy after you throw your back out during the dive. The water is cool and clean; this makes it excellent for swimming.

The cool, clear water is also excellent for fish. Harrington Creek has the most and the biggest fish that I have seen in a creek. There are at least one hundred fish in the swimming hole alone. The creek runs for miles and through some places that no man can get to except by air, and there are hundreds of little and big holes where fish swim almost untouched by predators. The average sized fish is around ten inches long and weighs about one-half a pound. There is a story that an old man pulled out a five pound trout from one of the areas that is hard to get to. Seeing for myself some of the trout that were pulled out of the creek, I believe that story.

The swimming hole is a great spot to skin dive. The water is deep, and under little rocks and in crevices lay dozens of crayfish that are fun to catch. There are so many fish at the bottom that they swarm around you when you go under. It's fun to take a net down and try to catch one of the trout. It's also challenging because those buggers are fast.

This is why I like Harrington Creek. Anyone who enjoys swimming, high diving, skin diving, fishing, or just a peaceful setting will love Harrington Creek.

Sometimes it can be effective to use your thesis statement all by itself as your introductory paragraph, and sometimes an addition such as Rod made is all that is really necessary. Concluding paragraphs are different from the developmental paragraphs we've been discussing, and your focus in the first draft needs to be on developing your body paragraphs. We will explore techniques for writing introductions and conclusions after this next Writing Activity.

Writing Activity 10.4

☐ Write a rough draft of your essay. Don't worry at first about a good introduction or conclusion. Just get your ideas down in paragraph form.

☐ Write a brief introductory paragraph. It may consist of only your thesis, but be sure your thesis is in the introduction you write.

☐ Write a one- or two-sentence paragraph that will bring your essay to a close. A short summary such as Rod's is often effective.

Writing the Introduction

The introductory paragraph serves three main functions. First, it captures your reader's interest—it serves as a lead, or "grabber." In Chapter 4 you already studied examples of openings that grab the reader's interest (pages 52–53). Second, the introductory paragraph contains the thesis or controlling idea of the essay and shows the writer's attitude toward the subject. You have already studied a great deal about how controlling ideas work in paragraphs. The thesis just controls a greater number of paragraphs. Third, the introductory paragraph can show how the essay will be organized. Rod's opening sentence is an excellent example of how an introduction can show the order in which the ideas will be discussed in the essay.

The introduction should be brief but still grab the reader's attention. Commonly used openings are:

- An anecdote or brief story. This might give your reader a brief glimpse of something or someone you will discuss later in your essay.

- A quotation. A line from a song or a well-known statement by a famous person can be an excellent attention grabber.

- A question or startling fact. Arousing your reader's curiosity is the best attention grabber of all, but your question or fact must be carefully chosen. Be sure it will, in fact, make your reader curious about what you will say in the paper.

- Background information. Sometimes the reader needs just a little background to really understand an essay, and the introduction is an excellent place to provide this.
- Scene setting. Especially in descriptive essays, it is often effective to paint a verbal picture that will put your reader in the place you want to describe.

Your introduction should be appropriate for the essay you write, and there's no way to give you a formula for choosing a type of introduction to use. If you can't decide how to introduce your essay, write two or three possible introductions based on our suggestions and choose the one you like best.

Writing the Conclusion

The conclusion brings the paper smoothly to a close. It should be short, and it should leave your reader with a sense of completeness. Rod's conclusion is typical in that it restates the thesis. Many of the same techniques you use for introductions can be used to conclude your essay. Common conclusions are:

- A restatement of the thesis with a summary of the main points.
- A statement of the importance of your subject.
- A quotation or an anecdote that seems to illustrate your main point and leave the reader with something to ponder.
- A personal note or a lesson that can be learned from your essay.

As for an introduction, there is no set formula for a conclusion. Think of your reading audience, and think about the idea that you want to leave in your readers' minds. The important thing is that your reader feels that the essay has not just stopped but has come naturally to an end.

 Writing Activity 10.5

- Write at least two possible introductions for your essay from activity 10.4.
- Write at least two possible conclusions for your essay.

□ Choose the introduction and the conclusion you like best and include them in your essay.

STEP 5:
Revising the Essay

Let's look now at Rod's revision, noticing especially how he changed his introduction to set the scene. Our notes on the revised essay and our discussion afterward explain how Rod's changes improve the essay.

ROD'S FINAL DRAFT

From the hill above the creek, the view is breathtaking. Rolling golden wheat fields ripple in the wind, giant rock formations dot the hillside, and mountains rise in the background. On a hot day, though, I don't notice the view anymore, because I'm thinking about other things. Harrington Creek is one of my favorite places to go because it has a perfect swimming hole, good fishing everywhere, and it is deep enough in spots to skin dive.

— good attention-getter

— expanded introduction to set the scene

From the hill the creek falls ten feet into a deep pool. This pool is a perfect swimming hole, thirty feet in diameter, eight feet in the shallow end, and fifteen feet in the deep end. Directly above the deep end is a twenty-foot cliff that is a spectacular diving platform. If you swim under the waterfall and sit on the rocky ledge, the pounding water will massage your back. This comes in handy when you throw your back out in a dive. The water in this pool is cool and clean. It is perfect for those hot summer days, but it's not so cold that it takes your breath away and freezes your extremities when you dive in.

— new sentence gives clearer picture

— ties back to "hot day" in introduction

The cool clean water is also excellent for fish. Harrington Creek has the most and the biggest fish that I have seen in a creek. There are at least 100 fish in the swimming hole alone. The creek runs for miles and through some places that man can't get to except by air, and there are hundreds of holes where fish swim almost untouched by predators. The average-sized fish is ten inches long and weighs about one-half a pound. There is a story that an old man pulled out a five-pound trout from one of the areas that is hard to get to. Seeing for myself some of the trout that have been pulled out of the creek, I believe that story.

> good use of specific detail

> adds interest to essay

The swimming hole is a great spot to skin dive. The water is deep and there are many rocks and crevices at the bottom. I have been down to the bottom with a mask several times, and I haven't found any two dives the same. Each time I find a new little crevice or a little hole where a fish or a little crayfish is hiding. It's also fun to take a net down and try to catch a fish, but it is more of a challenge than you would first expect because those little rascals are fast.

> shows his experience with skin diving in the creek

The reason why I like Harrington Creek is that there are so many things to do. Anyone who enjoys swimming, high diving, skin diving, fishing, or just a peaceful setting will love Harrington Creek.

> focuses on thesis

Now let's look at some of the changes Rod made in his revision. First of all, he combined the first and second paragraphs of his rough draft to make a new introduction. This combination sets the scene and draws the reader into the essay by putting the reader *at* Harrington Creek in the very first sentence. The visual picture prepares us for Rod's thesis, that the creek is one of his favorite places.

In the first body paragraph of his revision, Rod paid most of his attention to word choice and addition of detail. Using the word "pool" instead of "hole" in the first and second sentences adds a bit of variety, and changing "great" to "spectacular" in his description of the diving platform more effectively shows how he feels about it. Adding "It is perfect for those hot summer days" ties this paragraph nicely back to the introduction and thus improves coherence. Rod left his second body paragraph mostly unchanged from the rough draft, and that's just fine because the paragraph is detailed, interesting, and very effective.

In the skin diving paragraph, Rod worked mainly on developing the details from his personal experience. Adding these details focuses the reader's attention back on the idea that the creek is Rod's favorite place. The change in the first sentence of his concluding paragraph, too, improves coherence because it is more like a rephrasing of the thesis.

Before you begin your own revision, read the next example of a student essay. It is a paper we really like because it is a good example of the writing and revision processes. Student Nick Roussos used listing as a brainstorming technique for this paper, and his list led him to the following outline:

Thesis:

My last voyage as a crew member on an ocean-going oil tanker turned out to be an unforgettable, miserable experience.

Thesis question:

How was my last voyage unforgettable and miserable?

Answers:

1. **My friend and shipmate Jim was severely injured while attempting to cross the walkway on the deck to reach the bridge.**
2. **The injuries I suffered while searching for Jim, although only temporary, were very painful.**
3. **Although the weather started to show improvement, there were still more troubles ahead for all of us.**

Because the experience was so vivid in Nick's memory, he didn't include specific details in his outline, as Rod had. As he wrote, Nick was careful to follow the outline format and to use each of his answers as a topic sentence. While this is generally good practice, notice as you read the rough draft that it makes his exciting story too stiff and formal.

MY LAST VOYAGE, DRAFT 1

Many people cross the ocean for pleasure, but for some the crossing of the ocean is their occupation. It's a dangerous way to make a living. The ship's mighty turbines were operating at dead slow. The ship's autopilot, electronic gyro and radar were all turned off, and only the magnetic compass was available for navigation. The helmsman at the wheelhouse was struggling to maintain the heading ordered by the captain. Although it was a cold night, he was sweating profusely. With waves up to 60 feet high and winds well over 100 miles per hour, his attempts to maintain the correct heading proved to be an impossible task. We were in the middle of a typhoon. At this point it was all too clear to us that the ship and crew were at the mercy of the Pacific Ocean. My last voyage as a crew member on an ocean-going oil tanker turned out to be an unforgettable experience.

My friend and shipmate Jim was severely injured while attempting to cross the walkway on the deck to reach the bridge. It was one hour before midnight, and Jim and I were standing in the hallway behind a tightly sealed steel exit door. Looking through the window with the phone receiver pressed to my ear I waited for the all clear signal from the bridge to open the door. We were talking about the lousy weather when the man on the other end of the phone said, "Now." I pulled the steel bar on the door to the open position, and I flipped the high power light switch on. Jim, without saying a word, stepped out and engaged the hook of his safety belt to the rails. I pulled the door shut and locked it, engaging all locking bars. I immediately looked through the window and saw him being swept away by the crashing waves. He was thrown clear off the walkway against the steel tank openings on the deck. I pulled the alarm switch, the powerful loud electronic siren came on, and the entire crew reported to the exit within seconds. Using all available safety gear, we started searching for Jim. Three hours later we found him jammed between two steel pipes. He was frozen stiff and unconscious. But we soon discovered our troubles were not over yet.

The injuries I suffered while searching for Jim, although only temporary, were very painful. Wearing my leather safety belt, the minimum amount of clothing and secured to a nylon rope held by five crewmen, I was lowered onto the deck. I started searching for Jim, but it was a very slow process. The high wind forced me to crawl. Using the steel pipes on the deck I pulled myself forward a few feet at a time. The waves were another problem; millions of gallons of sea water were crashing on top of me. Sometimes I was thrown against a steel wall, and the pain in my back was unbearable. As I was attempting to get up and move to another area, I was hit on my side by a swinging crane beam. That hit catapulted me about fifteen feet and five feet up. Luckily for me, the deck was under three feet of water at that time, so when I came down, I didn't suffer any more injuries. By that time I wasn't feeling any pain, only numbness, so I kept searching for Jim. When the search was over, I went inside, my body started to warm up, and the pain in my back and side was more than I could stand.

Although the weather started to show improvement, there were still more troubles ahead for all of us. Twelve hours later the worst had passed, but we found ourselves in a new predicament. The wind subsided, the sea was calmer and the sky was clear. The change of the weather allowed us to turn on the navigation instruments. It didn't take long for us to discover that we were eighty miles off course and one-hundred miles back from our last known position. This was of no help at all for Jim's condition. It would take five days to get back to our last position and about ten more days before we could get any medical help for Jim. Our troubles appeared to have no end. We discovered our drinking water was contaminated with salt, oil and rust. Immediately we focused our attention to the fresh water converter unit. This unit converts sea water to drinking water. It was a relief to discover it was in working order. By that time we were saying "enough is enough." But to make our situation even worse, it was discovered one of the oil tanks was leaking. It wouldn't have been so bad if it had been crude oil leaking, but the leaky tank was holding the oil used to operate the boilers. Without it we couldn't go anywhere. After several hours and a lot of hard work, the oil was transferred to another tank, and we continued our voyage toward our final destination.

Take my advice, next time you decide to cross the ocean, take a submarine. It could be safer. We reached our final destination with no more problems, but upon a physical examination, Jim's head injuries were diagnosed as severe and permanent. He was sent home immediately. The injuries I received were temporary and needed only time to heal. I was hospitalized for only a few days. The day I got off the ship was the last I saw of crew and ship. The ship was a disaster inside and out. It was sent to a dry dock for a complete overhaul. As for me, the experience helped me make up my mind never again to cross the ocean on a ship.

When we learn that this essay will be about an experience, we expect to see the events in the order in which they actually happened. The topic sentences that appear in the outline, however, caused the writer to jumble the order of some of the events. For example, in the first body paragraph of the first draft the writer discusses how Jim got lost and ends that discussion with finding Jim. The topic sentence of the next paragraph is about the writer's own injuries, but he has to go back in time and talk about the search for Jim in order to show how those injuries occurred. There seems to be no good reason for these shifts in time.

Sometimes an outline can lock a writer into a pattern that is not the best way to develop a subject. Use your outline as a tool to help you plan the paper, but don't let it hurt your paper. Even before he began his revision, Nick had a feeling that the topic sentences didn't fit and were forcing him to do some things he didn't want to do. The outline had helped him decide which events of the experience were most important, but when he revised his paper to show the events in the order in which they actually happened, Nick found that while the ideas didn't change, the manner in which they were expressed improved greatly. Here's Nick's final draft.

MY LAST VOYAGE

Many people cross the ocean for pleasure, but for some the crossing of the ocean is their occupation. It's a dangerous way to make a living, and it isn't always pleasant. My last voyage as a crew member on an ocean-going oil tanker turned out to be an unforgettable, miserable experience.

— shortened introduction gets right to the point

The ship's mighty turbines were operating at dead slow. The ship's autopilot, electronic gyro and radar were all turned off, and only the magnetic compass was available for navigation. The helmsman at the wheelhouse was struggling to maintain the heading ordered by the captain. Although it was a cold night, he was sweating profusely. With waves up to 60 feet high and winds well over 100 miles per hour, his attempts to maintain the correct heading proved to be an impossible task. We were in the middle of a typhoon. At this point it was all too clear to us that the ship and crew were at the mercy of the Pacific Ocean.

information moved from introduction clearly sets the scene here

It was one hour before midnight, and Jim and I were standing in the hallway behind a tightly-sealed steel exit door. Looking through the window and pressing the phone receiver to my ear, I waited for the all clear signal from the bridge to open the door. We were talking about the lousy weather when the man on the other end of the phone line said, "Now." I pulled the steel bar on the door to the open position, and I flipped the high power light switch on.

change to strict chronological sequence shows action more clearly and keeps reader interested

Jim, without saying a word, stepped out and engaged the hook of his safety belt to the rails. I pulled the door shut and locked it, engaging all locking bars. I immediately looked through the window and saw Jim being swept away by the crashing waves. He was thrown clear off the walkway against the steel tank openings on the deck. I pulled the alarm switch, the powerful, loud electronic siren came on, and the entire crew reported to the exit within seconds. Using all available safety gear, we started searching for Jim.

Wearing my leather safety belt and a minimum amount of clothing and secured

reordered details build tension and excitement

to a nylon rope held by five crewmen, I was lowered onto the deck. I started searching for Jim, but it was a very slow process. The high wind forced me to crawl. Using the steel pipes on the deck, I pulled myself forward a few feet at a time. The waves were another problem: millions of gallons of water were crashing on top of me. Sometimes I was three feet under water. All of a sudden it happened. I was thrown against a steel wall, and the pain in my back was unbearable. As I was attempting to get up and move to another area, I was hit on my side by a swinging crane beam. That hit catapulted me about fifteen feet along the deck and five feet in the air. Luckily for me, the deck was under three feet of water at that time, so when I came down, I didn't suffer any more injuries. By that time I wasn't feeling any pain, only numbness, so I kept on searching for Jim. Three hours later we found him jammed between two steel pipes. He was frozen stiff and unconscious. When the search was over, I went inside. My body started to warm up, and the pain in my back and side was more than I could stand.

we see why the experience was unforgettable

Twelve hours later the worst of the weather and my pain had passed, but we found ourselves in a new predicament. The wind subsided, the sea was calmer and the sky was clear. The change of the weather allowed us to turn on the navigation instruments. It didn't take long for us to discover that we were 80 miles off course and 100 miles back from our last known position. This was of no help at all for Jim's condition. It would take two days to get back to our last position and about ten more days before we could get any medical help for Jim. Our troubles appeared to have no end. We discovered our drinking water was contaminated with salt, oil and

we see why the experience was miserable

rust. Immediately we focused our attention on the fresh water converter unit. This unit converts sea water into drinking water. It was a relief to discover it was in working order. By that time we were saying, "Enough is enough." But to make our situation even worse, it was discovered one of the oil tanks was leaking. It wouldn't have been so bad if it had been crude oil leaking, but the leaky tank was holding the oil used to operate the boilers. Without it we couldn't go anywhere. After several hours and a lot of hard work, the oil was transferred to another tank, and we continued our voyage toward our final destination.

Take my advice: next time you decide to cross the ocean, take a submarine. It could be safer. We reached our final destination with no more problems, but upon a physical examination, Jim's head injuries were diagnosed as severe and permanent. He was sent home immediately. The injuries I received were temporary and needed only time to heal. I was hospitalized for only a few days. The ship was a disaster inside and out. It was sent to a dry dock for a complete overhaul. This experience helped me make up my mind never again to cross the ocean on a ship.

> smooth transition to conclusion

> conclusion wraps up details of story—it answers all our questions

You may never have had an experience this exciting, but your experiences, whatever they are, are unique. Only *you* have seen your experiences from your point of view. If you write about things that are significant to you or that stand out in your memory for some reason, and if you explore your subjects to understand why they are important to you, your reader will come away from your essay with a new understanding.

 Writing Activity 10.6

☐ Revise your essay from activities 10.4 and 10.5.

The Opinion Essay: An Example

The two essays we have examined in this chapter describe a place and narrate an experience, but much college writing asks that you state and support an opinion. Other writing courses teach the opinion essay, and our final chapter, "Writing Responses to Essay Tests," also discusses some techniques of stating and supporting opinions. Here, however, we close with an example of a longer essay that also does an effective job of stating and supporting an opinion.

Our final example is an essay by one of our students, Gary Maddio, that was later published as a citizen editorial in the local newspaper. The essay is an example of a personal opinion paper, and it is effective because Gary is clearly writing from a position of authority on the subject. He not only has personal experience with the subject, but he also has facts, figures, and information about the experience of others and the success of the program. He includes many examples of his personal experience and knowledge to support his opinion.

A COSTLY MISTAKE

Funding cuts by the state of Washington forced the closure last week of the Eastern Washington Alcoholism Center (EWAC) in Spokane. That was a mistake, and my own life proves it. A state official was quoted as saying the funding cut was necessary to pump more dollars into the shorter, intensive alcoholism programs, which he claimed provide the same services for much less money. But for chronic, late-stage alcoholics, short-term treatment has not helped. For them, alternatives such as EWAC must remain open.

thesis stated emphatically; prepares us to see personal experience

The philosophy of EWAC is simple and realistic: to allow the clients the time that is so necessary to rebuild their self worth and dignity and to formulate a positive plan for re-entering society through activities such as furthering their education or

first two paragraphs summarize the situation and show the problem finding employment. It is impossible for a chronic, late-stage alcoholic to accomplish this in a 28-day, short-term program. The time permitted by EWAC's long-term treatment is vital if chronic, late-stage alcoholics are to readjust and become productive members of society.

Long-term treatment was my final hope for a life free from alcohol. Before I entered treatment at EWAC, my life was nonproductive and, at best, a dismal failure. I was the product of two divorces, 110 drinking-related arrests, many hospitalizations, a two-year term in prison, and 14 get-fixed-quick short-term programs. I was 36 going on 66, and the most gracious of doctors said my prognosis was poor. I had been through nearly 16 years of self-destruction by alcoholism.

shows personal experience in specific detail

I thought I was a unique drunk, but at EWAC I found forty men and women who were just like me, and now I know that is not surprising. A profile of the average clients in long-term treatment done by the staff at EWAC shows they are 35 years of age, divorced twice, ex-felons, and have been in short-term treatment four times. They also are unemployed and on welfare.

moves from personal experience to that of others; shows he wasn't alone with his problem

However, welfare wasn't bearing all of the burden. The cost to Washington taxpayers for the lifestyle of chronic, late-stage alcoholics is astronomical: extra police to patrol the skid roads, emergency room treatment in hospitals, and welfare to house and feed them. We pay for our disease physically and mentally, but the state of Washington pays for our slow death financially. A 28-day, short-term treatment doesn't even give the chronic, late-stage alcoholic time to dry out. Without the vital time provided in EWAC's program, the chronic alcoholic has no choice

shows that we *all* share the problem

but to return to skid road and his continued dependency on the taxpayer.

But with EWAC, he had a chance to become a productive member of society. EWAC's long-term program had an excellent success rate in treating the chronic, late-stage alcoholic. For example, I am currently enrolled in my fourth quarter of college with a 3.61 grade point average. I also manage a 24-unit apartment complex and do volunteer work with other recovering alcoholics. Three fellow EWAC clients with whom I am in contact also have made the transition to positive lifestyles. Two of them have enrolled in college, and the other is a counselor at an alcoholic treatment program in Idaho.

offers proof that EWAC is a good solution

In fact, the majority of clients whom I know who successfully completed the EWAC program show remarkable gains in sobriety, employment, and family stability. This is a population that repeatedly failed in short-term programs. During the last eighteen months, I have had two short-lived experiences with alcohol. They were short-lived because my time in the EWAC long-term treatment program allowed me to reconstruct my life and to set new goals. And I wasn't going to throw those goals away.

reinforces proof

EWAC was the only long-term program in Eastern Washington that offered late-stage, chronic alcoholics a way out of their living hell and a chance to become productive members of their communities. The other alternative is to remain society's outcasts and to be buried in a pauper's grave. I thank God that EWAC was available to me.

concludes with summary and strong statement of opinion

This essay is a good example of how a writer can use personal experience as strong support for an opinion. This is a powerful essay because the writer is obviously writing about a subject he knows and cares about.

In closing this chapter, let's review the steps in the process of writing an essay; they are very similar to the steps of writing a paragraph. First, brainstorm for ideas, choose your topic, and then do some focused brainstorming. Develop a possible thesis statement from your brainstorming list; the thesis will control your essay. Next, write an outline by turning the thesis statement into a question and answering that question. Remember that each answer could form a topic sentence for the body paragraphs of your essay. Next, write your rough draft, letting your thesis statement and outline guide your writing. Let your rough draft rest for a day, and then read it carefully, noticing whether each body paragraph does indeed support your thesis statement. Do as many revisions of your essay as necessary to communicate your ideas effectively.

Other Suggestions for Writing

1. Write an essay explaining how or why a specific incident changed your life.
2. Write an essay explaining how your experience shows the wisdom or foolishness of some law or rule.
3. Write an essay showing the things your job requires of you.
4. Write an essay about a problem you are directly involved with that you think should be solved. Choose something like a problem you see in your neighborhood, your school, or your work.
5. Write an essay about the high degree of self-discipline it takes to excel at demanding activities such as ballet, figure skating, classical guitar, or sports.

Terms to Remember

body paragraph   A paragraph that clearly develops one major section of the thesis statement.

concluding paragraph   The final paragraph of an essay. Its purpose is to leave the reader with a sense of completeness.

essay   A collection of paragraphs that focus on and develop a single idea.

introductory paragraph   A paragraph that introduces the essay, usually by catching the reader's interest, stating the thesis, and showing how the essay will be organized.

thesis statement   The controlling idea of an essay.

Preview for Chapter 11

Look for the following words and phrases in Chapter 11.

1. Responses	10. Trace
2. In-class essay tests	11. List
3. Out-of-class essay tests	12. Define
4. Predict	13. Evaluate
5. Direction words	14. Illustrate
6. Discuss	15. Summarize
7. Compare	16. State
8. Describe	17. Test strategy
9. Explain	

It's a good idea to develop a system for marking a textbook chapter as you read. You can, for example,

- circle unfamiliar words
- underline definitions of words
- number ideas if you need to remember them in sequence
- draw a star next to important ideas
- write a question mark near confusing ideas
- make notes to yourself in the margins ("ask instructor")
- develop your own shorthand ("impt" for "important")

11

WRITING RESPONSES TO ESSAY TESTS

The writing process you have studied can be used in most tasks that require writing, but some tasks call for a slight change in the process. Chapters 8 and 9 show how the process can be adapted for the task of writing summaries. This chapter will show you how it can be adapted for the task of writing **responses** to essay tests.

Essay tests may be given as in-class assignments or as out-of-class assignments, but writing the responses to such assignments is not really much different from writing any other paragraph or essay. **In-class essay tests** usually ask several questions, and you must answer each question by writing one or more paragraphs or short essays during a class period of one or two hours. **Out-of-class essay tests** usually ask fewer questions, but they often require that you write one or more longer essays. You may be given days or weeks to complete the out-of-class assignments. Your grade on an essay test often counts as a large part of your grade in a college course, so knowing how to deal with such tests can improve your grades.

Responses to these assignments are usually written for a very specific audience: the teacher who assigns them. Also, the responses must be written for a very specific purpose. A teacher gives such assignments with two questions in mind:

1. Can the student find or remember certain facts or ideas?
2. Does the student have the thinking skills necessary to put those facts and ideas together?

Your purpose in writing essay tests and assignments, then, must be to show that you do, indeed, have the knowledge and thinking skills the teacher wants to see.

In order to show your knowledge and your thinking skills, you must:

- *prepare for the test ahead of time* so that you know what to write
- *manage your time wisely during the test* so that you can complete the test in the time allowed
- *do exactly what you are assigned to do* so that your instructor doesn't have to guess about what you know

The steps in writing essay test answers help you be sure that you do those three important things.

IN-CLASS ESSAY TESTS

STEP 1:
Preparing for the In-class Essay Test

To prepare for a test, you must study, of course, but this does not mean that you stay up all night and cram. From the beginning of the course, keep up with your reading, review your reading assignments and class notes frequently, and ask questions when you don't understand something. If you know the material over which you'll be tested, you'll be less nervous about the test. Your mind will be clearer. You'll be able to remember more.

As you study, **predict** the questions you might find on the exam. A test situation demands that you think and respond quickly, and you think and respond most quickly when you are not surprised. If you have asked yourself a question and answered that question before you get to the test, you'll be on familiar ground if you see it on the test. Your instructor's lectures and comments will help you predict questions. The main headings and review questions in your textbooks will also help you predict, as will your knowledge of the skills that are being taught in the course.

As we said in our introduction to this chapter, college courses teach thinking skills as well as give information. As a result, your responses to essay tests must show that you know the information and that you have the thinking skills required to explain them. You show that you know the information by the facts or ideas you include in your answer to the question. You show your thinking skills by the way in which you put those facts and ideas together to form a paragraph or essay. Essay test questions almost always tell you what information to include and how to put it together, so understanding the question is almost as important as studying.

Most essay questions are not really questions. They are sentences that tell you what to do, and they commonly use **direction words**—usually verbs—that tell you what information to include in your answer and in what patterns to organize that information. For example, an essay question might say,

> Compare the benefits of jogging with the benefits of cross-country skiing.

The question requires that your paragraph include the important similarities of the two sports, and that the ideas be arranged in the comparison pattern.

Because the direction word tells you exactly what to do, you must be able to identify direction words and know what they mean. Here is a list of some of the most common direction words and a description of what each tells you to do.

DIRECTION WORD	WHAT IT TELLS YOU TO DO
Discuss	Tell in detail what you know about all important aspects of the subject.
Compare	Talk about the similarities. Sometimes instructors will also expect you to talk about differences, so if you have any doubts, ask.
Describe	Tell in detail how something looks or happens, or show in detail what occurs.
Explain	Show your understanding by giving specific information, including examples, illustrations, and reasons.
Trace	Start from the beginning and go to the end in chronological order.
List	Write a list. A numbered list is usually sufficient as a response to this direction word.
Define	Give a definition of a word or concept.

Evaluate	Make a value judgment about the subject. Explain why it's good or bad, strong or weak, important or unimportant.
Illustrate	Give examples to demonstrate or clarify.
Summarize	Write a summary that states the main points about the subject.
State	Tell the specific fact or idea that the question asks for.

If you study for the test, predict the questions you're likely to see on the test, and know what the direction words mean, you'll walk through the door on test day ready to do your best.

Writing Activity 11.1

- Using a textbook from one of your classes, predict two or three possible essay test questions.
- Begin each test question with a direction word.

STEP 2:
Planning Test Strategy

Because time is scarce during in-class exams, planning how you will spend your test time is vital. You must, therefore, develop a **test strategy**, or a way to approach the exam. There are three steps to developing a test strategy.

First, quickly read the whole test before you answer any question. This gives you an overview of the exam and allows you to identify those questions you are sure you can answer. Also, one question might suggest the answer to a question you're not sure of, so the preview can build your confidence and improve your performance.

Second, budget your time. Look at the number of questions and the point value of each. Obviously, you'll want to spend most of your time on the questions that will earn you the most points. Also, estimate how long it will take you to answer the questions you're sure of, and plan to answer those first. Now decide how much time you can afford to spend on each question, and pace yourself accordingly. Allow a few minutes before the end of the period to proofread your answers.

Third, decide on the specific order in which you'll answer the questions, and begin taking the exam.

On most essay tests, developing your test strategy will take only a couple of minutes, but your strategy will help you be sure that you finish the test in the time you are given and have spent enough time on those questions that really count.

STEP 3:
Stating the Controlling Idea

Most in-class essay questions require a paragraph or a short essay in response, but some do not. A question like this, for example, would not require a paragraph:

> List five digestive enzymes and state the type of food that each digests.

Two parallel lists, one naming the digestive enzymes and one naming the type of food that each digests, would be an adequate answer.

For most in-class essay test questions, though, a paragraph or short essay is the only appropriate response, and your statement of the controlling idea (the topic sentence of a paragraph or the thesis statement of an essay) will be the most important sentence in your response. Because it controls what goes into the paragraph and what stays out of the paragraph, your topic sentence will help you be certain that you do exactly what the direction word of a question tells you to do. Let's look at some examples.

> Compare the main characters of *The Catcher in the Rye* and *A Separate Peace* to show how they are examples of troubled youths.

The direction word is "compare," and it requires you to write about what the two characters have in common. The last part of the question focuses or limits the assignment even more sharply, for it requires that you discuss only the similarities which show how the characters are "troubled youths." The best way to be sure that your answer does exactly what the assignment asks is to change the question into your topic sentence or thesis statement of your answer. This step is simply the reverse of what you do in the paragraph outline when you turn your topic sentence into a question. Be sure to use as many of the words from the assignment as you can. Here, for example, is a possible topic sentence or thesis for a response to the above assignment.

Holden Caulfield in *The Catcher in the Rye* and Gene in *A Separate Peace* have four main similarities that show how they are examples of troubled youths.

The word "similarities" shows that the writer will compare, and the writer has specifically stated what the comparison will show.

Here is a question from a biology class.

Describe what happens when a bear goes into hibernation.

The direction word "describe" means to show in detail. In this case, you must show what happens to the bear when it goes into hibernation. Since your answer will be detailed, your topic sentence should be a general statement that controls the paragraph. Here's an example.

There are several major changes that take place when a bear goes into hibernation.

This topic sentence would help you be sure that you describe or show in detail only the changes that take place when a bear hibernates.

A history exam might ask this question:

Trace the major events of the late 1930s and early 1940s that led to America's entry into World War II.

The direction word "trace" requires that you start from the beginning and go to the end of the period in question, showing how the events relate to one another. If you were not immediately certain about which events to include, your topic sentence could be general:

Several major events beginning in the late 1930s and ending in the early 1940s led to America's entry into World War II.

If you were more certain of what your answer should contain, your topic sentence could be more specific:

Major events of the late 1930s and early 1940s that led to America's entry into World War II began with Hitler's rearming of Germany and ended with Japan's attack on Pearl Harbor.

Either of these two topic sentences gives a specific focus on the time period being covered and on the fact that the writer will state and discuss the events in chronological order. Each sentence limits the answer to the *major* events.

Often you will see questions with more than one direction word, and you must be sure that you do what each of the direction words tells you to do. Here, for example, is a test question from a class on human sexuality:

What determines whether a child will be a boy or a girl? Explain and discuss.

The first direction word is implied, not directly stated. It is "state." Your first task, then, would be to state a direct answer to the question:

The sex of a child is determined by the presence or absence of a Y chromosome in the sperm that fertilizes the ovum.

The second direction word, "explain," requires that you tell *why* or *how* the presence or absence of a Y chromosome determines the child's sex. The third direction word, "discuss," gives you a chance to talk about why and how these facts are important. Two paragraphs would be an appropriate response to this assignment: one that states and explains, and one that discusses. The topic sentence of the explaining paragraph will immediately follow the sentence that states the direct answer, and it would be something like this:

The female's cells carry two X chromosomes, but the male's cells carry one X and one Y chromosome; if the Y chromosome happens to be in the sperm that fertilizes the ovum, the child will be male.

The paragraph will consist of several sentences that explain how and why the Y chromosome may or may not be present in the sperm that fertilizes the ovum.

"Discuss" is a direction word that usually leaves you a great deal of freedom, so what you include in the discussion paragraph is largely up to you, though it must deal with the subject in some important way. Class discussions, lectures, your outside reading, and so on will tell you what kinds of things you might discuss. The topic sentence of the discussion paragraph could be,

> **Up to now, having a boy or a girl has been mostly a matter of luck, but some medical researchers are trying to give people the ability to choose the sex of their children.**

Or it could be,

> **According to the laws of chance, there should be an equal number of males and females in the world, but the numbers are not equal for several reasons.**

There are many more possibilities, of course, but the discussion paragraph would contain several sentences to develop the topic sentence.

You must be certain that you do what every direction word in an essay question tells you to do because ignoring or overlooking a direction word will cost you points on the exam. If you are careful to write at least one sentence that responds to each direction word, you can be sure that your answer will be as complete as you can make it.

 Writing Activity 11.2

☐ Write a topic sentence for a possible answer to each of the following questions. Be as specific as possible.

1. Trace the process of writing a paragraph.

2. Discuss the ways in which your writing has improved since you began this course.

3. Explain why brainstorming is an important step in the writing process.

STEP 4:
Exploring and Planning the Answer

Step 4 combines focused brainstorming and outlining; the topic sentence you write in Step 3 provides your focus for brainstorming. For example, consider this question asked in a psychology class:

> Discuss the main limitations of intelligence tests.

The direction word "discuss" and the rest of the question ask you to tell all you know about the *main limitations* of intelligence tests. To focus your thinking, then, you might turn the question into this topic sentence:

> **Intelligence tests have _____ main limitations.**

Or this one:

> **Intelligence tests have two main limitations.**

Or this one:

> **The main limitations of intelligence tests are language handicaps and cultural differences.**

Any one of these three topic sentences about limitations of intelligence tests will provide an excellent guide for Step 4, planning your answer. Even the first sample topic sentence,

> **Intelligence tests have _____ main limitations,**

provides a sharp focus by reminding you that you need to discuss some number of main limitations of intelligence tests, even if you're not sure how many there are. To get yourself thinking clearly about them, you might list, cluster, or freewrite around the idea of limitations of intelligence tests. If you were sure enough of the limitations to write something like the third sample topic sentence,

> **The main limitations of intelligence tests are language handicaps and cultural differences,**

you might need only to focus your brainstorming on the details about language handicaps and cultural factors. If, however, you were already completely sure of your facts and details, you might not need to write anything at all in Step 4.

How much brainstorming or outlining you do for an essay test answer will depend on how well you know the material and how much time you have. If you are having trouble remembering the material, list, freewrite, or cluster to help yourself remember. If you're not sure how to organize the answer, outline it by turning your topic sentence into a question and answering that question. If you know the material well and have a good idea about how it should be organized, Step 4 will take you very little time to complete.

The question we gave about intelligence tests happened to be the third part of a three-part question, and there were two other questions to be answered in a two-hour period. The student was a little uncertain of the details about language handicaps and cultural factors, so she made a quick list of the limitations she remembered from her reading:

> **Language handicap—differences in vocabulary or language, physical/psych. problems.**
> **Cultural factors—experiences, what's important in home and society.**

Her brainstorming list became the outline for her answer.

 Writing Activity 11.3

□ Choose one of the topic sentences you wrote for Writing Activity 11.2 and plan your answer for it.

□ Time yourself as you do this. You should spend no more than three minutes on this step for an assignment of this nature.

STEP 5:
Writing the Answer

Writing the answer to an essay question that requires a paragraph is no different from writing the kinds of paragraphs you have already studied. All you need to do is write down the topic sentence, follow that with a sentence that states your first main point, and write one or more sentences that develop or explain that main point. Next, state and develop your second main point, and so on. Keep an eye on the clock so that you don't get carried away and spend too much time, and be aware of mechanics— sentence structure, punctuation, and spelling. You won't have much time for proofreading.

Here is our student's response to the question, "Discuss the main limitations of intelligence tests."

The main limitations of intelligence tests are language handicaps and cultural differences. Language handicaps may result if a person grows up in a home where English is not spoken or where an unusual English vocabulary is used. A person may also have a physical or psychological problem that will affect his use of language. As a result, he can't understand or respond to the questions even though he may know the answer, and therefore his intelligence is not being tested. Cultural factors can also interfere. If a child has grown up in a home or society that doesn't give him the experiences that most American children have, he might not do well on a test that includes those experiences. Someone growing up on New York City streets develops a different set of skills from those of an Iowa farm boy. Different things are important in the two cultures, and intelligence tests do not always allow for these cultural differences.

- topic sentence
- first main point
- second main point
- development of second main point
- third main point
- development of third main point
- example for third main point
- summary statement for third main point

Notice especially how the student relates her details back to the idea of limitations: "his intelligence is not being tested," "he might not do well on a test," and "tests do not always allow for these cultural differences." She clearly shows the instructor that she remembers and understands the material.

Writing Activity 11.4

☐ Using your work from Writing Activity 11.3, write an answer to the question you have chosen.

☐ Again, time yourself. Five or ten minutes is probably the most you should allow.

STEP 6:
Checking Your Work

There is seldom time for revision or careful proofreading during an in-class essay exam, and teachers usually take this into account when reading them. Still, the teacher usually reads the exams fairly quickly and wants to see whether the students know and can handle the material. As a result, an answer that is clearly stated and properly spelled and punctuated is likely to earn a higher grade than one in which the teacher has to guess at meanings. We advise students to plan to leave five minutes at the end of an exam period to reread their answers, looking for obvious gaps in information or for obvious mechanical errors. Pay special attention to the spellings of words, names, or terms that are important to the course. It's hard to convince a teacher that you really know the material if you can't spell the words.

Writing Activity 11.5

☐ Quickly check the work you did in Writing Activity 11.4.

☐ Make necessary corrections neatly.

In closing this section, let us review the process of responding to an in-class essay examination. First, because tests usually determine your grade in a class, prepare by studying and reviewing frequently from the first day of the class. Predict the questions and direction words you will see. Second, during the test, plan a test strategy by reading all of the questions, deciding upon the order in which you will answer the questions, and estimating how much time you can spend on each. Third, as you answer each question, turn it into a topic sentence, paying close attention to the direction words and to other key words. Fourth, explore what you know about the question and plan your answer. Fifth, write the best answer you possibly can, remembering that the teacher is your reading audience and that she is looking for specific knowledge and skills. Finally, quickly check your work, making neat, readable corrections.

OUT-OF-CLASS ESSAY TESTS

Out-of-class essay tests vary. They may differ only slightly from in-class essay tests, or they may differ greatly. For example, you might be required to review a concert; read, summarize and respond to an article; analyze a novel; or even write an extensive research paper. Still, most of these tests will require that you write a paper in order to show your knowledge of a body of material and your mastery of certain thinking skills.

One example of an out-of-class essay test is this one-question exam worth one-fourth of the final grade in an American civilization class. We've underlined the direction words.

> <u>Compare</u> the New England, Middle, and Southern colonies as to the types of *economies* they developed. In so doing, <u>explain</u> how the New England colonies solved their balance of trade problem of buying large quantities of manufactures and other products from England, especially as difficulties emerged in lumbering. <u>Explain</u> why Pennsylvania was such an economic success, why land-jobbing was not the biggest part of the economy of the Middle colonies, and why the Middle colonies evolved craft production. For the Southern colonies, <u>explain</u> why tobacco evolved in Virginia and rice in South Carolina, how the development of slavery differed in these two colonies and why.

The main direction word for this question is "compare," but the instructor announces in class that he wants students to discuss both similarities and differences. The word "explain" is repeated three times within the assignment, and the teacher is very exact about what he wants the students to explain. The process of writing an out-of-class essay test is much the same as writing an in-class essay test, except that Steps 1 and 2 are reversed. That is, for out-of-class assignments, plan your test strategy *before* you prepare for the test.

STEP 1:
Planning Test Strategy

You can't do a good job on an assignment if you wait until the last minute to start, so you must plan and control your time. Ask yourself these questions:

- How many days do I have before the assignment is due?
- How much time per day do I have available to spend on this assignment?

Think about your other classes, your family responsibilities, your job, and any other activities that demand your time. Remember that you must eat and sleep. Write a study schedule for yourself, predicting times you will work on your paper, and post your written schedule where your room-mates or family can see it. Explain to others why your schedule is important, and do your best to stick with your schedule. If you find that you are not sticking with your schedule, something must change. Either revise your schedule so that you *will* stick with it, or think of ways to be more responsible.

Finally, starting from the due date of your paper and working backward, write a schedule of when you plan to complete each step of the writing process. The amount of time you schedule for preparation depends on your knowledge and the requirements of the test. When possible, give yourself at least a day or two to write the rough draft. Schedule a day to let the rough draft get cold before you begin your revision. Give yourself a day or two for the revision, and schedule a day to let the revision get cold before you proofread it. If possible, allow more time for the revising process, as you will probably need more than one rewrite.

STEP 2:
Preparing for the Test

For a test such as our example about the economies, you'd probably need to do quite a bit of reading, so you'd need to decide at once where to go to get the information necessary to answer the question. The assignment sheet itself or your instructor will usually tell you. If you need only your course textbook, decide which chapters you will need to read. If you need to get information from the library, go there at once. The books you need may already be checked out, or you may need to order some material, so it is important that you get started immediately.

As you read, keep the test assignment in front of you, and when you find information that will help you answer the question, write it down. Review your lecture notes for material that might be helpful. For our sample assignment, you would look for and write down facts and ideas about the economies of the three areas, and you would especially look for information about balance of trade, land-jobbing, slavery, and so on.

STEP 3:
Stating the Controlling Idea

For our sample question, you would need to write an overall thesis statement that says something about the similarities and differences among the economies. Remember that the main direction word is "compare," and that the word "economies" puts strict limits on what is to be compared. Here is a sample thesis for the question:

> **While the underlying economic activity of most Americans in all colonies was self-sufficient agriculture, the three groups of colonies differed in important ways. The New England colonies specialized in commercial activities, the Middle colonies specialized in crafts, and the Southern colonies specialized in cash crop production.**

STEP 4:
Planning the Answer

Outline your essay to be sure that each section of the essay addresses each of the required points. For our sample, you would surely plan to write at least a paragraph about the New England colonies, a paragraph about the Middle colonies, and a paragraph about the Southern colonies. Each of the sentences containing the direction word "explain" would guide and limit the topic sentence for the main body paragraphs.

Because the question and the thesis are complex, and because the parts of the question are so specific, the best approach in planning the answer to this question is to plan four parts to your essay, one to discuss the basic similarity of the colonies (self-sufficient agriculture) and one each to discuss the specific economic characteristics of each of the three groups of colonies. Controlling ideas for the four parts might be stated as follows:

1. **The basic reason why the colonies were able to specialize is that agriculture allowed families and communities to support themselves while they engaged in other activities.**

2. **The New England colonies developed a commercial economy, and they solved their balance of trade problem by creating a trade surplus with the West Indies that enabled them to pay off their trade deficit with England.**

3. **Land-jobbing was not a large part of the economy of the Middle colonies because land had been granted to specific individuals, but the colonies were an economic success because their favorable rents, religious freedom, and geographic advantages attracted both farmers and craftsmen.**

4. **In the Southern colonies, tobacco and rice, both large-income crops, were natural crops for the respective lands and climates of Virginia and South Carolina, and each colony's geographic characteristics, together with the origins of their settlers, also contributed to the fact that slavery was much harsher in South Carolina than in Virginia.**

STEP 5:
Writing a Rough Draft of the Answer

The only difference between writing the rough draft of an essay for an out-of-class essay test and drafting the kind of essay you wrote in Chapter 10 is that the essay test assignment must help guide your answer. As you draft your essay, reread the question and draw a line through each section of the question as you answer it. Doing this will help you to be certain that you have completely answered the question. If you can't think of a good way to open your essay, use only your thesis statement as an introductory paragraph. Your concern in the rough draft step is to show your reading audience (your teacher) that you have gathered the necessary information, that you have thought about that information, and that you understand the similarities and differences among the important pieces of that information.

STEP 6:
Revising and Checking Your Work

If you have controlled your time well, you can let your essay get cold before you revise. Begin by reviewing your body paragraphs to be sure that they contain the necessary information. Again, use the test question as a guide. Next, ask whether you have stated the information clearly, and whether you have developed each main point with enough specific detail to show your reader that you know what you're talking about. When you know that the body paragraphs are in good shape, write an introductory paragraph that will catch your reader's interest and that clearly states your thesis. When that is done, write a concluding paragraph that brings the essay smoothly to a close. Review Chapters 4 and 10 if you are unsure about how to introduce and conclude your paper. Finally, let your paper get cold, and then check it for spelling, punctuation, and sentence structure problems. If you make large changes, write or type a new draft. If the changes are small, make them neatly in ink.

Sample Out-of-class Essays

To illustrate a good out-of-class essay test answer, we have chosen a response to a question that is simpler and less technical than the sample question we have followed in Steps 1–6. The essay was written by student Donna Quale in response to this out-of-class exam question from a political science class:

> In the America of the 18th century Benjamin Franklin played a dramatic role in shaping the thoughts and actions of his fellow colonials. In many ways he was the ideal man of the 18th century. Explain how Franklin exemplified the 18th century as we have come to know it.

Donna's research came from a single book about Ben Franklin which had been assigned as one of the course texts. The students were expected to read it on their own. The course text and lectures had discussed the characteristics of the 18th-century man. The instructor wanted to see that her students had read and understood the book about Franklin, that they had understood the characteristics of people in the 18th century, and that they had the thinking skills necessary to see how a person's actions could reflect the values of the time in which he lived.

Our notes on Donna's paper show how she took the information from her reading and her course work and presented it in such a way as to show her teacher that she had learned both the information and the thinking skills.

Benjamin Franklin was a revolutionary man in a revolutionary age. He had visions of a prosperous future for a growing nation. He is a perfect example of the characteristics for which the 18th century is known.

strong opening statement

thesis directly responds to essay question

The 18th century saw the development of small, fast ships that made traveling long distances in a relatively short time a possibility. Franklin was a traveler in this new age of travel. By the time he was nineteen, he had sailed to England with plans to purchase needed materials to set up his own printing business in Philadelphia. Later in his life he spent years in England trying to persuade the British government and the English people of the benefits of a free and democratic America. He also traveled to France to win that country's sympathy for his emerging nation. He signed the alliance with France that was crucial to our success in the revolution, and he signed the Treaty of Paris that ended the revolution and doubled the size of our country. Because of his travels and knowledge of foreign languages, he became America's ambassador to Europe.

1st major point to support thesis

good, specific examples support topic sentence

The 18th century sparked the glimmer of what was to become, in the 19th century, the industrial revolution. The revolution of politics between England and America

2nd major point

demanded that the people of the colonies make and grow what they needed.
Benjamin Franklin encouraged the growth
of this independence. He sponsored ap-
prentice printers in setting up their own
shops, and in doing so he was always
careful to arrange precise contracts between himself and his partners so as to
avoid future problems.

section could use more examples

    The 18th century was a time of vision
and a belief in reason. Franklin wrote, "I
have always thought that one man of tol-
erable abilities will work great changes
and accomplish great affairs among man-
kind." Franklin's signature is on both the
Declaration of Independence and the
Constitution. He opened the first public library in the United States. His newspaper
was written with the goal of encouraging
thought and discussion among the common people. He was civic-minded and was
always busy with projects which would
benefit all—from the lowly activity of de-
vising a method of keeping the streets
clean and the street lamps unsmoked to
the lofty accomplishment of founding the
American Philosophical Society and the
academy which later became the University of Pennsylvania. Ben Franklin worked
to improve the quality of man's life.

3rd major point

good, specific examples illustrate topic sentence

    The 18th century was the age of en-
lightenment. Modern scientific ideas were
being developed and acknowledged, and
Benjamin Franklin was America's first scientist. He discovered and proved that elec-
tricity has both negative and positive
charges. He noticed that light colors reflect
heat and that dark colors absorb it, so he
experimented by placing swatches of
black and white fabric in the snow and
saw that the black fabric sank as the snow
melted under it. He also invented or devel-

4th major point

good, specific examples show us that Franklin was a scientist oped many mechanical devices. He worked to develop a stove which would burn more efficiently. He invented the odometer for measuring the distance a wagon traveled. He invented the harmonica, a mechanical hand (for getting books off a high shelf), and the bifocal eyeglasses. He refused to patent his inventions because he felt, as many in this "age of enlightenment" did, that knowledge should be shared. He wrote, "As we enjoy great advantages from the inventions of others, we should be glad of an opportunity to serve others by any invention of ours; and this we should do freely and generously."

Benjamin Franklin was truly a man of the 18th century—a man of revolutionary vision and reason, a man with a whole world approach to the social, political, economic, scientific, and practical problems of his day.

conclusion ties paper together, brings it to an interesting end

The instructor may be reading an essay like this as one of forty or fifty papers on the same subject, and he wants to learn quickly whether the student has discussed all the main points. Donna's opening paragraph clearly states her controlling idea, and it gets right to the point. Each of her paragraphs states and develops a single main point so that the reading audience, her teacher, can clearly follow her ideas. Her short concluding paragraph restates her main idea, though in a more specific way.

Some out-of-class assignments, of course, are less complex than what we've discussed so far. Here, for example, is an assignment from a course in nutrition.

> Read an article from a current nutrition journal. Write a summary of the article (approximately half a page), and then write your personal response to the article (same length).

Since you studied summary writing in Chapters 8 and 9, you know how to handle the first part of this assignment, and the second part simply asks that you use your paragraph writing skills. Here are student Nona Jones' summary and response.

"SULFITES: FDA DRAGS HEELS WHILE TOLL RISES"

In this September 1984 <u>Nutrition Action</u> article, author Mitch Zeller points out that the average person is unaware of the use of sulfites in our foods. This article discusses the use and effects of sulfites. With the use of sulfites in our food, beverages and drugs, many people are having reactions such as tightness in the chest, wheezing, loss of consciousness, or even death. Sulfur dioxide and sodium bisulfite are used the most in our foods to keep them fresher looking, more appealing to the eye, and to give them a longer shelf life. This is a very inexpensive method; therefore, most restaurants have used them for their fresh vegetables and fruits, especially when they have a salad bar. Even though the FDA has been sent petitions for the past two years to ban the use of sulfites, the only thing it has accomplished is to set up two advisory committees to study the situation. Mr. Zeller feels that this is just a "delaying tactic to avoid having to make a decision." The FDA has considered putting the information about sulfites on the labels of foods, but this would not help the people who eat in restaurants or drink wine which Mr. Zeller says, "are the most dangerous sources."

author, source, controlling idea

effects

reasons for use

FDA action

Personal Response

Before I read this article, I knew that sulfites were a problem, but I hadn't thought much about the problem of public awareness. Since this article was published, people have been made somewhat more aware of the side effects related to the use of sulfites, and I'm glad that this is happening. I read in the paper that restau-

topic sentence

discussion of awareness

rants were told to stop using sulfite on fresh vegetables, especially on the salad bars. I cannot help but wonder if the restaurants are being checked for use of sulfites on the baked potato that has become such a popular fad at the fast food restaurants. Due to the fast pace of our society, many more people are eating in restaurants, and that makes the use of sulfites even more dangerous because the consumption is greater. I realize that it is a difficult problem to keep foods safe and still be able to have every type of food in every season. As the article points out, it takes a very long time to have the FDA take any action on the use of dangerous additives to our foods, but if the public were made more aware of how the FDA is run, there may be more pressure put upon them by the consumer instead of by the politician and the manufacturer. I feel that we would all be more aware if there were more publications dealing with food and nutrition. I was unable to find <u>Nutrition Today</u> and many of the other recommended magazines on the shelves of bookstores. The only place they were available was the library, and not too many people are going to take the time to go to the library for magazines.

discussion of danger to health

recognition of restaurants' problems

discussion of FDA

two recommendations for increasing awareness

   In a summary and personal response assignment, a teacher expects to see evidence that you can read, understand, and state the major details of an article about the subject being studied. The summary shows that you have these abilities. The teacher also expects to see that you understand how the concepts of the article relate to everyday life, and this is where the response comes in. The response may include your emotions as well as your thoughts.

   To write a personal response, think about what you knew before you read the article and what you thought and felt as you read and thought about what the article had to say. Think about the main points that the article makes about the subject. Why did you choose this article in the first place? Why does the subject interest you? Does the article discuss a problem? Why is it a problem? How does it affect you or those you care about? What might happen in the future if the problem continues? These and other questions can lead you to a statement about your response to the article, and that statement can become a topic sentence for a paragraph that discusses your response.

In this section, we have seen three examples of out-of-class essay tests. One was a complex question requiring very specific information for its answer, one a simpler but more general question that required the student to select details for her answer, and one that required a summary and response. In the chapter as a whole, we have seen that essay tests are not much different from other writing assignments. To remind you of their differences and similarities, however, let us briefly review what you must keep in mind as you approach an essay test.

When you write an answer to any essay test question, whether in class or out of class, your purpose is to show your reading audience—your teacher—that you have the information and the thinking skills that the course is designed to teach. Preparation is critical: you must have and understand the information before you begin to write. Planning, too, is critical. You have only a limited amount of time in which to answer the question or questions, and you must do exactly what you are told to do, so budgeting your time and understanding the question, especially the direction words, is necessary. The rest is not easy, for writing and thinking are always hard work, but the writing skills which you are developing can help you be sure you accomplish your purpose. State your controlling idea, and make an outline as necessary to be sure your response will include all the required information. Write your answer and check it to be sure you have done what you set out to do and that you have expressed yourself clearly. Revise when you have time, since no first draft is ever perfect, and check the mechanics of your writing.

Finally, don't let the words "essay test" frighten you. An essay test is little more than just another writing assignment. Because you have worked hard on your writing skills and because you now know a process you can use in any writing task, you can approach an essay test or any other writing task with confidence.

Other Suggestions for Writing

1. List the steps followed in writing an essay.
2. Describe several things you should do when previewing a textbook chapter.

3. Explain how to write a summary.

4. Using information from "The Bad News Grizzlies" (page 181), compare the status of the grizzly bear today with its status in the nineteenth century.

5. Using information from "Leaving the Office Behind" (page 162), trace a logical sequence of steps one might take to get rid of job tensions after getting home.

6. Discuss the reasons why the narrator in "Climbing Kilimanjaro" (page 167) decides to climb the mountain.

Terms to Remember

compare A direction word that tells you to show the similarities. Sometimes "compare" is used to mean compare and contrast, or to discuss both the similarities and the differences. If you are not sure whether the teacher wants both, just ask.

define A direction word that tells you to give the meaning of a word or term.

describe A direction word that tells you to show what something looks like, tell how it feels, tell how something happened. Use specific detail to allow the reader to create a mental picture of the object or event.

direction word A word that tells you what to do.

discuss A direction word that tells you to talk about all important aspects, characteristics, or main points. Give as much relevant information as possible.

evaluate A direction word that tells you to make a value judgment and to explain the reasons for your judgment.

explain A direction word that tells you to show your understanding by giving specific information including examples, illustrations, and reasons.

illustrate A direction word that tells you to use examples.

in-class essay tests Tests taken under a time limit and usually requiring a paragraph or essay in response to each test item.

list A direction word that tells you to write your answer in list form. Items in a list usually do not have to be stated in complete sentences. Your answer may look more like a grocery list than a paragraph.

out-of-class essay tests   Assignments that are done as tests outside of class and that usually require an essay. Time limits for these tests may be days or weeks.

predict   To say what may happen in the future. When you predict questions your instructor may ask on a test, you are making an educated guess about what will happen.

responses   Any answers you write to test questions.

state   A direction word that tells you to write a statement.

summarize   A direction word that tells you to write a summary.

test strategy   The plan you devise for using your time during a test.

trace   A direction word that tells you to describe the development or progress of something, often in chronological order.

APPENDIX

THE MECHANICS OF WRITING

Guide to the Appendix

You need to know at least the most basic elements of sentence structure and punctuation in order to express your thoughts clearly and completely. Part I of this appendix explains the most basic parts of the sentence, and Part II shows how you can combine the parts to make your meaning clear. Part III shows you how to correct some common problems that can interfere with meaning, while Part IV explains how sentences are punctuated, and Part V discusses spelling.

This appendix will be most useful to you if you study only one section of it at a time and use the information in that section to help you check or improve something you are writing. When you read the sections, have a piece of your own writing beside you. Use the following guide to locate sections that will teach those rules and ideas that will most help you improve your writing. If you have trouble deciding where to go, your instructor can lead you to the sections that will help you the most.

IV PUNCTUATING SENTENCES

I

PARTS OF THE SENTENCE

The sentence is the basic building block of the paragraph, and the sentence is, of course, made up of words. We use a specific vocabulary to talk about the words in sentences, and you need to understand that vocabulary in order to understand what you are doing when you write or revise your work.

SECTION 1:
Some Definitions

A **sentence** is a group of words that has a subject and a verb and that expresses a complete thought. It begins with a capital letter and ends with a period, question mark, or exclamation point. In the English language, a sentence can do one of four things.

- The *declarative sentence* makes a statement or a declaration about something:

  The team won the game.

- The *interrogatory sentence* asks a question:

  Did the game last long?

- The *exclamatory sentence* expresses a strong emotion:

  We won!

  An exclamation can be considered a complete sentence even without a subject and verb:

  Oh, no!

I

- The *imperative sentence* gives an order or command:

    Watch the game.

The subject of an imperative sentence is not written in the sentence. Since it tells someone to do something, its subject is understood to be "you":

    (You) Watch the game.

Each word of a sentence can be identified as a specific part of speech. Let's look at the parts of the sentence.

1.1 Noun

A **noun** is a word that names a person, a place, a thing, or an idea. The nouns are underlined in the following examples:

    <u>Fred</u> works in <u>Newport</u> in a <u>garage</u> that's a real <u>antique</u>.
    <u>Stacey</u> made the <u>decision</u> that she wouldn't go to <u>school</u>.

1.2 Pronoun

A **pronoun** is a word that can take the place of a noun. Pronouns are underlined in this example:

    Jeff liked <u>his</u> ice cream, so <u>he</u> ate <u>it</u>.

Every complete sentence has at least one noun or pronoun in it. A noun or pronoun will be the subject of the sentence, but there may be other nouns and pronouns in the sentence. See Sections 13.1 and 13.2 for further discussion of pronouns.

1.3 Subject

A **subject** is a noun or pronoun that names what the sentence is about. The subject is underlined in these examples:

    <u>Cats</u> scratch.
    My <u>cats</u> scratch each other when they fight.
    <u>I</u> don't know why I keep cats as pets.
    <u>They</u> are a real nuisance.

See Section 6 for a complete discussion of subjects.

I

1.4 Verb

A **verb** is a word that shows an action or a state of being. Verbs are underlined twice in the following examples.

> **Clarita <u>runs</u>.**
>
> **Sylvia <u>hit</u> a home run and <u>was</u> very excited.**
>
> **Jan <u>feels</u> happy today.**

Every complete sentence has at least one verb in it. The main verb of the sentence tells what the subject does or is. We discuss verbs at length in Sections 2–5.

1.5 Adjective

An **adjective** is a word that gives more information about (or modifies) a noun. Adjectives are underlined in the example.

> **Wanda's <u>large</u>, <u>yellow</u> Buick was parked on the <u>dead</u> lawn.**

Chapter 5 discusses the use of adjectives and nouns in writing descriptions.

1.6 Adverb

An **adverb** is a word that gives more information about (or modifies) a verb, an adjective, another adverb, or even a whole sentence. Adverbs are underlined in the examples.

> **The sun shone <u>brightly</u>.** (modifies the verb "shone")
>
> **The day became <u>too</u> hot.** (modifies the adjective "hot")
>
> **We tired <u>very</u> <u>quickly</u>.** ("very" modifies the adverb "quickly," and "quickly" modifies the verb "tired")
>
> **<u>Unfortunately</u>, we had picked the wrong day to run.** (modifies the whole sentence)

Chapter 6 discusses the use of adverbs and verbs in writing about action.

1.7 Preposition

A **preposition** usually shows how a noun or pronoun relates to another word in the sentence. It usually answers the question where or when

I

and often shows the *position* of something. Prepositions are underlined in the example.

<u>On</u> the table was a picture <u>of</u> my mother sitting <u>under</u> a tree.

Here is a complete list of prepositions:

about	beyond	outside
above	by	over
across	down	past
after	during	since
against	except	through
along	for	throughout
among	from	to
around	in	toward
at	inside	under
before	into	until
behind	like	up
below	near	upon
beneath	of	with
beside	off	within
between	on	without

1.8 Article

An **article** is one of three words, "a," "an," or "the," that comes before a noun. Articles are underlined in the examples.

<u>The</u> cow is in <u>the</u> pasture. ("The" is called a *definite article* because it limits the noun to one specific thing. One specific cow is in one specific pasture.)

<u>A</u> cow is in <u>a</u> pasture. ("A" is an *indefinite article* because it is less limiting. One cow is in one pasture, but it could be *any* cow, and it could be *any* pasture. "A" is used before nouns that begin with consonant sounds.)

<u>An</u> apple is on <u>the</u> tree. ("An" is also an indefinite article. "An" is used before words that begin with a vowel sound.)

I

1.9 Conjunction

A **conjunction** is a word that joins ideas and shows how they are related to each other. They are divided into three groups. (See Section 12 for a thorough discussion of how conjunctions are used in sentences.)

1.9.1 *Coordinating conjunctions* are used to join ideas that are equally important. The coordinating conjunctions are:

for	or
and	yet
nor	so
but	

I found this pocket knife in the parking lot, <u>and</u> it has all the features I like in a knife.

George watches wrestling, <u>but</u> Frank reads books.

1.9.2 *Subordinating conjunctions* are used to show that one idea is less important than another. Here is a list of subordinating conjunctions:

after	if	until
although	in order that	whatever
as	provided	when
as if	since	whenever
because	so that	where
before	supposing	whereas
even if	though	wherever
even though	till	whether
ever since	unless	while

We have planned a trip to the coast several times <u>although</u> our plans never seem to work out.

<u>If</u> the television is on, Frank goes to the kitchen to read.

1.9.3 *Adverbial conjunctions*, also called conjunctive adverbs, show how ideas are logically related to each other. Here is a complete list:

I

accordingly	indeed	otherwise
also	instead	similarly
besides	likewise	still
consequently	moreover	then
furthermore	namely	therefore
hence	nevertheless	thus
however	nonetheless	

You won't be here for my birthday; <u>therefore</u>, I'll celebrate the day alone.

He likes to read; <u>however</u>, he sometimes prefers to draw.

Section 2:
What Verbs Do

2.1 Show action

Some verbs show action. Verbs are underlined twice in the examples.

The quarterback <u>passed</u> the ball.
Alicia <u>sings</u> Country and Western songs.
Darol <u>will plant</u> potatoes.
Wanda <u>wept</u>.
Suleo <u>drives</u> too fast.
Good runners <u>stretch</u> before running.

2.2 Link ideas

Some verbs show a state of being rather than an action. They are said to link ideas. Verbs are underlined twice in the examples.

Bernie <u>felt</u> ill.
Debbie <u>is</u> pregnant.
The roses <u>will smell</u> better in the afternoon.

These verbs are called **linking verbs** because they link the subject of the sentence with something that tells more about the subject. The most common linking verbs are forms of the verb "be." "Be" has eight forms:

am	were
is	be
are	been
was	being

Other linking verbs are the words:

act	get
appear	grow
become	seem
continue	stay

and the verbs that have to do with the senses:

feel	sound
look	taste
smell	

2.3 Show tense

All verbs change to show time or tense. There are many tenses of English verbs; here are some of the most common. In each example, the verb is underlined twice.

PAST: **I looked**. (The action took place in the past.)

PRESENT: **She looks**. (The action is taking place right now.)

FUTURE: **They will look**. (The action will take place in the future.)

PAST PERFECT: **We had looked**. (The action took place at some specific time in the past.)

PRESENT PERFECT: **You have looked**. (The action took place in the past but is completed now.)

FUTURE PERFECT: **They will have looked**. (The action will be completed at a specific time in the future.)

PAST PROGRESSIVE: **It was looking**. (The action happened in the past, but it was temporary.)

PRESENT PROGRESSIVE: **He is looking**. (The action is happening now, but it is temporary.)

See Section 4 for an example of verb tenses.

I

2.3.1 Some verb tenses require **helping verbs**. In our examples, the verbs that have more than one word are using helping verbs. The last word is the *main verb,* and the word or words that come before it are the helpers. A helping verb can help either an action verb or a linking verb. In the following examples, "she" is the subject. The main verb and its helping verbs are underlined twice.

She <u>is walking</u>.   She <u>was walking</u>.

She <u>should be walking</u>.   She <u>should have been</u>

She <u>will have been walking</u>. <u>walking</u>.

She <u>had walked</u>.   She <u>could have walked</u>.

She <u>was growing</u> rapidly.   She <u>might walk</u>.

She <u>is being</u> good.

Commonly used helping verbs are:

be	been	should
am	will	would
is	shall	have
are	can	has
was	may	had
were	could	do

Sometimes words are used between the main verb and its helpers:

<u>Have</u> the children <u>eaten</u> yet?

No, they <u>have</u> not <u>eaten</u>.

We <u>may</u> never <u>be</u> entirely <u>finished</u> with this meal.

2.3.2 Verbs change their tenses in regular and irregular patterns. Regular verbs always form the past and past participle with an "-ed" ending, but irregular verbs do not follow that consistent pattern. The child who says "I digged a hole" is being very logical in forming the past tense. He just hasn't learned that "dig" is an irregular verb, with "dug" as its past tense.

	Present	*Past*	*Past Participle*	*Present Participle*
Regular	lift	lifted	lifted	lifting
Irregular	eat	ate	eaten	eating

See Section 5 for a list of irregular verbs.

I

2.4 Change to match subjects

Verbs sometimes change to match their subjects. That is, when a verb is used with a third person singular subject such as "he," "she," or "it" (see Section 13.1), the verb must have an "s" added to it. This happens only in the present tense. Here are some examples:

SINGULAR: **The girl plays**. (The verb adds an "s" so that both the noun and the verb show singular.)

PLURAL: **The girls play**. (The verb drops the "s" when the noun becomes plural.)

SINGULAR: **She cares**. (Verbs often add "s" when used with a singular noun.)

PLURAL: **They care**. (The "s" is not used when the verb is used with a plural noun.)

SINGULAR: **Giff feels happy**. (singular subject and verb)

PLURAL: **Giff and Jeff feel happy**. (plural subject and verb)

Some helping verbs make a similar change, but only with a singular subject (note, also, that these occur in tenses other than the present):

I have played. (present perfect)

You have played.

She has played.

I am playing. (present progressive)

You are playing.

He is playing.

And finally, the verb "be" changes to match a singular subject in the present and past tenses:

Present	*Past*
I am	**I was**
You are	**You were**
She is	**He was**

See Section 13.3 for further discussion of noun–verb agreement.

I

SECTION 3:
How to Find Verbs

3.1 Look for tense

An important aid in finding the verb in a sentence is to look for the word you would change in order to change the time (or tense) of the sentence from, say, past to present. The word you change will be either a main verb or a helping verb.

PAST:	I <u>smelled</u> smoke.
PRESENT:	I <u>smell</u> smoke.
PAST:	David <u>was driving</u> too fast.
PRESENT:	David <u>is driving</u> too fast.

3.2 Look for all action or state of being words

Sometimes a sentence will have more than one verb. To find all of the verbs, read each sentence carefully, looking at all the words that show action or state of being.

We <u>went</u> to the fair and <u>had</u> a great time. (We did more than one thing.)

Dawn <u>loves</u> sailing, <u>likes</u> driving, and <u>is</u> scared to death of flying. (Dawn responds to these three things.)

3.3 Look at what the words do

Sometimes words are verbs in one sentence but not in another, so look carefully at what the words do.

The girl <u>was laughing</u>. ("Laughing" is the main verb, and "was" is a helping verb. They describe what the girl was doing.)

The laughing girl <u>sat</u> down. ("Laughing" is not a verb. It is an adjective that describes which girl sat down.)

3.4 "-ing" words

A word ending in "-ing" cannot be the verb in a sentence unless it has a helping verb in front of it.

I

> **We <u>were swimming</u> and <u>splashing</u>.** ("Were" is a helping verb that helps both main verbs, "swimming" and "splashing."
>
> **Swimming and splashing <u>were</u> our favorite activities.** ("Swimming" and "splashing" work as nouns in this sentence.)

3.5 "to" verbs

No verb with "to" in front of it will be the main verb unless it has a helping verb in front of "to."

> **She <u>has to work</u>.** ("She" is the subject, "has to" is a helping verb, and "work" is the main verb.)
>
> **She <u>is</u> ready to work.** ("She" is the subject, "is" is a linking verb. Since "to work" has no helper, we know it is not part of the verb.)
>
> **We <u>told</u> them to go.** ("We" is the subject, "told" is the verb. Since "to go" has no helping verb, we know it is not a part of the verb.)
>
> **We <u>used to be</u> able to do that.** ("We" is the subject, "used to be" is the verb. Since "to do" does not have a helping verb in front of it, it cannot be part of the verb of the sentence.)

 Editing Activity A.1

- ☐ Take a short piece of your own writing, and rewrite it to change the tense (that is, if it is about the past, rewrite it so that it is about the present).
- ☐ As you do this, underline each verb. Be sure to underline the helping verbs as well as the main verbs.

SECTION 4:
Tenses of Verbs

The following list shows the common tenses of three verbs. We include the verb "be" (the verb that tells what something is) because it changes more than any other verb. We also include an irregular verb, "drink," and a regular verb, "jump." In each example, the verb is underlined twice.

I

Past Tense

Singular

I <u>was</u>, I <u>drank</u>, I <u>jumped</u>
You <u>were</u>, You <u>drank</u>, You <u>jumped</u>
She <u>was</u>, It <u>drank</u>, He <u>jumped</u>

Plural

We <u>were</u>, We <u>drank</u>, We <u>jumped</u>
You <u>were</u>, You <u>drank</u>, You <u>jumped</u>
They <u>were</u>, They <u>drank</u>, They <u>jumped</u>

Present Tense

Singular

I <u>am</u>, I <u>drink</u>, I <u>jump</u>
You <u>are</u>, You <u>drink</u>, You <u>jump</u>
He <u>is</u>, She <u>drinks</u>, It <u>jumps</u>

Plural

We <u>are</u>, We <u>drink</u>, We <u>jump</u>
You <u>are</u>, You <u>drink</u>, You <u>jump</u>
They <u>are</u>, They <u>drink</u>, They <u>jump</u>

Future Tense

Singular

I <u>will be</u>, I <u>will drink</u>, I <u>will jump</u>
You <u>will be</u>, You <u>will drink</u>, You <u>will jump</u>
It <u>will be</u>, She <u>will drink</u>, He <u>will jump</u>

Plural

We <u>will be</u>, We <u>will drink</u>, We <u>will jump</u>
You <u>will be</u>, You <u>will drink</u>, You <u>will jump</u>
They <u>will be</u>, They <u>will drink</u>, They <u>will jump</u>

I

Past Perfect Tense

Singular

I had been, I had drunk, I had jumped

You had been, You had drunk, You had jumped

She had been, He had drunk, It had jumped

Plural

We had been, We had drunk, We had jumped

You had been, You had drunk, You had jumped

They had been, They had drunk, They had jumped

Present Perfect Tense

Singular

I have been, I have drunk, I have jumped

You have been, You have drunk, You have jumped

He has been, It has drunk, She has jumped

Plural

We have been, We have drunk, We have jumped

You have been, You have drunk, You have jumped

They have been, They have drunk, They have jumped

Future Perfect Tense

Singular

I will have been, I will have drunk, I will have jumped

You will have been, You will have drunk, You will have jumped

She will have been, He will have drunk, It will have jumped

Plural

We will have been, We will have drunk, We will have jumped

You will have been, You will have drunk, You will have jumped

They will have been, They will have drunk, They will have jumped

I

Present Progressive Tense

Singular

I <u>am being</u>, I <u>am drinking</u>, I <u>am jumping</u>

You <u>are being</u>, You <u>are drinking</u>, You <u>are jumping</u>

It <u>is being</u>, He <u>is drinking</u>, She <u>is jumping</u>

Plural

We <u>are being</u>, We <u>are drinking</u>, We <u>are jumping</u>

You <u>are being</u>, You <u>are drinking</u>, You <u>are jumping</u>

They <u>are being</u>, They <u>are drinking</u>, They <u>are jumping</u>

Past Progressive Tense

Singular

I <u>was being</u>, I <u>was drinking</u>, I <u>was jumping</u>

You <u>were being</u>, You <u>were drinking</u>, You <u>were jumping</u>

She <u>was being</u>, It <u>was drinking</u>, He <u>was jumping</u>

Plural

We <u>were being</u>, We <u>were drinking</u>, We <u>were jumping</u>

You <u>were being</u>, You <u>were drinking</u>, You <u>were jumping</u>

They <u>were being</u>, They <u>were drinking</u>, They <u>were jumping</u>

Section 5:
Irregular Verbs

As an aid in using verbs and helping verbs correctly, here is a list of commonly used irregular verbs showing each of the four principal parts, or how the verbs change from tense to tense. If you want to use a verb and are not sure of its parts, consult a dictionary. The participle forms of verbs always take helping verbs:

> I <u>arise</u> most mornings at 5:00.
>
> I <u>arose</u> yesterday at 7:30.
>
> I <u>have arisen</u> early for ten years.
>
> I <u>am arising</u> early to get to work on time.

Some Irregular Verbs

Present	*Past*	*Past Participle*	*Present Participle*
arise	arose	arisen	arising
beat	beat	beaten	beating
become	became	become	becoming
begin	began	begun	beginning
blow	blew	blown	blowing
break	broke	broken	breaking
bring	brought	brought	bringing
build	built	built	building
burst	burst	burst	bursting
buy	bought	bought	buying
can	could	been able	being able
catch	caught	caught	catching
choose	chose	chosen	choosing
come	came	come	coming
cut	cut	cut	cutting
deal	dealt	dealt	dealing
dig	dug	dug	digging
dive	dove (or dived)	dived	diving
do	did	done	doing
draw	drew	drawn	drawing
drink	drank	drunk	drinking
drive	drove	driven	driving
eat	ate	eaten	eating
fall	fell	fallen	falling
feed	fed	fed	feeding
feel	felt	felt	feeling
fight	fought	fought	fighting
find	found	found	finding
fly	flew	flown	flying
forget	forgot	forgotten	forgetting
forgive	forgave	forgiven	forgiving

I

Some Irregular Verbs (continued)

Present	*Past*	*Past Participle*	*Present Participle*
freeze	froze	frozen	freezing
get	got	got (or gotten)	getting
give	gave	given	giving
go	went	gone	going
grow	grew	grown	growing
have	had	had	having
hear	heard	heard	hearing
hide	hid	hidden	hiding
hit	hit	hit	hitting
hold	held	held	holding
hurt	hurt	hurt	hurting
keep	kept	kept	keeping
know	knew	known	knowing
lay	laid	laid	laying
lead	led	led	leading
leave	left	left	leaving
let	let	let	letting
lie	lay	lain	lying
lose	lost	lost	losing
make	made	made	making
meet	met	met	meeting
pay	paid	paid	paying
put	put	put	putting
quit	quit	quit	quitting
read	read	read	reading
ride	rode	ridden	riding
ring	rang	rung	ringing
rise	rose	risen	rising
run	ran	run	running
say	said	said	saying
see	saw	seen	seeing

Some Irregular Verbs (continued)

Present	*Past*	*Past Participle*	*Present Participle*
seek	sought	sought	seeking
sell	sold	sold	selling
send	sent	sent	sending
set	set	set	setting
shake	shook	shaken	shaking
shine	shone	shone	shining
show	showed	shown	showing
shut	shut	shut	shutting
sing	sang	sung	singing
shrink	shrank	shrunk	shrinking
sink	sank	sunk	sinking
sit	sat	sat	sitting
sleep	slept	slept	sleeping
speak	spoke	spoken	speaking
spend	spent	spent	spending
spring	sprang	sprung	springing
stand	stood	stood	standing
steal	stole	stolen	stealing
strike	struck	struck	striking
swim	swam	swum	swimming
take	took	taken	taking
teach	taught	taught	teaching
tear	tore	torn	tearing
tell	told	told	telling
think	thought	thought	thinking
throw	threw	thrown	throwing
understand	understood	understood	understanding
wake	woke (or waked)	woken (or waked)	waking
wear	wore	worn	wearing
win	won	won	winning
write	wrote	written	writing

I

I

Section 6:
How to Find Subjects

6.1 Find the main noun or pronoun

Find the noun or pronoun that names what the sentence is about. Not every noun in a sentence will be the subject, but every subject will have a noun or pronoun in it.

> **A <u>dog</u> was in the room**. ("Dog" and "room" are both nouns, but "dog" is the subject. The sentence says something about the dog.)

6.2 Find the verb

Find the verb and ask "Who or what does the action of the verb?" The answer will be the subject of the sentence.

> **<u>Jill</u> skis**. (Who skis? Jill does, so "Jill" is the subject.)

> **<u>Jill</u>, my friend from Vermont, skis**. (Who skis? Again, Jill does, and "Jill" is the subject of the second sentence also.)

6.3 Look at the middle or end

Often the subject is found at the beginning of the sentence. Sometimes, though, you must look at the middle or end of a sentence for the subject.

> **There is the black <u>dress</u> I've always wanted.**

> **There was a <u>dog</u> in the room.**

> **Here is a <u>picture</u> of a fountain.**

> **Here is Nicki and Helen's new <u>computer</u>.**

Many students want to call "there" and "here" the subjects of the samples above, but "there" and "here" are not nouns or pronouns, so they cannot be subjects. The sentences say that something (the subject) was there or here.

6.4 Plural subjects

Some sentences have a plural subject, that is, more than one subject. In cases like that, the subject is every noun that names what the sentence is talking about.

> **<u>Daisy</u> and <u>Laurel</u> spent the afternoon talking**. (Who spent the afternoon talking? Daisy and Laurel did.)

> **<u>Champagne</u>, <u>cheese</u>, and <u>pears</u> make a wonderful appetizer combination**. (What makes a wonderful appetizer combination? Champagne, cheese, and pears do.)

> **My <u>sister</u> and <u>I</u> are good friends**. (Who are good friends? Sister and I.)

6.5 Subjects and prepositional phrases

Remember that the subject is *never in a prepositional phrase*. A prepositional phrase is a phrase that begins with a preposition (see Section 1.7) and ends with a noun. The following are all prepositional phrases:

> **on the table**

> **on the dining room table**

> **on the large, round, oak dining room table**

In each of these examples, "on" is the preposition that begins the phrase, and "table" is the noun that ends it. In

> **across the wide, bumpy street**

"across" is the preposition that begins the phrase, and "street" is the noun that ends it. A prepositional phrase always begins with a preposition and ends with a noun, but that noun is *never* the subject of the sentence.

In the examples that follow, the subject of each sentence is underlined once, the verb is underlined twice, and the prepositional phrases are in parentheses. Identifying and ignoring prepositional phrases is an easy way to reduce a sentence to its essentials. Then you can more easily spot the subject.

Either (of these lawnmowers) is a good buy. ("Of" is the preposition that starts the prepositional phrase, and "lawnmowers" is the noun that ends it.)

There were a box (of apples), four erasers, and two bags (of brownies) (on the back seat).

(In the red house) (on the hill), three people live (with seven dogs) but (without running water).

 Editing Activity A.2

□ Choose a short piece of your writing.

□ Put parentheses around each prepositional phrase.

□ Underline the subject of each of your sentences. If you can't find a subject for each sentence, or if you're unsure about something, check with your instructor.

II

BUILDING SENTENCES

Every sentence must have at least one independent clause, but sentences can be made up of a variety of words, phrases, and clauses. If you have a basic understanding of how clauses and phrases can be combined, and if you know how to find and correct the most common errors in building sentences, your ability to write good clear sentences will improve.

SECTION 7:
Independent Clauses

A **clause** is a group of related words that has a subject and a verb. An **independent clause** can stand (independently) on its own as a sentence. It does not depend on another clause to make it a complete thought. An independent clause always expresses a complete thought. The subjects and verbs are underlined in the following examples of independent clauses.

> **People** often **do** silly things.
> **Fishing** the Salmon River **is** exciting.
> **There were** six **princesses**.

Each example has a subject and a verb, and each expresses a complete thought and can thus stand independently on its own.

Independent clauses are also called **main clauses**, for they express the main or most important ideas of sentences. A sentence may have more than one independent clause, but every sentence has at least one indepen-

II

dent clause. Here are examples of sentences with more than one independent clause. The independent clauses are underlined.

> <u>**People often do silly things**</u>, but <u>**they can do intelligent things, too**</u>.
>
> <u>**Fishing the Salmon River is exciting**</u> because it is such a wild place; however, <u>**it can be dangerous**</u>.

Remember this: Every complete sentence needs at least one independent clause.

SECTION 8:
Dependent Clauses

A **dependent clause** cannot stand on its own. It has a subject and a verb, but it does not express a complete thought. It needs (or depends on) another clause to finish its thought.

> **After <u>Lil</u> <u>bought</u> the roller skates**
>
> **Since <u>I</u> <u>gave</u> my geraniums to Shirley**

Remember this: A dependent clause written by itself is not a complete sentence.

8.1 Made by subordinating conjunctions

A clause that begins with a word such as "although," "after," "unless," "because," "since," "if," "while," "until," or "before" is a dependent clause. These words are called *subordinating conjunctions*. A complete list of them appears in Section 1.9, and they are discussed at length in Section 12.3.1. Words like these show relationships between ideas, and thus they make a reader or listener expect more information. They create dependent clauses because the writer or speaker needs to supply that information to make the sentence complete.

Consider the following dependent clauses:

Although I enjoy her company

If she would just call

"I enjoy her company" is a complete sentence—an independent clause—but the word "although" makes it dependent. "Although" shows a relationship between two ideas, and we need to know the second idea before the thought is complete. This second idea must be an independent clause. Here's one way to make the thought complete (the dependent clause is in parentheses, and the subject and verb are underlined in both the dependent and the independent clause):

(Although I enjoy her company), I don't see her very often.

The sentence is now complete.

The dependent clause "If she would just call" gives us the same problem. What would happen "if she would just call"? Again, we need an independent clause to make the thought complete:

I'd invite her out (if she would just call).

8.2 Made by relative pronouns

Some dependent clauses are made by *relative pronouns* such as "who," "which," "whom," "whose," and "that," and such dependent clauses may also be called **relative clauses**. (See Section 12.3.2 for further discussion of relative pronouns.) In the examples that follow, the dependent clauses are in parentheses, and the subject and verb are underlined in both the dependent and independent clauses.

The old woman (who lives next door to me) will be 93 tomorrow.

"Who lives next door to me" has a subject (who) and a verb (lives), but it cannot stand alone as a complete thought. It is a dependent clause. The independent clause, "The old woman will be 93 tomorrow," is a complete thought, but the dependent (relative) clause gives more information about the woman.

Yesterday my daughter did something (that upset me very much).

"That" is the subject of the dependent clause and "upset" is the verb, but "that upset me very much" is not a complete thought. The independent clause, "Yesterday my daughter did something," is a complete thought, but the dependent clause adds information that clarifies or explains the thought.

II

Dependent clauses that begin with relative pronouns are not quite as easy to pick out as are dependent clauses that begin with subordinating conjunctions, but if you memorize the five relative pronouns, "who," "which," "whose," "whom," and "that," you will be able to identify most relative clauses. Check for a subject and a verb, and let your ear and your sense of the language guide you in distinguishing between dependent and independent clauses:

Whose hat is this? (This is a question and a complete sentence.)

Whose hat is on the chair (Unless this is asked as a question, it does not express a complete thought and thus is not an independent clause.)

Whose hat this is (Clearly, this does not express a complete thought.)

The chief thing to remember is that a dependent clause written by itself is not a complete sentence. To show clearly the relationships among the ideas of your paragraphs, you must write in complete sentences.

 Editing Activity A.3

□ Choose a piece of your writing that you would like to check for complete sentences.

□ Read through your paragraph and underline each dependent clause. If you have a dependent clause that begins with a capital letter and ends with a period, it is not a complete sentence. It can probably be joined to the sentence before it or to the sentence after it.

□ Rewrite any problem sentences to make them complete. Section 11, Sentence Fragments, discusses incomplete sentences in detail. If you have questions, see your instructor.

SECTION 9:
Phrases

A **phrase** is a group of related words that does not have both a subject and a verb. A phrase does not express a complete thought; it is only a part of a complete sentence. A phrase looks like this:

with the warm brown eyes

rising confidently

to write the letter

Phrases are used in sentences to add information to, or modify, the sentence or some part of it. Phrases are underlined in these examples:

My friend <u>with the warm brown eyes</u> is sitting <u>in the cafeteria</u>.

<u>Rising confidently</u>, Elizabeth answered the question perfectly.

She kindly consented <u>to write the letter</u>.

Remember that phrases are different from clauses. A clause is a group of related words with both a subject and a verb. A clause may express a complete thought and be able to stand alone as a complete sentence. A phrase *does not* have both a subject and a verb, and it can *never* stand alone as a complete sentence. It can, however, work as an important part of a sentence, adding information that helps both the reader and the writer to understand more clearly what is being discussed. See Section 6.5 for a discussion of a particular kind of phrase, the prepositional phrase.

SECTION 10:
Run-on Sentences

Read the following sentence. Does it cause you some confusion?

I left without my coat on the bus I tripped and fell.

The sentence is confusing because it needs punctuation to clarify the ideas it expresses. A sentence written this way is called a **run-on sentence**. There are two independent clauses (see Section 7), so there are actually two sentences here. Each is made up of one independent clause and one phrase (see Section 9). The independent clauses are underlined, and the phrases are in parentheses.

<u>I left</u> (without my coat). (On the bus) <u>I tripped and fell</u>.

10.1 Definition

A run-on sentence is two independent clauses written together with no punctuation or with just a comma between them. (Another name for two independent clauses written together with just a comma is "comma splice.")

II

RUN-ON: **Tomorrow is a holiday let's go to the beach.**

RUN-ON: **Tomorrow is a holiday, let's go to the beach.**

Run-on sentences are incorrect because they can confuse a reader, so let's look at some ways of correcting them.

10.2 Correcting run-on sentences

There are four ways to correct run-on sentences.

RUN-ON: **We decided to fix up the old Chevrolet it had been in the family for years.**

10.2.1   Use a period between two independent clauses.

CORRECTED: **We decided to fix up the old Chevrolet. It had been in the family for years.**

When you use a period, you must capitalize the first word that follows it since that word begins a new sentence.

10.2.2   Use a semicolon between two independent clauses.

CORRECTED: **We decided to fix up the old Chevrolet; it had been in the family for years.**

When you use a semicolon, do not capitalize the word that follows it. Use a semicolon only when the ideas are closely related.

10.2.3   Use a comma and a coordinating conjunction ("for," "and," "nor," "but," "or," "yet," "so") between the independent clauses.

CORRECTED: **We decided to fix up the old Chevrolet, <u>for</u> it had been in the family for years.**

The first letters of the coordinating conjunctions spell FAN BOYS—For, And, Nor, But, Or, Yet, So. Use a comma *and* one of the FAN BOYS to join independent clauses. Do not capitalize the conjunction. Do not use a comma *after* the conjunction. (See Section 12.2.1 for a complete explanation of coordinating conjunctions.)

10.2.4   Use a subordinating conjunction ("since," "although," "because," "when," "if," "before," and so on) to make one of the independent clauses into a dependent clause (see Sections 1.9 and 12.3.1).

CORRECTED: **<u>Since</u> it had been in the family for years, we decided to fix up the old Chevrolet.**

II

Punctuation note: A comma usually follows a dependent clause when the dependent clause *begins* a sentence. There is usually no comma between an independent and a dependent clause when the dependent clause *ends* the sentence:

We decided to fix up the old Chevrolet since it had been in the family for years.

10.3 More examples

RUN-ON:	**We bought fresh flowers and sourdough bread at the market we would enjoy them during dinner that night by the fire.**
RUN-ON:	**We bought fresh flowers and sourdough bread at the market, we would enjoy them during dinner that night by the fire.**
CORRECTED:	**We bought fresh flowers and sourdough bread at the market. We would enjoy them during dinner that night by the fire.**
CORRECTED:	**We bought fresh flowers and sourdough bread at the market; we would enjoy them during dinner that night by the fire.**
CORRECTED:	**We bought fresh flowers and sourdough bread at the market, and we would enjoy them during dinner that night by the fire.**
CORRECTED:	**We bought fresh flowers and sourdough bread at the market because we would enjoy them during dinner that night by the fire.**

All of the corrected examples above are properly punctuated, but some are more effective than the others. When you separate or combine your sentences, think about how you can best show what you really want to say.

RUN-ON:	**Jim and Linda have a large family they can easily form two teams for a baseball game.**
CORRECT:	**Jim and Linda have a large family; they can easily form two teams for a baseball game.**
BETTER:	**Jim and Linda have a large family, so they can easily form two teams for a baseball game.**

II

RUN-ON:	**Walking around a shopping mall usually bores me, I have fun at one when I'm with you.**
CORRECT:	**Walking around a shopping mall usually bores me, but I have fun at one when I'm with you.**
BETTER:	**Although walking around a shopping mall usually bores me, I have fun at one when I'm with you.**

 Editing Activity A.4

□ Underline each independent clause in a paragraph you want to check for run-on sentences. Look for the punctuation that comes between them.

□ If there is no punctuation between two independent clauses, you have written a run-on sentence that must be corrected in one of the four ways shown in Section 10.2.

□ If there is a comma between two independent clauses, check to see that it is followed by a coordinating conjunction (one of the FAN BOYS). If it is not, you have written a run-on sentence that must be corrected in one of the four ways shown in Section 10.2.

SECTION 11:
Sentence Fragments

A **fragment** is a part of something, and a sentence fragment is a part of a sentence. It does not express a complete thought. Remember that a complete sentence must have a subject and a verb and must express a complete thought. A sentence fragment may or may not have a subject and verb, but it never expresses a complete thought.

11.1 Finding sentence fragments

The best way to check a paragraph for sentence fragments is to look at it sentence by sentence. As you read what you have written, you get caught up in the flow of ideas and may not notice a sentence fragment. If you write and read each sentence separately, you can often spot a fragment and even see how to correct it.

A complete sentence *names* something or somebody and *tells* something about what it names. The naming part of the sentence contains the subject, and the telling part contains the verb. We'll show you a sample paragraph that has some sentence fragments; then we'll write each sentence of that paragraph separately to show you a way of checking to see whether each one has a subject (or naming part) and a verb (or telling part) and whether each one expresses a complete thought.

> **My uncle Bill dresses very strangely. His shoes usually don't match. I suspect he wears special devices inside them. He always wears a cowboy hat. And an outdated business suit. His ties look as if he bought them at the Salvation Army. I always get embarrassed when I'm seen with him. Because he's so strange. I think anybody would be embarrassed.**

Now let's look at the sentences separately.

> **My uncle Bill dresses very strangely.** (The sentence names "Bill," tells that he dresses strangely, and expresses a complete thought.)
>
> **His shoes usually don't match.** (The sentence names "shoes," tells that they usually don't match, and expresses a complete thought.)
>
> **I suspect he wears special devices inside them.** (The sentence names "I," tells that the subject suspects something, and expresses a complete thought.)
>
> **He always wears a cowboy hat.** (The sentence names "he," tells that he wears something, and expresses a complete thought.)
>
> **And an outdated business suit.** (This is a phrase. It does not have a subject and a verb and does not express a complete thought. It logically belongs to the telling part of the previous sentence.)

CORRECTED SENTENCE: **He always wears a cowboy hat and an outdated business suit.**

> **His ties look as if he got them at the Salvation Army.** (This sentence names "ties," tells how they look, and expresses a complete thought.)

II

I always get embarrassed when I'm seen with him. (This sentence names "I," tells that the subject gets embarrassed, and expresses a complete thought.)

Because he's so strange. (This dependent clause names "he," tells that he's strange, but doesn't express a complete thought. It could be combined with either the preceding sentence or the following one.)

CORRECTED SENTENCE: **I always get embarrassed when I'm seen with him because he's so strange.**

CORRECTED SENTENCE: **Because he's so strange, I think anybody would be embarrassed.**

I think anybody would be embarrassed. (This sentence names "I," tells what the subject thinks, and expresses a complete thought.)

Looking at each sentence in isolation from the others and then asking specifically whether it names a subject, tells something about its subject, and expresses a complete thought can help you identify sentence fragments. Often, this exercise helps you see how the fragments can be corrected.

11.2 Correcting clause fragments

Every clause has a subject and a verb, but not every clause can stand independently as a complete sentence. A dependent clause (see Section 8) written by itself is a sentence fragment and must be corrected. There are two types of clause fragments.

11.2.1 Clauses that begin with words like "because," "although," "after," and "if" (*subordinating conjunctions*, see Sections 1.9 and 8.1) are dependent clauses that need further information before they can express a complete thought. Usually you can correct this type of fragment by joining it with an independent clause, but sometimes it's better to rewrite the dependent clause to make it independent. Our examples show how these fragments might appear in your paragraphs. The dependent clause is underlined in each.

EXAMPLE WITH FRAGMENT: **We walked through the rain and mud all that day. <u>Because we had no choice</u>. The drill instructor wouldn't let us stop.**

CORRECTED:	**We walked through the rain and mud all that day <u>because we had no choice</u>. The drill instructor wouldn't let us stop.**
EXAMPLE WITH FRAGMENT:	**We finally arrived in Denver. <u>After we had driven for sixteen hours</u>.**
CORRECTED:	**We finally arrived in Denver <u>after we had driven for sixteen hours</u>.**
CORRECTED:	**<u>After we had driven for sixteen hours</u>, we finally arrived in Denver.**
EXAMPLE WITH FRAGMENT:	**Most of the time, the best way to learn is through experience. Although that can be painful.**
CORRECTED:	**Most of the time, the best way to learn is through experience. Those experiences can be painful.** (Rewriting the dependent clause to make it independent helps to emphasize the idea it expresses.)
FRAGMENT:	**<u>If I could just talk to him for ten minutes</u>.**
CORRECTED:	**I wish I could just talk to him for ten minutes.** (In conversation, we use "if" to mean "I wish," and our voice tones make the meaning clear. In writing, however, meaning must come from the words on the page, not voice tones. "If" fragments should often be rewritten as complete sentences.)

11.2.2   Clauses that begin with words like "who," "which," and "that" (*relative pronouns*, see Section 8.2) must be rewritten or else combined with an independent clause. Such clauses are underlined in the examples.

FRAGMENT:	**A room in my house <u>that looks like a second-hand store</u>.** (The subject is "room," but the only verb, "looks," is the verb of the dependent clause. "That" is the subject of the dependent clause. There is no independent clause because there is no verb that goes with "room.")

CORRECTED:	**I have a room in my house that looks like a second-hand store**. (The independent clause, "I have a room in my house," combines with the dependent clause to make a complete sentence.)
CORRECTED:	**A room in my house looks like a second-hand store**. (The relative pronoun "that" is dropped. "Room" becomes the subject of the independent clause and "looks" is the verb.)
EXAMPLE WITH FRAGMENT:	**Felicia has been looking for work for more than a month. Yesterday, she finally made an appointment with a job counselor. Who says he can help her find a job**.
CORRECTED:	**Felicia has been looking for work for more than a month. Yesterday, she finally made an appointment with a job counselor who says he can help her find a job**. (The dependent clause is combined with the previous sentence.)
CORRECTED:	**Felicia has been looking for work for more than a month. Yesterday, she finally made an appointment with a job counselor. He says he can help her find a job**. (The dependent clause is rewritten to make it an independent clause.)

11.3 Correcting phrase fragments

Some fragments are not clauses but are phrases. Like clause fragments, these phrase fragments must be combined with a complete sentence or else rewritten so that they have a subject and verb and express a complete thought. Fragments are underlined in the examples.

EXAMPLE WITH FRAGMENT:	**We finally saw the lost dog. Running along the street**.
CORRECTED:	**We finally saw the lost dog running along the street**.
EXAMPLE WITH FRAGMENT:	**The four of us spent the afternoon fishing. Crammed into a rubber boat built for two people**.

CORRECTED: **The four of us spent the afternoon fishing. Unfortunately, we were crammed into a rubber boat built for two people.**

II

Editing Activity A.5

□ To check the sentences in a piece of your writing, write your first sentence on a separate piece of paper.

□ Read your sentence carefully to be sure that it names something or someone, tells something about that person or thing, and expresses a complete thought.

□ Continue by writing each sentence on a separate line and reading each one separately. Copy and examine just one sentence at a time. Writing each sentence separately lets your mind see each sentence as a separate unit without getting caught up in the flow of ideas.

□ Does each sentence <u>name</u> something and <u>tell</u> something about it? Does each express a complete thought? If so, you're ready to look at your next sentence. If not, try to change it so it does.

SECTION 12:
Four Sentence Types

Clauses and phrases can be combined into four different types of sentences that offer writers an almost endless variety of ways to combine and present ideas to a reading audience. Read through this section to become familiar with the four sentence types. As you write, experiment with them. As you read, watch how other writers use them.

12.1 The simple sentence

A **simple sentence** has one independent clause (see Section 7):

Beverly likes soft drinks.

II

A block diagram of the simple sentence looks like this:

| Independent clause | .

The simple sentence focuses the reader's attention on just the one idea expressed by the independent clause:

Emily Dickinson wrote more than 1,000 poems.

The simple sentence might contain a great deal of information in addition to the independent clause, but its center of interest and information will be in the single, independent clause that forms its heart:

Emily Dickinson, Amherst's reclusive but now famous poet, wrote more than 1,000 short, untitled poems in her 56-year lifetime.

The words and phrases that are added to the independent clause may clarify the sentence and make it more interesting, but they are not of primary importance.

12.2 The compound sentence

A **compound sentence** has more than one independent clause. It focuses the reader's attention on two or more ideas that are closely related and of equal importance:

Beverly likes soft drinks, but she only drinks them with ice.

| Independent clause | , but | independent clause | .

She likes only two brands; she refuses to buy any others.

| Independent clause | ; | independent clause | .

She worries about her weight; therefore, she buys only diet soda.

| Independent clause | ; therefore, | independent clause | .

12.2.1   The two or more independent clauses may be joined by a comma and a coordinating conjunction.

Western Montana has severe winters, but its summers can be warm and pleasant.

Independent clause	, for	independent clause
	, and	
	, nor	
	, but	
	, or	
	, yet	
	, so	

II

A coordinating conjunction is a joining word which shows a logical relationship between two ideas of coordinate or equal importance. The coordinating conjunctions are "for," "and," "nor," "but," "or," "yet," and "so." When they are used to join two independent clauses, these words are always preceded by a comma (see Section 17.6). It is important to understand the relationships shown by these words.

- "For" and "so" show a cause and effect relationship between the two ideas expressed in a sentence. They show what happened and why it happened.

  We ran (effect), for the ball had gone through a large window (cause).

  It rained for three days (cause), so we called off the outdoor concert (effect).

- "And" is like a plus sign. It adds information.

  I try to get to work on time, and I usually do.

- "Nor" and "or" offer choices. "Nor" offers a negative choice while "or" offers a positive choice.

  It wasn't warm in Anchorage, nor was it warm in Chicago.

  I'll do that tomorrow, or I might put it off until Monday.

- "But" and "yet" show contrasts. They join ideas that seem opposite to each other.

  We didn't expect the house to sell, but it sold for twice what we paid for it.

  The fishing was slow, yet we still had fun.

12.2.2 A compound sentence may be formed by joining independent clauses with a semicolon (Sections 10.2.2 and 18.1), and the semicolon may be used either with or without a connecting word. The connecting word with a semicolon should not be a coordinating conjunction.

II

WRONG: **She loves concerts; but her husband thinks they're a waste of money.**

RIGHT: **She loves concerts; her husband thinks they're a waste of money.**

RIGHT: **The card game was interesting; nevertheless, the television soon attracted my attention.**

When the relationship between two ideas is obvious, use the semicolon by itself. When you want to call your reader's attention to the relationship, use one of the following words to introduce an independent clause (These words are called **adverbial conjunctions** or **conjunctive adverbs**; see Section 1.9):

- Use "also," "besides," "furthermore," and "moreover" to show the addition of ideas.

  I don't have time to do it; besides, I don't really want to.

  This machine can do everything; moreover, it does it in half the time.

- Use "however," "instead," "nevertheless," "nonetheless," "otherwise," and "still" to show contrast or opposition.

  We expected you at eight; however, you arrived at twelve.

  I'm glad I drove; otherwise, I'd have been fogged in for three days in Atlanta.

- Use "accordingly," "consequently," "hence," "therefore," and "thus" to show cause and effect.

  The plane's engine caught fire shortly after takeoff; consequently, the pilot turned back.

  We needed to get there quickly; hence we took Route 92.

- Use "likewise" or "similarly" to show comparison.

  The wedding was spectacular; likewise, the reception was superb.

- Use "then" to show a time relationship.

  Finish these exercises; then take the test.

- Use "namely" or "indeed" to introduce a specific example or other specific information.

There was a lot of work to do; namely, there were pipes to repair, brush to cut, and a garage to rebuild.

Things looked bad; indeed, they couldn't have looked worse.

Punctuation note: When one of these joining words joins two independent clauses, it *must* be preceded by a semicolon and is *usually* followed by a comma. Since most of these words can also be interrupters in a sentence (see Section 17.2), be sure that there is an independent clause on each side of the word before you use a semicolon in front of it.

Write,

Fran wanted to walk; however, Almut chose to drive.

| Independent clause | ; however, | independent clause | . |

But write,

Fran wanted to walk; Almut, however, chose to drive.

| Independent clause | ; | independent clause with interrupter | . |

Write,

The brakes failed; therefore, the car rolled swiftly down the hill.

| Independent clause | ; therefore, | independent clause | . |

But write,

The car, therefore, rolled swiftly down the hill.

| Independent clause with interrupter | . |

12.3 The complex sentence

A **complex sentence** has one independent clause and one or more dependent clauses (see Section 8). Dependent clauses are in parentheses in the following example.

(Because Beverly likes soft drinks), she always has one in her hand.

| Dependent clause | , | independent clause | . |

She's constantly buying them (although I don't know how she can afford to).

| Independent clause | dependent clause | . |

The dentist (that she goes to) wants her to quit drinking soft drinks.

| Independent | dependent clause | clause | . |

While a compound sentence shows relationship between two ideas of equal (or coordinate) importance, a complex sentence shows one main idea and one or more other ideas that are subordinate to or less important than the main idea. For that reason, dependent clauses are also called **subordinate clauses**.

12.3.1 *Subordinating conjunctions* are words like "because," "although," and "if" (see Section 1.9.2 for a complete list). They introduce dependent (or subordinate) clauses (Section 8.1). In our examples, the dependent clauses are in parentheses.

(Although I had invited her), Karen didn't come to the party.

(Although Karen didn't come to the party), I had invited her.

The first sentence calls attention to the fact that Karen didn't attend the party because that information is placed in the independent clause. The second sentence places information about the *invitation* in the independent clause, so it stresses the fact that Karen had been invited. The word "although" is called a subordinating conjunction, and it is used to show contrast or opposition. Other words show different relationships.

- Use "as," "because," "since," or "whereas" to show cause and effect.

   (Since the band was one we liked), we decided to go to the dance.

- Use "as" or "as if" to show a comparison.

   (As Maine goes), so goes the nation.

- Use "after," "as," "before," "ever since," "til," "until," "when," "whenever," "where," "wherever," and "while" to show time or place relationships.

  (After we had eaten dinner), we felt better.

  (Wherever you go), that's where I'll go.

- Use "even if," "even though," "if," "provided," "supposing," "though" "unless," "whatever," and "whether" to show a condition or a possibility.

  (Even if I manage to save the money), I probably won't go to Japan this summer.

  (Supposing that you are accepted by all three colleges), which one will you choose?

- Use "in order that" or "so that" to show a purpose.

  (So that we can finish more quickly), we'll each do a different part of the experiment.

We have started our example sentences with the dependent clause, but the dependent clause may come at either the beginning or the end of the sentence.

Because we ran out of ink, we didn't finish the printing job.

| Dependent clause | , | independent clause | . |

We didn't finish the printing job because we ran out of ink.

| Independent clause | dependent clause | . |

Remember, too, that the idea you want to emphasize must go in the independent clause; the ideas in the dependent clauses are subordinate to the idea of the main or independent clause in a complex sentence.

12.3.2   Rather than show a logical relationship, the relative clause (Section 8.2) adds information that is related to some part of the independent or main clause of the sentence. The subject of a relative clause may be a *relative adjective*—"what," "whatever," "whichever," "whose," and "whosoever"; a *relative adverb*—"where," "when," "why," and "how"; or a *relative pronoun*—"who," "whose," "whom," "which," "what," "that," "whoever," "whomever," and "whatever." Here are some complex sen-

II

tences with one independent clause and one relative clause. The relative clause is in parentheses in each.

> **You can take (whichever seat you want).**
>
> **We wondered (why the mistake had been overlooked).**
>
> **The man (who runs this department) is a real tyrant.**
>
> **My uncle, (who is chairman of the board,) will visit Texas next month.**
>
> **We all took music lessons, (which were very costly).**

Punctuation note: Notice that some of the relative clauses have commas around them while others do not. In each of the first three examples, the relative clause is obviously necessary to the meaning of the sentence; hence it is not set off by commas. In the fourth example, the relative clause is not essential to the meaning of the sentence, and thus it is set off with commas. In the fifth example, the comma shows that the writer intends the relative clause as a kind of afterthought. Had he wanted to emphasize the cost, he could have left the comma out. We discuss this further in Section 17.4.

12.4 The compound-complex sentence

A **compound-complex sentence** has two or more independent clauses and one or more dependent clauses:

> **Because Beverly likes soft drinks, she always has one in her hand, and she doesn't hesitate to share it with others.**

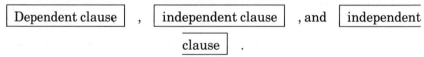

| Dependent clause | , | independent clause | , and | independent clause | . |

The punctuation rules remain the same as those for compound and complex sentences. Here's another example.

> **Denny often visits the whitewater streams of the Northwest because he thinks kayaking is the king of sports, but he also likes sailing, so he spends a lot of time on Cape Cod where he has a cottage.**

(This sentence has three independent clauses: "Denny often visits the whitewater streams of the Northwest," "he also likes sailing," and "he spends a lot of time on Cape Cod." It has two dependent clauses: "because he thinks kayaking is the king of sports," and "where he has a cottage.")

The pattern here is

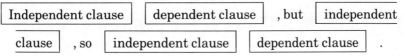

Here's a final example.

My cousin Doris, who lives on a ranch in Wyoming, is a joy to visit, for she's interested in everything, reads anything she can get her hands on, and loves to talk. (Here we have an independent clause interrupted by a dependent clause and joined to a second independent clause with a comma and a coordinating conjunction.)

The pattern is

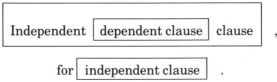

Editing Activity A.6

□ In a piece of your own writing, identify the sentence types which you have used.

□ If most of your sentences are of the same type, create sentence variety by rewriting or combining some of your sentences.

III

IMPROVING YOUR SENTENCES

When you have learned to combine phrases and clauses into sentences, you are ready to take a closer look at your sentences. Part III discusses some of the more common problems that interfere with meaning in sentences.

SECTION 13:
Agreement

Nouns and pronouns must agree in person, and subjects and verbs must agree in number. Thus, if you use a third person singular noun such as "John," any pronoun you use to refer to John must also be third person singular ("he," for example). Likewise, if you use a singular subject, your verb must also be singular.

13.1 Noun–pronoun agreement

Nouns and the pronouns that refer back to them must always agree with each other. For example, we write,

Justin left Roseburg because <u>he</u> couldn't stand the rain. (We use the singular pronoun "he" to refer to the singular noun "Justin.")

Gabe and Justin left Roseburg because <u>they</u> wanted freedom. (We use the plural pronoun "they" to refer to our plural subject, "Gabe and Justin.")

We speak of pronouns as being *first, second,* or *third person* and of being singular or plural.

	Singular	Plural
First person	I	we
Second person	you	you
Third person	he, she, it	they

In making sure that pronouns agree with their nouns, remember that the subject is never found in a prepositional phrase (see Section 6.5).

> **<u>Each</u> of the women <u>owns</u> <u>her</u> own home.** (This sentence is correct because the subject "each" is singular and therefore the verb "owns" and the pronoun "her" must also be singular.)

> **<u>All</u> of the women <u>own</u> <u>their</u> own homes.** (This is correct because the subject "all" is plural and therefore the verb "own" and the pronoun "their" must be plural.)

13.2 A note on pronouns

You'll hear and see a great deal of variation in the use of pronouns because of a problem with the English language. We do not have a third person singular pronoun that we can use to refer to people without identifying them as male or female.

For many years, people wrote, "In his work, a doctor must always be sure that he advises his patients carefully," or, "A good first grade teacher will always be sure her students are quiet at rest time." This use of our language contributed to sex stereotyping: we thought of doctors as men and of first grade teachers as women. Here are some commonly used solutions to the problem.

- Use plural nouns and pronouns.

  Good first grade teachers will be sure their students are quiet at rest time.

- Leave out the pronoun.

  A good first grade teacher will be sure students (or the students) are quiet at rest time.

- Alternate male and female examples.

  One teacher might ask her students to sing, while another may have his students dance.

III

Some solutions are awkward and should be avoided in writing.

■ Don't use "he or she," "s/he," and similar forms.

AVOID: **In his or her work, a doctor must always be sure that he or she advises his or her patients carefully.** (You can see that this form can become awkward and annoying.)

USE: **In their work, doctors must always be sure that they advise their patients carefully.**

USE: **In her work, a doctor must always be sure she advises her patients carefully.**

■ Don't use a plural pronoun to refer to a singular noun.

AVOID: **When you see the judge, tell them you're sorry and won't do it again.**

USE: **When you see the judge, say that you're sorry and that you won't do it again.**

USE: **When you see the judge, tell him you're sorry and won't do it again.**

Of course, if you're writing about a male, use masculine pronouns, and if you're writing about a female, use feminine pronouns. The rule is to avoid sex stereotyping and to recognize the equality of women and men in your writing.

 Editing Activity A.7

□ Take a piece of writing to check for noun–pronoun agreement. Underline each pronoun. (Remember that a pronoun is simply a word that takes the place of a noun.)

□ Next, draw an arrow to the noun that the pronoun replaces, like this:

Each (of my nephews) has his own way (of speaking). ("Of my nephews" and "of speaking" are prepositional phrases, so they can't be the subject. We put them in parentheses to make it easier to spot the subject.)

□ If you see that your nouns and pronouns disagree in either number or person, change your sentence to correct the error.

13.3 Subject–verb agreement

The subject of each sentence must agree with its verb. If the subject is plural, the verb must be plural; if the subject is singular, the verb must be singular (see Section 2.3 for a discussion of plural and singular verbs). If you're a native speaker of English, your ear will tell you that you should write "Mark is going," not "Mark are going," or to write "Mark and Doug are going," not "Mark and Doug is going." The singular form of the verb "is" agrees with the singular subject "Mark." The plural form "are" agrees with the plural subject "Mark and Doug."

SINGULAR: **There <u>was</u> a <u>box</u> of apples on the back seat.**

PLURAL: **There <u>were</u> a <u>box</u> of apples and a French <u>horn</u> on the back seat.**

In the first example, there was only one thing on the back seat, a box, so our verb is the singular form: "was." In the second example, there were two things on the back seat, a box and a horn. The verb, then, is plural: "were."

Here's another pair of sentences to illustrate number agreement.

Here <u>are</u> two <u>wrenches</u> and a <u>hammer</u>.

Here <u>are</u> a <u>hammer</u> and two <u>wrenches</u>.

The first sentence sounds just fine because a plural noun follows a plural verb. The second, though, sounds a little odd because the plural verb is followed by a singular noun. Nevertheless, the plural verb must be used in both cases because the subject of each sentence ("two wrenches and a hammer," and "a hammer and two wrenches") is plural.

Several pronouns are always singular and therefore require singular verbs. These pronouns are always singular:

anybody	neither
anyone	no one
each	nobody
either	one
everybody	somebody
everyone	someone

When one of these pronouns is the subject of your sentence, use a singular form of the verb.

<u>Neither</u> of them <u>anticipates</u> a problem.

<u>Everyone</u> at the party <u>is having</u> a good time.

Because of illness, <u>each</u> of the boys <u>has to stay</u> at home.

III

 **Editing
Activity
A.8**

☐ In each sentence of a piece of writing that you want to examine for subject–verb agreement, underline your subject once and your verb twice. (See Sections 2–6 on subjects and verbs if you have trouble doing this.)

☐ If you have a plural subject with a singular verb or a singular subject with a plural verb, correct the sentence. You may wish to look back at the list of verb forms in Section 4.

SECTION 14:
Shifts

14.1 Shifts in tense

One writing problem that can cause a reader to become confused is a **shift in tense** or time within a sentence or paragraph. Note how the following sentence shifts from past to present.

> **Jean and Richard went to Florida last winter because Minnesota was too cold. Later, they wish they'd gone to Arizona.**

The verb "went" is in the past tense, and it is clear that the second sentence is also about something that happened in the past. The verb "wish," however, is in the present tense, and so there is a shift in tense or time. If you start writing in the past tense, stay in the past tense. Don't shift from past to present or from present to past. Here's how we would correct our example:

> **Jean and Richard went to Florida last winter because Minnesota was too cold. Later, they wished they'd gone to Arizona.**

Here's another example:

WRONG: **He gives her pearl earrings to match her pearl necklace, and she smiled with delight.**

RIGHT: **He gives her pearl earrings to match her pearl necklace, and she smiles with delight.**

14.2 Shifts in person

A **shift in person** often causes problems in writing and can confuse your reader.

> **If a student is writing a paper, you might find a word proces-sor helpful**.

Here the shift is from third person ("a student") to second person ("you"). (See Section 13.1 for a discussion of first, second, and third person pronouns.) Here are three ways to correct the sentence.

WRONG: **If a student is writing a paper, you might find a word processor helpful.**

RIGHT: **If a student is writing a paper, he might find a word processor helpful.**

RIGHT: **If students are writing papers, they might find word processors helpful.**

RIGHT: **If you are writing a paper, you might find a word processor helpful.**

Use second person (you) only if you are addressing your reader directly. To make a general statement about people, use third person. (See the discussion in Section 13.1.)

14.3 An example

We have underlined verbs and pronouns in the following paragraph. Before you read our corrected version, see if you can spot and correct the shifts in tense and person on your own.

> **Last winter <u>we</u> <u>had</u> a record snowfall, and that <u>makes</u> for the best sledding ever. One weekend in particular <u>had</u> perfect weather, so <u>I</u> <u>get</u> on the phone and <u>invite</u> all my friends. Soon the house <u>was</u> full of kids, adults, dogs, and coats, but not for long. <u>Everyone</u> <u>has</u> toboggans, inner tubes, sleds, and flying saucers, so <u>you</u> all <u>go</u> out to the pasture to slide. After an hour or two of flying down hills, narrowly missing fences and trees, crashing into each other, and generally having a grand time, <u>you</u> all <u>end</u> up by the fire again. <u>I've</u> never <u>had</u> a better time than that.**

Here is our corrected version. We've kept everything in the past tense because it's about an event that happened in the past. We've also eliminated the shift from first to second person.

Last winter <u>we</u> <u>had</u> a record snowfall, and that <u>made</u> for the best sledding ever. One weekend in particular <u>had</u> perfect weather, so <u>I</u> <u>got</u> on the phone and <u>invited</u> all <u>my</u> friends. Soon the house <u>was</u> full of kids, adults, dogs, and coats, but not for long. <u>Everyone</u> <u>had</u> toboggans, inner tubes, sleds, and flying saucers, so <u>we</u> all <u>went</u> out to the pasture to slide. After an hour or two of flying down hills, narrowly missing fences and trees, crashing into each other, and generally having a grand time, <u>we</u> all <u>ended</u> up by the fire again. <u>I've</u> never <u>had</u> a better time than that.

 Editing Activity A.9

□ Look carefully at the verbs and pronouns in your paragraph.

□ If you have shifts in either time or person, correct them.

SECTION 15:
Modifiers

To modify something is to change it. A **modifier** is a word or group of words that changes an idea by giving additional information about it.

15.1 One-word modifiers

We have already seen how adjectives (Chapter 5) and adverbs (Chapter 6) can work as modifiers, but let's take another look at how these one-word modifiers can help a sentence.

The car stopped.

This sentence simply states an action. It gives no visual image. See how much more effective this sentence becomes with the addition of just one adjective to modify "car" and one adverb to modify "stopped":

The battered car stopped jerkily.

Modifiers can help explain or clarify ideas, and where we place modifiers can change the meaning of a sentence. Compare the following two sentences.

We almost spent all our money.

We spent almost all our money.

The placement of the modifier "almost" changes the meaning of the sentences. If we came close to spending the money and then changed our minds, the first sentence would be accurate, but if we had actually spent the money and had spent nearly all of it, the second would be our choice.

Where we put a modifier can make a large difference in meaning. As another illustration, try placing the word "only" at different places in the following sentence:

I hit him in the eye yesterday.

III

15.2 Longer modifiers

We often use one-word modifiers to help the reader visualize a scene or understand an idea, but we also use clauses and phrases to do the same thing.

Running onto the field, I frantically waved my arms.

The first group of words, "Running onto the field," modifies the second, for it gives additional information about what the speaker did. "Running onto the field" modifies the subject of the independent clause that follows it. It modifies "I."

15.3 Correcting misplaced modifiers

If they're used improperly, modifiers can confuse or amuse the reader. Modifiers become confusing in a sentence when they are **misplaced**, that is, not placed close enough to the word they modify.

Soaring above Nantucket Harbor, Bob watched the great blue heron.

This says Bob—not the heron—was actually doing the soaring. The sentence should read like this:

Bob watched the great blue heron soaring above Nantucket Harbor.

Here are more examples.

MISPLACED MODIFIER: **The North Cascades attract climbers with challenging peaks.**
(says climbers have challenging peaks)

III

CORRECTED:	**With their challenging peaks, the North Cascades attract climbers.** (says North Cascades have challenging peaks)
MISPLACED MODIFIER:	**A diamond earring hung from her earlobe that shone brilliantly.** (says her earlobe shone brilliantly)
CORRECTED:	**A diamond earring that shone brilliantly hung from her earlobe.** (says the earring shone brilliantly)
CORRECTED:	**Shining brilliantly, a diamond earring hung from her earlobe.** (says the earring shone brilliantly)
MISPLACED MODIFIER:	**The dress hung on the hanger torn to shreds by the cat's claws.** (says the hanger was torn to shreds)
CORRECTED:	**Torn to shreds by the cat's claws, the dress hung on the hanger.** (says the dress was torn to shreds)
CORRECTED:	**The dress, torn to shreds by the cat's claws, hung on the hanger.** (says the dress was torn to shreds)

One way to analyze a sentence you're having trouble with is to break it down into its simplest parts. In the last example above, we have four main ideas:

1. The dress was hanging.
2. It was on a hanger.
3. It was torn to shreds.
4. The cat's claws had torn it.

Seeing the ideas separately can help us decide how to arrange them clearly. How the ideas are arranged in a sentence is up to the writer, but the writer's aim must always be to communicate ideas clearly.

15.4 Correcting dangling modifiers

Modifiers are called **dangling** when there is no word in the sentence for them to modify.

DANGLING MODIFIER: **Cheering wildly, the team won the game with a last-second touchdown.**

A modifier in the position of "Cheering wildly" will modify the subject of the independent clause which follows it. The subject of that independent clause is "the team." Was the team cheering wildly? Probably not, at least not while the play was going on. It was probably the crowd that was cheering, but the sentence doesn't say so. "Cheering wildly" is called a dangling modifier because it modifies the incorrect noun "team"; the sentence has no word that "cheering wildly" correctly modifies. We need to say who was doing the cheering to eliminate any confusion. We can change either the modifier or the main sentence to make the meaning clear.

MODIFIER CHANGED: **While the crowd cheered wildly, the team won the game with a last-second touchdown.**

MAIN SENTENCE CHANGED: **Cheering wildly, the crowd watched the team win the game with a last-second touchdown.**

Here are more examples:

DANGLING MODIFIER: **Angry about the delay, the reservations were cancelled.** (says the reservations were angry)

MODIFIER CHANGED: **Because we were angry about the delay, the reservations were cancelled.** (says we were angry)

MAIN SENTENCE CHANGED: **Angry about the delay, we cancelled the reservations.** (says we were angry)

DANGLING MODIFIER: **Never having done any surfing before, the waves looked threatening.**

MODIFIER CHANGED: **Since I had never done any surfing before, the waves looked threatening.**

MAIN SENTENCE CHANGED: **Never having done any surfing before, I thought the waves looked threatening.**

Again, breaking the sentence into its parts can help:

1. I had never done any surfing before.

2. The waves looked threatening.

Breaking the sentence into its parts shows that there are two subjects, "I" and "waves." The example with the dangling modifier leaves out "I," but the two corrected versions include both subjects.

III

 Editing Activity A.10

□ Read over a sample of your work. Any time you are unsure about where to place a modifier in a sentence, list the ideas of the sentence separately.

□ Write two or three versions of the sentence, putting the ideas in different order. Try writing the modifier as a dependent clause, and try moving the modifier as close as you can to the word it modifies.

□ For your final draft, choose the sentence that expresses your ideas most clearly or effectively.

Section 16: Parallel Structure

One writing technique that helps make the relationships of ideas clear to a reader is the use of **parallel structure**. All this means is that sentences or parts of sentences have the same form. Here's an example of a sentence without parallel structure:

Gracie enjoys hiking in Tibet, elephant riding in Nepal, and to backpack in New Zealand.

Once you have set up a pattern in a sentence, stick with that pattern. The pattern in our example is "Gracie enjoys. . . ."

Gracie enjoys hiking

Gracie enjoys elephant riding

Gracie enjoys to backpack

See the problem with the last part of the sentence? It's easily corrected by making the last part parallel with the first two parts:

Gracie enjoys hiking in Tibet, elephant riding in Nepal, and backpacking in New Zealand.

Here's another example:

I'd like to be an engineer, a lawyer, or go into banking.

The pattern here is "I'd like to be. . . ."

I'd like to be an engineer

I'd like to be a lawyer

I'd like to be go into banking

Again, there's a problem with the last part. Here's the sentence rewritten to give it parallel structure:

I'd like to be an engineer, a lawyer, or a banker.

Here are a few more examples.

NOT PARALLEL:	**She wanted to know whether I could type and my ability to take shorthand.**
PARALLEL:	**She wanted to know whether I could type and take shorthand.**
NOT PARALLEL:	**We looked for a car with power steering, air conditioning, new tires, and it had to have a good stereo.**
PARALLEL:	**We looked for a car with power steering, air conditioning, new tires, and a good stereo.**
NOT PARALLEL:	**Alexis is witty, charming, tells jokes, and polite.**
PARALLEL:	**Alexis is witty, charming, funny, and polite.**

Editing Activity A.11

□ In your sentences, look for patterns that you have begun. Check to see that you have continued the patterns and thus have parallel structure.

IV

PUNCTUATING SENTENCES

When people read what you write, they cannot see your facial expressions and gestures, and they cannot hear the tones of your voice. These expressions and tones are the signals—the punctuation, if you will—that we use when we speak. When we write, then, we must use a different set of signals to tell the reader when a thought is changing, and the signals we use are **punctuation marks**. Part IV shows you how to use punctuation for effective communication.

SECTION 17:
The Comma

17.1 In dates and addresses

Use commas to separate the parts of most dates and addresses.

COMMAS
REQUIRED:
June 27, 1983, is a day I will never forget.

I'd just as soon forget December 2, 1985.

Milford, New Hampshire, is a pleasant town.

I like it better than Akron, Ohio.

London, England, is a huge city.

NO
COMMAS:
I joined the Army on 16 April 1981.

May 1968 was a cold month.

The town of Ione in California is a little bigger than the town of Ione in Washington.

17.2 With interrupters

Put commas before and after names or other words that interrupt sentences.

COMMAS REQUIRED:	**I'm sure, Jinny, that the cold won't bother you.**
	Dress warmly, however.
	We find, therefore, that the defendant is guilty.
	I suggest, my dear child, that you come home before midnight.
	I think, darn it, that there's more to it than that.
	Listen carefully, my fine friend.
NO COMMAS:	**My dear child is always home before midnight.**
	Jinny won't be bothered by the cold.

17.3 In a series

Put commas between items in a series. A series is usually three or more words, phrases, or clauses. Here are some examples:

COMMAS REQUIRED:	**I have lived in Duluth, Laramie, Wallace, and Butte.**
	Every day we arrived at work, ate doughnuts, laughed in meetings, and otherwise enjoyed ourselves.
	Bill cooked the chicken, Jan made the salad, and Jim fixed the lemonade.

Sometimes a connecting word ("and," "but," "or") is repeated before each item of a series. When it is, no comma is used to separate the items:

NO COMMAS:	**Bill cooked the chicken and Jan made the salad and Jim fixed the lemonade.**

Be sure to stop using commas when you've stopped listing.

INCORRECT:	**Snow, sleet, ice, and rain, caused our plane to turn back.** (The four items in the series form the subject of the sentence, and placing a comma after "rain" puts a comma between the subject and the verb of the sentence. Be careful not to do this.)

CORRECT: **Snow, sleet, ice, and rain caused our plane to turn back**. (Only the items in the series are separated by commas.)

17.4 With unnecessary material

Put commas before and after material that is not necessary to the meaning of the sentence.

My youngest brother, who is an accountant, really enjoys fishing.

Note that the dependent clause "who is an accountant" is not necessary to the meaning of the sentence. It is simply added information, and we set it off in two commas, as if it were in parentheses. In another sentence, the same clause might be necessary to the meaning:

My brother who is an accountant really enjoys fishing.

Here the clause is necessary to identify which brother; it distinguishes him, for example, from my brother who is a teacher and my brother who is a truck driver.

Unnecessary information needs commas both before *and* after it. Many students want to put a comma after "accountant" in the last example because there is a tendency to pause there. That single comma, however, separates the subject and the verb. *Do not use a single comma between the subject and the verb.*

WRONG: **Riding the ferries that travel Puget Sound, is exciting.**

RIGHT: **Riding the ferries that travel Puget Sound is exciting.**

Remember, commas are used in pairs when you set off unnecessary material in the middle of a sentence. Here are more examples:

COMMAS
REQUIRED: **In this society, where athletes are important, baseball players earn high salaries.**

People, who usually live in houses, are a common life form on this planet.

Betty Jean, a girl I dislike, finally left town.

NO
COMMAS: **Baseball players earn high salaries in a society where athletes are important.**

People who usually live in houses outnumber those who usually live in caves.

A girl I dislike finally left town.

Phrases and clauses like those in the examples above are sometimes referred to as **restrictive** or **nonrestrictive** modifiers. A modifier gives additional information about part of a sentence; a restrictive modifier restricts, or limits, the noun it modifies. In the sentence,

All students who do their homework are sure to pass.

the modifier "who do their homework" is restrictive; it limits the group of students who are sure to pass. However, in the sentence,

Jennifer and Katie, who do their homework, are sure to pass.

the modifier "who do their homework" is nonrestrictive. The subject tells us which people are sure to pass. The modifier gives us additional but unnecessary information about why those people are sure to pass. Again, commas go before and after material that is not necessary to the sentence.

17.5 With introductory material

Put a comma after a dependent clause that introduces an independent clause and after other introductory words and phrases that do not flow smoothly into the sentence. Here are some examples of introductions that need to be set off by commas.

COMMAS
REQUIRED:

If I go tomorrow, I'll have to miss class.

Above, the sky was clear and blue.

In the dark shadows of the skyscrapers, a cold wind howled.

Meanwhile, J. R. waited at the office.

Satisfied, Bobby walked in with Sue Ellen.

For several good reasons, we decided not to run the marathon.

To mention just one, our knees protested violently with every step we took.

Walking up the stairs, we became convinced we had made the right decision.

When a sentence contains both a dependent clause and an independent clause, use a comma only when the dependent clause comes first:

| Dependent clause | , | independent clause |

| Independent clause | | dependent clause |

COMMA: **Because I could not stop, I ran into the wall.**

NO COMMA: **I ran into the wall because I could not stop.**

COMMA: **When I ran down my icy driveway, I slipped and broke my right leg.**

NO COMMA: **I slipped and broke my right leg when I ran down my icy driveway.**

COMMA: **Even though it was snowing heavily, we had a picnic near the river.**

NO COMMA: **We had a picnic near the river even though it was snowing heavily.**

17.6 With coordinating conjunctions

Put a comma before "for," "and," "nor," "but," "or," "yet," or "so" when one of these words joins two independent clauses.

Independent clause	, for	independent clause
	, and	
	, nor	
	, but	
	, or	
	, yet	
	, so	

This rule is a little easier to remember than it looks. The first letters of the seven words that need a comma in front of them—For, And, Nor, But, Or, Yet, So—spell FAN BOYS. If you use one of the FAN BOYS to join two independent clauses, put a comma in front of it like this:

He left, for she had hurt him.

She had hurt him, and she was glad.

He didn't want to leave, nor did she want him to go.

Always check to be sure you do, in fact, have two independent clauses. The sentence

She had hurt him and was glad.

for example, wouldn't take a comma before "and" because "was glad" is not an independent clause. The easiest way to check is to put parentheses around all the words on each side of the connecting word, like this:

(She had hurt him) and (was glad).

If the words within each set of parentheses form an independent clause, you need a comma before the connecting word.

17.7 Misuses of the comma

The best general rule for punctuation is this: *Do not use a comma or any other punctuation mark unless you can state a definite reason for doing so.* There are some more specific cautions about commas to keep in mind, though.

17.7.1   Do not separate the subject from the verb with one comma.

> WRONG: **Some people who go to school, enjoy the social life.**
>
> RIGHT: **Some people who go to school enjoy the social life.**

Be particularly careful of this when using one of the FAN BOYS ("for," "and," "nor," "but," "or," "yet," "so") to join two verbs rather than two independent clauses.

> WRONG: **He studied all night, but worked all the next day.**
>
> RIGHT: **He studied all night but worked all the next day.**
>
> RIGHT: **He studied all night, but he worked all the next day.**

17.7.2   Do not use just a comma between two independent clauses. This use is called a *comma splice*. Avoid comma splices. (See Section 10.)

> WRONG: **He was late for dinner, we decided to eat without him.**
>
> RIGHT: **He was late for dinner. We decided to eat without him.**
>
> RIGHT: **He was late for dinner; we decided to eat without him.**
>
> RIGHT: **He was late for dinner, so we decided to eat without him.**
>
> RIGHT: **Because he was late for dinner, we decided to eat without him.**

17.7.3   Do not use a comma between an independent clause and a dependent clause when the independent clause starts the sentence.

> WRONG: **We were glad to see him, because he had brought gifts.**
>
> RIGHT: **We were glad to see him because he had brought gifts.**

17.7.4   Do not use a comma before the first word or after the last word in a series.

WRONG: **He brought, tuna fish, eggs, milk, and honey, from the store.**

RIGHT: **He brought tuna fish, eggs, milk, and honey from the store.**

IV

Editing Activity A.12

☐ Examine your paragraph for problems with each comma rule.

☐ Look carefully at your paragraph for any use of dates or addresses. Check your comma use and correct it as necessary.

☐ Look for names or other words that interrupt your sentences. Check your comma use and correct it as necessary.

☐ Look at any use of items in a series. Check your comma use and correct it as necessary.

☐ Look carefully at each sentence. Is there material that is not necessary to the meaning of the sentence? Is it set off with a comma on each side? Have you incorrectly used commas to set off necessary material? Correct your comma use as necessary.

☐ Look at each independent clause. Does it have a dependent clause or some other introductory element? If so, read it aloud. Does it flow smoothly into the independent clause? If not, set it off with a comma.

☐ Look again at each independent clause. Is it joined to another independent clause with no punctuation or with just a comma? If so, correct the run-on sentence.

☐ Look for any unnecessary commas. Can you state a rule for each comma you have used? Eliminate any unnecessary commas.

□ If you make large changes, write a corrected version of your paragraph and check it with your instructor.

SECTION 18:
The Semicolon

There are only two rules for using semicolons, one to join independent clauses and the other to separate items in a series.

18.1 With independent clauses

Use a semicolon (;) to join two independent clauses. A semicolon is like a period in that it can separate two independent clauses. It is used to show a closer relationship between ideas than that suggested by a period. It is not followed by a capital letter.

| Independent clause | ; | independent clause |

Here are two examples:

Daisy and Laurel worked night and day on the drawings; they were determined to meet the deadline.

I hate being late for work; my boss always gives me such a bad time about it.

Words like "however," "therefore," "finally," "nevertheless," "likewise," and "furthermore" are sometimes used to join independent clauses. When they are, they must be preceded by a semicolon, although a period is sometimes used instead. These joining words are called *adverbial conjunctions* (see Sections 1.9 and 12.2.2) and are usually followed by a comma.

| Independent clause | ; therefore,
 ; however,
 etc. | independent clause |

We had forgotten to eat breakfast; consequently, we collapsed in the afternoon.

Lifting weights is good exercise; therefore, most coaches prescribe it.

I used plenty of yeast in the bread dough; however, it didn't rise.

Think of the joining word as simply the first word of the second independent clause.

When you use the semicolon to join independent clauses, check to see that you do, indeed, have two independent clauses. Words like "however" and "therefore" are often used as interrupters in a sentence, and in such a case they are set off with commas.

AS INTERRUPTER:	**We left early, however, to avoid the rush.**
AS JOINER:	**We left early; however, we didn't avoid the rush.**
AS INTERRUPTER:	**The project, therefore, was stalled by a computer breakdown.**
AS JOINER:	**The computer broke down; therefore, the project was stalled.**
AS INTERRUPTER:	**We will, instead, have dinner at the Space Needle.**
AS JOINER:	**We planned to eat at the wharf; instead, we will have dinner at the Space Needle.**

18.2 In a series

Use a semicolon to separate items in a series when the items themselves contain commas. That sounds more complicated than it actually is. Here are some examples:

> **I have lived in Duluth, Minnesota; Laramie, Wyoming; Wallace, Idaho; and Butte, Montana.**

> **Marcia heated, reheated, and reheated the pizza; Glen and Ed had it for breakfast, lunch, and dinner; and Stacey and Jeff ignored it all.**

This use of the semicolon can keep a reader from getting confused in complicated lists.

SECTION 19:
The Colon

Use a colon after a complete thought to introduce a word, list, quotation, or explanation which follows.

> **There is only one thing I want in life: love.**
>
> **I have several favorite activities: skiing, bowling, reading, and tennis.**
>
> **My mother had a gentle way of forgiving people: "I'm sure he wanted to do the right thing."**
>
> **There was a good reason why he was late: he had three flat tires on the way.**

Do not use a colon if the list follows a verb.

WRONG:	**My favorite activities are: skiing, bowling, reading, and tennis.**
RIGHT:	**My favorite activities are skiing, bowling, reading, and tennis.**
WRONG:	**You should bring: warm coats, warm boots, and mittens.**
RIGHT:	**You should bring warm coats, warm boots, and mittens.**
WRONG:	**My brothers are: Sloan, Darol, and David.**
RIGHT:	**My brothers are Sloan, Darol, and David.**
RIGHT:	**I have three brothers: Sloan, Darol, and David.**

You may also, of course, use a colon in the way that we have used it after "WRONG" and "RIGHT" above.

SECTION 20:
Quotation Marks and Underlining

20.1 Word-for-word quotations

We use quotation marks to show word-for-word quotations from written or spoken sources.

IV

"I'm afraid I can't help you," Nora sighed.

Bev replied, "I guess I'll have to leave, then."

"Fine," Nora smiled, "but I wish I could have helped."

Columnist Dave Barry writes about Christmas, "A favorite tradition in our family is to try to find a parking space at the mall."

20.1.1 Do not put quotation marks around paraphrases and indirect quotations. To distinguish between a direct and an indirect quote, ask yourself whether you are stating the exact words another writer or speaker used.

> INDIRECT: **Cynthia said that artichokes are a marvelous addition to a salad.** (The sentence reports *what* Cynthia said, but not necessarily in the exact words she used.)

> DIRECT: **Cynthia said, "Artichokes are a marvelous addition to a salad."** (The sentence reports Cynthia's exact words.)

> INDIRECT: **Marty promised he would get his shopping done early this year.**

> DIRECT: **Marty promised, "I'll get my shopping done early this year."**

Think about what people say when they actually talk to you. Would Marty walk up to you and say, "He would get his shopping done early this year"? Of course not; it is therefore an indirect quotation.

Use a comma between the identification of the speaker or writer and the quotation itself, but do not use commas with indirect quotations.

> INDIRECT: **William Butler Yeats said that only God could love a certain woman for herself alone and not her yellow hair.**

> DIRECT: **William Butler Yeats said, "Only God, my dear, could love you for yourself alone and not your yellow hair."**

20.1.2 Commas and periods go inside the final quotation marks:

"It's twenty degrees," she shivered.

George complained, "I hate weather like this."

"If you don't like it," Bill said, "move to Arizona. That's what I plan to do."

This is known as "justice."

20.1.3   Colons and semicolons go outside final quotation marks:

Jeremiah said, "You really ought to do it"; therefore, we did.

Too late I remembered my mother's saying, "A fool and his money are soon parted": my wallet was empty, and my checkbook showed a balance of $1.26.

20.1.4   Question marks and exclamation points go inside or outside the ending quotes, depending on whether they punctuate the quotation itself or the whole sentence in which the quotation appears:

Andy yelled, "Get out of the water! There are alligators in there!"

I can't believe Elton said, "I've never been to California"!

Did he really say, "I'd like to visit Paris next year"?

Janet murmured, "Would you mind if I go with you?"

IV

20.2 Use in titles

Use quotation marks around the titles of poems, songs, short stories, magazine articles, newspaper articles, or other works that appear in longer publications. Underline the names of the longer publications.

"To the Head of the Class" in the December 9 <u>Sports Illustrated</u> talks about Michigan's win over Georgia Tech.

Of all the poems in Ann Darr's <u>Cleared for Landing</u>, I like "Relative Matter" best.

Two stories in James Joyce's <u>Dubliners</u> are "Araby" and "Counterparts."

SECTION 21:
The Dash and Parentheses

Use dashes or parentheses to show an abrupt interruption or change of thought. (On a typewriter, make a dash by typing two hyphens.)

IV

> **Mary was too tired to think—she'd worked hard all day.**

> **The man with the guitar—an excellent player—left rather quickly.**

> **My sister (who is really a good cook) rarely goes into the kitchen.**

> **We had dinner at a wonderful seafood restaurant (which happened to be where John Steinbeck once dined).**

Parentheses are always used in pairs, while the dash may be used singly at the end of a sentence. Use dashes if you want an interruption to stand out strongly; parentheses make the interrupter less forceful. If a sentence needs punctuation without parentheses, it still needs punctuation with the parentheses.

> **Tired of driving (she'd been at it all day), Anna pulled into a truck stop.**

> **The truck stop was crowded (it certainly couldn't have been because of the food); she had to share a booth with three strangers.**

If you put a complete sentence within parentheses, punctuate it as you would any other sentence.

> **Driving a car with a stick shift is hard for some people. (That says less about their intelligence than about their coordination.) My dearest friend is one such person.**

SECTION 22:
The Apostrophe

The apostrophe is a punctuation mark with only two uses. It shows contraction and it shows possession. A contraction is a shorter version of something, and we use contractions all the time. Only in a very formal situation would we say "I do not like her." We're much more likely to say, "I don't like her."

22.1 In contractions

In contractions, put an apostrophe where a letter or letters are left out. Often a contraction is a joining of two words, with the first letter or so of the second word left off, like this:

we have $\longrightarrow$ we've

they are $\longrightarrow$ they're

he will $\longrightarrow$ he'll

it is $\longrightarrow$ it's

Sometimes, though, the letters are left out of another part of the word, like this:

would not $\longrightarrow$ wouldn't

And one word changes quite a bit:

will not $\longrightarrow$ won't

Regardless of how the contraction is made, though, the apostrophe shows where letters have been left out.

22.2 In possessive nouns

In possessive nouns, use an apostrophe and an "s" to show possession or ownership. Possessives are a little bit tricky, but they're not really hard to master. You need to follow only two steps. First, decide whether there is possession. Second, decide whether the apostrophe must go before or after the final "s" in the possessive noun. Let's look at some examples of the possessive apostrophe, and then we'll explore the two steps.

John's house is the nicest on the block. (belongs to John)

It is much nicer than the Smiths' house. (belongs to the Smiths)

Frank Jones' house is nearly as nice, though. (belongs to Frank Jones)

All the yards are littered with children's toys. (belong to the children)

The girls' clubhouse stands in the vacant lot. (belongs to the girls)

Note that in each example, the possessive noun is followed by another noun: "John's house," "the Smiths' house," "Frank Jones' house," "children's toys," "girls' clubhouse." If a noun ending in "s" is closely followed by another noun, the first noun is probably possessive. Put another way, the second noun is probably the name of something that belongs to the first noun. There may be words between the two nouns, usually adjectives but sometimes adverbs as well, but the two nouns will be closely related. Here are two more examples.

IV

Carolyn's ancient, brown Volkswagen sat in the driveway. ("Ancient" and "brown" are adjectives that modify "Volkswagen," and the Volkswagen belongs to Carolyn.)

Ralph's carefully maintained tractor is a familar sight in the neighboring fields. ("Carefully" is an adverb that modifies "maintained," and "maintained" is an adjective that modifies "tractor." The tractor belongs to Ralph.)

Once you have determined that your sentence does have a possessive noun, you must decide whether to put the apostrophe before or after the final "s," and there's a foolproof way to do this. Teresa Ferster Glazier, in her book *The Least You Should Know About English*, says that you should ask "Who (or what) does it belong to?" If your answer ends in "s," put the apostrophe after the existing "s." If your answer doesn't end in "s," add an "s" and put the apostrophe before the "s."

The children's toys are on the rug. (Who do the toys belong to? They belong to the children. Our answer does not end in "s," so we add an "s" and put the apostrophe before the "s.")

The boy's trike is in the corner. (Who does the trike belong to? It belongs to the boy. Our answer does not end in "s" so we add an "s" and place the apostrophe before the "s.")

My mother's house is burning down. (Who does the house belong to? It belongs to my mother. Our answer does not end in "s," so we add an "s" and insert the apostrophe before the "s.")

The boys' championship soccer team lost its game. (Who does the team belong to? It belongs to the boys. Our answer ends in "s," so the apostrophe goes after the existing "s.")

The parents' party was ruined. (Who does the party belong to? It belongs to the parents. Our answer already ends in "s," so the apostrophe goes after the existing "s.")

James' new clothes were a mess. (Who do the clothes belong to? They belong to James. Our answer ends in "s," so the apostrophe goes after the existing "s.")

Be very careful to ask the question exactly. If you ask "Whose house is it," for example, your answer won't be in a form that will help you decide where the apostrophe goes. *Ask "Who does it belong to?"*

There are instances where the question sounds a little odd, but it still works.

a day's wages (Who do the wages belong to? They belong to one day. Our answer does not end in "s," so we add an "s" and put the apostrophe before the "s.")

two weeks' wages (Who do the wages belong to? They belong to two weeks. Our answer ends in "s," so the apostrophe goes after the existing "s.")

last Wednesday's assignment (Who does the assignment belong to? It belongs to last Wednesday. Our answer does not end in "s," so we add an "s" and place the apostrophe before the "s.")

Note that the possessive apostrophe is used only in nouns. Never use the apostrophe in these possessive pronouns:

yours	ours
his	theirs
hers	whose
its	

Joe's car runs well.	BUT	His car runs well.
The building is Mary's.	BUT	The building is hers.
The dog is Ada's and Sam's.	BUT	The dog is theirs.
The cat drank the cat's milk.	BUT	The cat drank its milk.

Use "it's" only for a contraction of "it is" or "it has." If you can't substitute "it is" or "it has" in your sentence, don't use an apostrophe in "its."

It's raining again today. ("It is" raining again today.)

It's been raining for weeks. ("It has" been raining for weeks.)

I like the coast, but I don't like its weather. (Can't substitute "it is" or "it has.")

SECTION 23:
Capitalization

23.1 In sentences

Always capitalize the first word in a sentence.

23.2 Proper names

Always capitalize names of people, nationalities, races, languages, and religions.

> **My friend Jim Pollard used to be a policeman.**
>
> **My Laotian friend Pao is very talented.**
>
> **My sister is Protestant, but her husband is Jewish.**

23.3 Names of places

Capitalize specific names of states, streets, cities, buildings, bodies of water, and so on.

> **I attend Kansas State University.**
>
> **She lives on Riverside Avenue.**
>
> **We visited New York City last year.**
>
> **His office is in the Paulsen Building.**
>
> **I've never seen the Atlantic Ocean.**

Don't capitalize names that are not specific.

> **I attend a state university.**
>
> **She lives on the avenue that runs between here and the railroad.**
>
> **We visited several cities last year.**
>
> **We saw many interesting buildings.**
>
> **Next year we'll go to the ocean.**

23.4 Names of times

Always capitalize names of months, days, and holidays.

> **We usually have good weather in June.**
>
> **Last Monday and Saturday were busy days.**
>
> **On the Fourth of July we swam in Ely Lake.**

23.5 Names of seasons

Never capitalize names of seasons.

> **Next fall we're going to Michigan.**
>
> **Our winter activities vary from year to year.**

23.6 Family names

Capitalize Mother, Grandfather, Uncle and so on if you use them as part of a name, but do not capitalize them otherwise.

> **I wish, Mother, that you'd stay home next week.**
>
> BUT
>
> **My mother loves to travel.**
>
> **My dad's brother, Uncle Harry, was a real cowboy.**
>
> BUT
>
> **My uncle was a real cowboy.**

23.7 Titles

Capitalize people's titles when they are used as part of a name, but do not capitalize them otherwise.

> **Good morning, Dr. Jones.**
>
> BUT
>
> **I said good morning to my doctor.**
>
> **I accidentally tripped Professor Hollowell in the hall.**
>
> BUT
>
> **The professor seemed a little startled.**

23.8 Courses and subjects

Capitalize names of specific courses, but not of academic subjects.

> **I'm not sure I can pass Physics 232.**
>
> BUT
>
> **I'm taking history this quarter.**

23.9 Book titles

Capitalize important words in titles. That is, capitalize all words except articles, prepositions, coordinating conjunctions, and "to" unless they're the first or last words of the title or unless they occur after a colon.

> **Even Cowgirls Get the Blues is a funny book.**
>
> **Elton John sings "I Guess That's Why They Call It the Blues."**
>
> **Dylan Thomas wrote "A Process in the Weather of the Heart."**

IV

23.10 Directions

Capitalize names of directions when they indicate a specific area but not when they merely show direction.

Let's spend next winter in the South.

BUT

Let's go south next winter.

V

WAYS TO IMPROVE SPELLING

Spelling is a problem for many people, and if it's a problem for you, there are several things you can do about it.

SECTION 24:
Things You Can Do

24.1 Keep a list

Since you probably consistently misspell the same words, keep a list of the words that give you trouble. (Chances are, you have fewer than fifty words that give you trouble.) Any time your instructor marks a spelling error, or any time you find one on your own, write the correct spelling of that word on your list. Don't just jot the spellings on envelopes or scraps of paper; make a formal list in a part of your notebook that you look at often. Review the list regularly.

24.2 Use index cards

A variation on keeping a list is using a stack of index cards. Write each word you need to learn on the blank side of a 3 × 5 card, and write the pronunciation and definition on the lined side. Carry the cards with you and review them regularly. Have a friend quiz you on the spellings.

24.3 Use a spelling dictionary

These are little books with titles such as *The Word Book II* or *Webster's New World 33,000 Word Book*, and they are available in most bookstores.   319

They give you spelling, show you how the words are broken into syllables, and distinguish between words that look or sound alike. They are small and easy to carry, and they show nearly 100 words per page so that you can usually find the word just by guessing fairly close to the correct spelling.

24.4 Use the visual motor method

In this method, you look carefully at the word, perhaps tracing over its letters with your finger or pencil. Cover the word and see if you can write it correctly; check *carefully* to see that you've got it right. When you can spell it right three times in a row, you probably have it. Practice to be sure.

24.5 Develop memory tricks

Develop a set of tricks to help you remember spellings. To remember the difference between "advice" and "advise," for example, you might remember the phrase "advice about ice." "Loose as a goose" might help you remember the difference between "loose" and "lose." "There's iron in the environment" can help you remember how to spell "env<u>iron</u>ment."

24.6 Use a dictionary

Develop the habit of using a dictionary regularly. The more you know about a word and its definitions and origins, the more likely you are to spell it correctly.

SECTION 25:
Problem Word Pairs

Some words look or sound alike, and it's easy to become confused about which one to use. Here is a list of the most common of these confusing word pairs.

accept, except	"Accept" means to approve of or to receive willingly.
	"Except" means "but" or "excluding."
	This sentence might help you remember the difference (the capitalized letters show similarities in spelling):

I'll Accept Advice from anybody EXcept my EX-wife.

advice, advise

The "s" in "advise" is pronounced like "z."

"advise" is always a verb.

I'd advise you not to go.

"Advice" is never a verb.

I took his advICE about the thin ice.

affect, effect

"Affect" is always a verb. It means to have an influence on.

Spring pollen always affects my sinuses.

"Effect" is almost always a noun. If you can put "a," "an," or "the" in front of it, spell it "effect."

The effect of spring pollen is often severe.

all ready,
already

"All" means "completely." If you can say "completely ready" or just "ready," use "all ready."

I'm all ready for bed. ("I'm completely ready for bed," or "I'm ready for bed" say the same thing.)

Use "already" if you can't leave off the "all" or say "completely" and have it make sense.

I've already told you five times.

all right

"All right" is the only form that is acceptable. Always spell it "all right."

a lot

"A lot" is the only form that is acceptable. Always spell it as two words: "a lot."

are, our

"Are" is always a verb.

We are having fun.

"Our" means something belongs to us.

We like our new car.

brake, break

The "brake" is what you push to slow your car or what you do when you push that pedal.

Put on your brakes; there's a stop sign ahead.

Don't brake hard on icy roads.

"Break" tells what happens to the glass that you drop. It means to shatter or to end. "Break" also means a pause.

> **The glass will break on that concrete floor.**
>
> **You'll break her heart if you break your engagement.**
>
> **Isn't it time for our coffee break?**

choose, chose

"Choose" is present tense, "chose" is past.

> **You must choose one of these gifts right now.**
>
> **Yesterday I chose not to go to school.**

clothes, cloths

You wear "clothes," but you use "cloths."

> **She always wears nice clothes.**
>
> **Use only soft cloths on your camera lens.**

coarse, course

Something that is "coarse" is rough or not fine.

> **Burlap is a very coarse cloth.**
>
> **Use coarse sandpaper on that rough board.**
>
> **That ground pepper is a little too coarse for my taste.**

Use "course" for all other meanings.

> **Did the river change its course?**
>
> **Of course it did.**
>
> **I learned that in my geology course.**

complement, compliment

"Complement" with an "e" means to complete something (as an outfit) or to make it perfect (as in a perfect combination).

> **That hat is the perfect complement to my new suit.**

"Compliment" with an "i" means to say nice things or to praise.

> **Be sure to compliment him on his hat.**
>
> **That's the nicest compliment I've ever received.**

Remember that a compl<u>E</u>ment compl<u>E</u>tes something and that <u>I</u> l<u>I</u>ke a compl<u>I</u>ment.

conscience, conscious

Your "conscience" is that little inner voice that tells you when you're doing wrong.

My conscience wouldn't let me lie to you.

If you are "conscious," you are awake and aware.

The boxer was no longer conscious.

She was suddenly conscious of someone else's presence.

If you are c<u>O</u>nsci<u>O</u>us, both your eyes are probably open, and the two "o"'s can remind you of two open eyes. If your co<u>N</u>scie<u>N</u>ce says something to you, it's probably "<u>N</u>o, <u>N</u>o," and the two "n"'s can help you remember that spelling.

desert, dessert

A "dessert" is what you eat after dinner. It is <u>S</u>o <u>S</u>weet that you want a second helping.

I'm gaining weight, so I shouldn't eat dessert.

"Desert" is used for all other meanings.

The desert is a hot, dry place.

He hated the army and wanted to desert.

do, due

To "do" is to act.

I do many things during the day.

If you do that again, you'll be in trouble.

What did he do to the car to make it run?

"Due" means owed or expected.

The rent is due on the fifth.

The paper is due tomorrow.

have, of

"Have" is a main verb or part of a helping verb.

I have time to do it now.

You should have been here last week.

We could have gone to the party.

When we say, "You should've been here," or "We could've gone," that *sounds* like "should of" or

V

"could of." It is *never* correct to use "of" as part of a helping verb.

"Of" is used only as the first word of a prepositional phrase (see Section 6.5).

This is a picture of my father.

Today is the fifth of December.

hear, here

"Hear" tells what you do with your ear. You hEAR with your EAR.

I can't hear the music.

"Here" identifies a place. HERE tells wHERE something is. If it's HERE, it's not over tHERE.

I like living here.

Here is your new coat.

it's, its

"It's" has only two possible meanings. It means "it is" or "it has."

It's time to go.

It's been a long time since I saw you.

"Its" is a possessive pronoun. It does not take an apostrophe (see Section 22.2).

The cat drank its milk.

knew, new

"Knew" is the past tense of "know," and both words deal with knowledge.

I knew the answer to that question.

I knew her when she was a child.

"New" means unused or not old.

She bought a new car, not a used one.

Isn't that a new shirt?

know, no

"Know" is the present tense of the verb that shows knowledge. (See "knew" above.)

He doesn't know how to do that.

"No" means refusal or "not any."

No, I don't plan to see her.

I have no way to get to her house.

loose, lose	"Loose" is the opposite of "tight." It also means "free."

> **That knot is too loose to hold.**
>
> **My horse was tied, but he got loose last night.**

We speak of someone being "loose as a goose," and remembering that phrase can help you remember that the word takes two "o"'s.

"Lose" is the opposite of "win." Remember that if you get <u>0</u> points you'll probably l<u>O</u>se the game.

> **I didn't think we could lose that game.**

passed, past	"Passed" is always a verb.

> **The car passed me on a curve.**
>
> **We always ran when we passed the grave-yard.**

"Past" is never a verb.

> **Let's forget about the past.**
>
> **We always ran past the graveyard.**

peace, piece	"Peace" is the opposite of war. We have pe<u>A</u>ce in the <u>A</u>bsence of w<u>A</u>r.

> **During the war, we prayed for peace.**

A "piece" is a part of something. We ask for a <u>PIE</u>ce of <u>PIE</u> when it's time for dessert. The two words share the letters "pie."

> **This puzzle is missing a piece.**

principal, principle	Something that is princip<u>A</u>l is very important. It comes first, just as the letter "<u>A</u>" comes first in the alphabet.

> **The principal called us to his office.**
>
> **Our principal problem is a lack of money.**
>
> **How much interest you earn depends on how much principal you invest.**

A princip<u>LE</u> is a ru<u>LE</u>.

> **He lived by one principle: be honest.**

I know how to work the problem, but I can't explain the principle.

quiet, quite, quit	"Quiet" means silent, and both words have two syllables, qu<u>I</u>-<u>E</u>t and s<u>I</u>-l<u>E</u>nt.

We spent a quiet evening together.

"Quite" means completely or very. It has only one syllable. Qu<u>I</u>te rhymes with b<u>I</u>te.

I'm not quite done.

It's quite cold outside.

"Quit" means to stop.

I wasn't finished, but I quit anyway.

real, really	"Real" means genuine.

We got a real deal on this house!

Is that a real diamond, or is it a fake?

"Really" means very.

My grandfather is really old.

It was really hot yesterday.

Don't use "real" when you mean "really."

right, write	Something that is "right" is correct.

I don't think that's the right answer.

"Write" means to record on paper. You <u>WRITE</u> with a pen or type<u>WRITE</u>r.

You should write to your mother more often.

than, then	"Th<u>A</u>n" is a word that comp<u>A</u>res things.

My car is much older than theirs.

"Th<u>E</u>n" always tells wh<u>E</u>n.

I started my homework; then my brother came by.

We'll do the dishes first, and then we'll go to the movies.

their, there, they're	"Their" is always a possessive pronoun.

They watched their daughter win the race.

"<u>THERE</u>" tells w<u>HERE</u> something is or it points something out.

If it's not here or there, I don't know where it is.

There were six vultures circling overhead.

"They're" is always a contraction of "they are."

They're sure to win if they practice.

threw, through

"Threw" is the past tense of "throw." It is always a verb.

I threw the rock.

Use "through" for any other meaning.

Are you through with your breakfast?

Don't walk through that door.

to, too, two

"Two" has only one meaning. It is a number.

There are two lions on the hood of the car.

"Too" has two "o"'s and two meanings. It means also, and it means more than enough.

Heather brought mustard, and Sara did, too.

That meant we had too much mustard.

Both meanings of "too" show that something is added. Remembering that can remind you to add the extra "o."

Use "to" for any meaning other than the three shown above.

I'd like to escape from here.

I think I'll go to China.

weather, whether

"Weather" is what happens outdoors. One form of we<u>A</u>ther is r<u>A</u>in.

The weather today is terrible.

"Whether" refers to a choice. It means "if."

I don't know whether to sleep or exercise.

Whether you do it is up to you.

V

were, where	"Were" is always a verb.

They were looking for their dog.

"Where" talks about a place. If you ask w<u>HERE</u> something is, you'll be told it's either <u>HERE</u> or t<u>HERE</u>.

Where have all the flowers gone?

who's, whose   "Who's" is always a contraction of "who is" or "who has."

Who's sleeping in my bed?

Who's been sitting in my chair?

"Whose" is a possessive pronoun.

I know whose woods these are.

She's the one whose sister is a surgeon.

you're, your   "You're" is always a contraction of "you are."

You're the one who broke it.

"Your" is a possessive pronoun.

Your brother is the one who broke it.

INDEX

A 6
B 7
C 8
D 9
E 0
F 1
G 2
H 3
I 4
J 5